Plate tectonics, volcanoes, and earthquakes

PLATE TECTONICS, VOLCANOES, AND EARTHQUAKES

DYNAMIC EARTH

PLATE TECTONICS, VOLCANOES, AND EARTHQUAKES

EDITED BY JOHN RAFFERTY, ASSOCIATE EDITOR, EARTH SCIENCES

IN ASSOCIATION WITH

Published in 2011 by Britannica Educational Publishing
(a trademark of Encyclopædia Britannica, Inc.)
in association with Rosen Educational Services, LLC
29 East 21st Street, New York, NY 10010.

Distributed exclusively by Rosen Educational Services.
For a listing of additional Britannica Educational Publishing titles, call toll free (800) 237-9932.

First Edition

Britannica Educational Publishing
Michael I. Levy: Executive Editor
J. E. Luebering: Senior Manager
Marilyn L. Barton: Senior Coordinator, Production Control
Steven Bosco: Director, Editorial Technologies
Lisa S. Braucher: Senior Producer and Data Editor
Yvette Charboneau: Senior Copy Editor
Kathy Nakamura: Manager, Media Acquisition
John P. Rafferty: Associate Editor, Earth Sciences

Rosen Educational Services
Alexandra Hanson-Harding: Editor
Nelson Sá: Art Director
Cindy Reiman: Photography Manager
Nicole Russo: Designer
Matthew Cauli: Cover Design
Introduction by Therese Shea

Library of Congress Cataloging-in-Publication Data

Plate tectonics, volcanoes, and earthquakes / edited by John P. Rafferty.
p. cm.—(Dynamic Earth)
"In association with Britannica Educational Publishing, Rosen Educational Services."
Includes index.
ISBN 978-1-61530-106-5 (lib. bdg.)
1. Plate tectonics. 2. Volcanoes. 3. Earthquakes. 4. Geodynamics. I. Rafferty, John P.
QE511.4.P585 2010
551.8—dc22

2009042303

Manufactured in the United States of America

Cover, pp. 12, 82, 302 © www.istockphoto.com/Julien Grondin; p. 22 © www.istockphoto.com/Árni Torfason; pp. 23, 307 © www.istockphoto.com; pp. 202, 305 © www.istockphoto.com/Yali Shi

CONTENTS

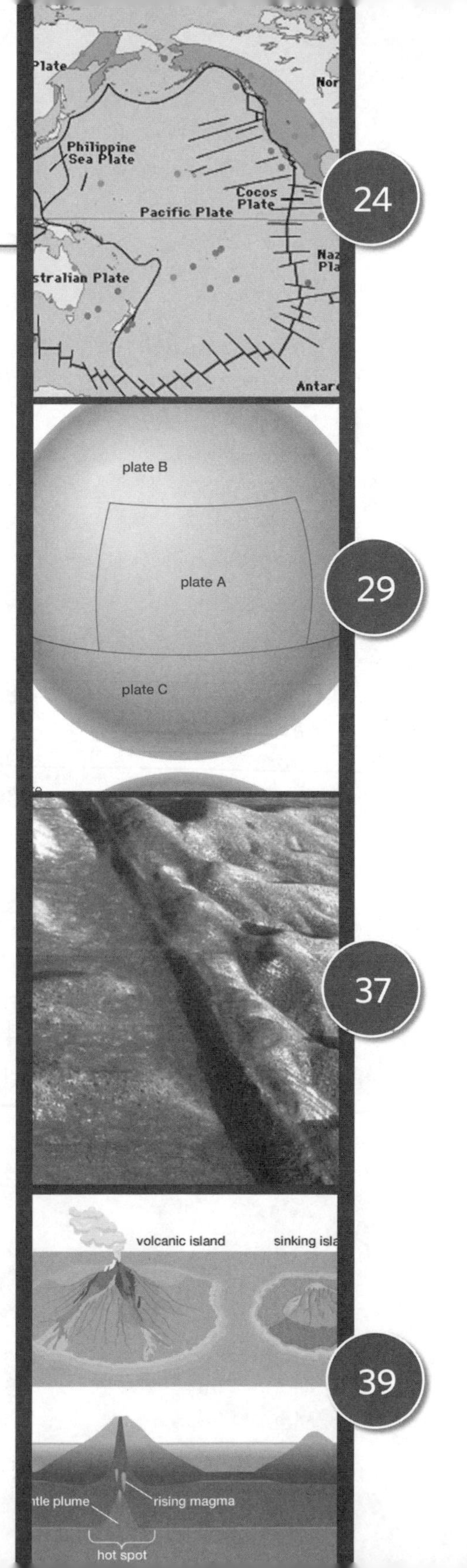

Philippine Sea Plate
Cocos Plate
Pacific Plate
plate B
plate A
plate C
volcanic island
rising magma
hot spot
24
29
37
39

141
153
158
161

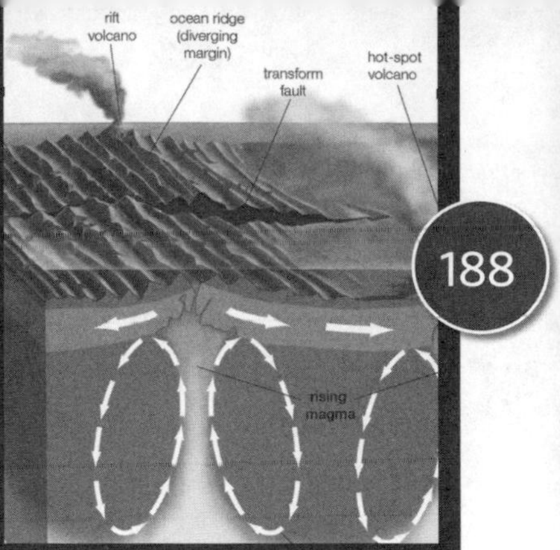
rift volcano
ocean ridge (diverging margin)
transform fault
hot-spot volcano
rising magma
188

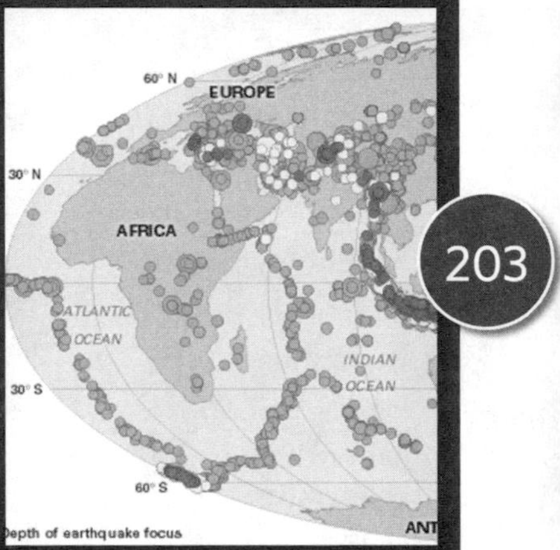
60° N
EUROPE
30° N
AFRICA
ATLANTIC OCEAN
INDIAN OCEAN
30° S
60° S
203

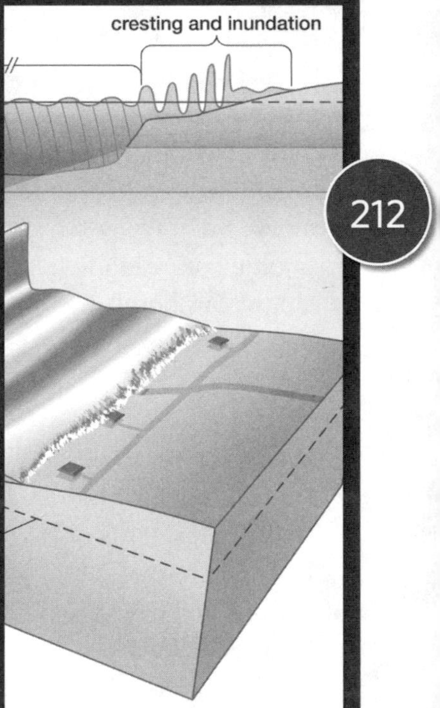
cresting and inundation
212

235
237
245

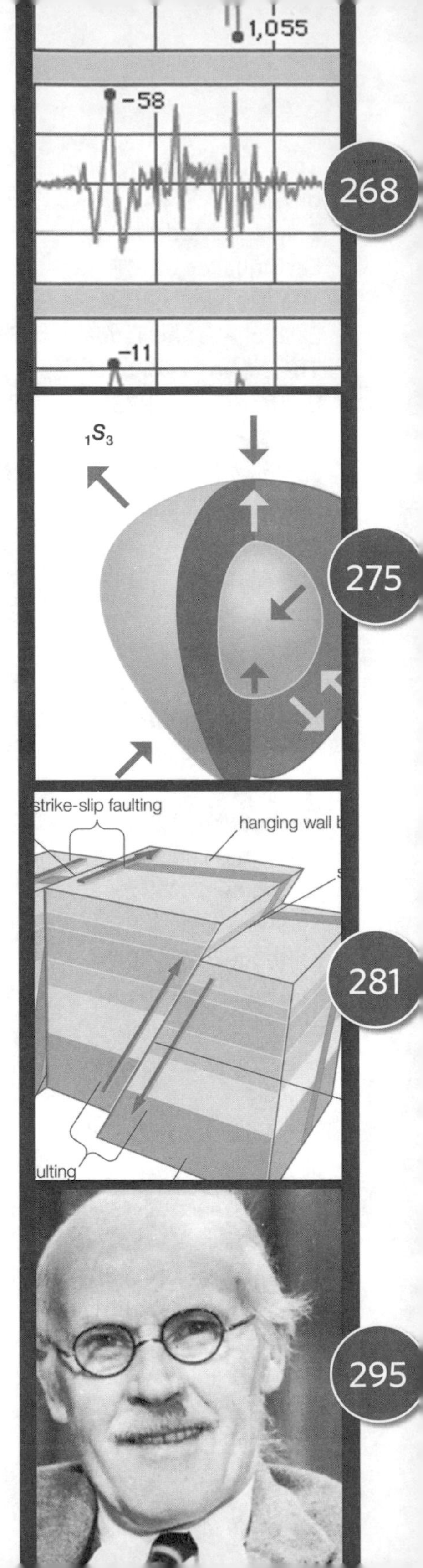
1,055
-58
-11
268
$_1S_3$
275
strike-slip faulting
hanging wall
281
ulting
295

INTRODUCTION

Humans live on unsteady ground. This fact was made abruptly apparent on January 12, 2010, when a magnitude 7.0 earthquake devastated the Caribbean island nation of Haiti. Because many buildings in this impoverished country were poorly constructed, they could not withstand the shaking and collapsed en masse, particularly in the capital city of Port-au-Prince, 15 miles from the quake's epicenter. Rescue workers desperately combed through rubble, hunting for survivors. By early February, Haiti's prime minister estimated that more than 200,000 people had been killed by the earthquake's effects. This type of earthquake, caused by two separate sections, or plates, of the Earth's crust sliding against each other is known as a strike-slip earthquake. It is just one example of the restlessness of Earth's surface.

This book will show how the movement of rock within the Earth is explained by the theory of plate tectonics, the idea that Earth's outer layer is broken into moving pieces. It will show how Earth adds and subtracts land over time. In addition, it will explain how and why volcanoes erupt and earthquakes shake the ground we live on.

As early as 1620, scholars noticed that the outlines of continents could fit together like puzzle pieces. In 1912, German scientist Alfred Wegener first explained the concept of "continental drift." He postulated that a single supercontinent, which he called Pangea, once existed, but broke apart into several pieces over geologic time. Wegener cited the existence of similar types of rocks and fossils found from separate continents as proof. He also used continental drift to explain the evidence of major climate and biological changes.

A volcano erupts on the island of Réunion in the Indian Ocean. © www.istockphoto.com/Julien Grondin

By the late 1960s, scientists had pieced together the "how" of plate tectonics. Earth's crust—the top layer of the lithosphere—is broken into pieces called plates. The plates rest on and slide over a layer of plastic and molten rock. As the plates move, they shape the features of Earth's surface above, including continents and oceans. Movement takes time—a mere 5 to 10 cm (2 to 4 inches) per year in some places, less in others. Hundreds of millions of years have passed since Pangea began to separate into the land masses we know today.

The surface of each tectonic plate is made up of continental crust and oceanic crust. The continental crust is less dense and thus floats higher than oceanic crust. It is also about 40 km (25 miles) thick. While oceanic crust averages about 6.4 km (4 miles) thick. Tectonic plates interact at convergent, divergent, and transform boundaries.

When the boundary of oceanic crust meets, or converges with, continental crust, the more buoyant continental crust stays afloat while the oceanic crust is forced beneath it—a process called subduction. The subducting crust melts under the pressure and heat of Earth's mantle, and the process offers an explanation of why continental crust is generally older than oceanic crust. When two oceanic plates meet, the older plate subducts under the younger one. In contrast, when two continental crusts meet, neither gives way. Instead, the earth is forced up, creating mountains. The thickness of the crust aids this process. The Himalayas were formed when the plate under India and the plate under Asia met. They are still applying enough pressure to cause the Himalayas to grow taller each year.

Two plates slide past each other at transform boundries. These plate interactions neither create nor destroy crust. Most transform boundries lie beneath the ocean:

however, some, such as the San Andreas Fault in California, occur on land. Faults associated with convergent and transform boundries appear as two huge masses of rock tensely locked in place. When the plates build up enough pressure to overcome the friction holding them, the releasing energy causes the ground to shake—an earthquake.

Earth's volume is a constant. As crust moves, subducts, and is consumed by the mantle, new crust is formed. When some plates move together, other plates move apart, or diverge. At divergent bundries, hot, liquid magma from Earth's mantle fills in the gaps and creates new crust. This process contributes to the spreading and expansion of the ocean floor. On land, between two diverging continental plates, the ascending magma creates a rift. The best example of continental rifting is the East African Rift Valley, and evidence suggests that the land east of the rift will separate from Africa one day.

Some scientists doubted Wegener because his ideas about the driving force behind plate movement were unsubstantiated. One of the leading modern theories contends that heat circulating within Earth's mantle, essentially convection, causes plate movement.

Paleoclimatologists, for example, provided evidence for plate tectonics. The splitting of Pangea into Gondwana and Laurasia kept Earth's polar areas much warmer than they are today. Between about 100 million and 70 million years ago, the poles were warm enough to support forests. Once the plates shifted, wind patterns and ocean currents changed to such a degree that polar ice sheets began to grow. Scientists have also speculated about the major effects of plate tectonics on evolution and diversity of life.

Theories of diverging and subducting plates have informed the study of volcanoes to a great degree. In the mid-1700s, *Encyclopædia Britannica* described volcanoes as "burning mountains." Today, it is commonly known that volcanoes function as vents that release magma and gases from beneath Earth's surface. The release is called an eruption.

About 80 percent of volcanoes are located in subduction zones. The line along which subduction occurs is called a trench, and these features, are the deepest areas on Earth. The pressure and water within oceanic crust cause the rock to melt from 70 to 200 km (40 to 120 miles) below the surface. Since the magma is less dense than the rock around it, it rises and melts more rock on its way to the surface. Under the ocean, volcanoes form along the trench, building crust and landforms called island arcs.

Some volcanoes occur where plates are diverging. Although rifting is a constant process, volcanoes only occur intermittently along the rift, when enough pressure has built up. In some places, "hot spots" form volcanoes in the middle of plates. The volcanoes of Hawaii are examples of hot spots.

Sometimes the magma flows out of pre-existing fissures in subducting and diverging plates. Sometimes it collects below a vent until it creates enough pressure to produce an explosive eruption. Where does this force come from? Besides rock, magma contains many gases. Rapid expansion of these gases can cause violent volcanic eruptions.

Naturally, the most violent, destructive volcanoes have the most gaseous magma. When magma reaches the surface, it is called lava. The more gas within the lava, the faster lava flows and spreads. Alone, volcanic gases—including carbon monoxide, carbon dioxide, and hydrogen sulfide—can quickly kill plants, animals, and people. In 1986, a gas cloud released through a volcanic crater lake took the lives of more than 1,700 people in Cameroon, West Africa.

Ash from volcanic eruptions ranges from fine dust to heavy blocks. The force of the volcanic blast can be so powerful that large pieces of rock have been thrown over 20 km (12 miles)! Ash falls can have negative repercussions on crop production near volcanoes. However, in the long run, ash makes soil very fertile. The ash from major volcanic explosions can reach such heights that they can reflect incoming sunlight and influence global climate. Krakatoa (1883), Mount Agung (1963), and Pinatubo (1991) were three volcanic eruptions that lowered the world's temperature by 0.5 °C (0.9 °F)! Pyroclastic flows are another feared element of volcanoes. These mixes of volcanic materials and gases travel down the slopes of volcanoes at speeds of 160 km (100 miles) an hour Since the material within pyroclastic flows may be as much as 1,300 °C (700 °F). they burn everything in their path.

The six degrees of eruptions in order from least to most explosive are: Icelandic, Hawaiian, Strombolian, Vulcanian, Pelean, and Plinian. The least explosive still have slow-moving-lava, which allows the gradual release of gases. At the other end of the spectrum, Plinian volcanoes produce the most damage, because the gases contained within them are released rapidly.

Most volcanoes are located on islands and mountains bordering the Pacific Ocean plate. This boundry is known as the "Pacific Ring of Fire," or the Circum-Pacific Belt. It is also home to most of the world's earthquakes, another by-product of plate tectonics. About 50,000 earthquakes happen each year, although usually only one or two cause major damage.

Plate tectonics is the process largely responsible for earthquakes. It does not cause all of them, however. Some are initiated by human activity, such as mining, whereas others can be triggered by large meteors crashing to Earth's surface. The most common source is the shearing of two plates of Earth's crust. These plates meet at faults, where they are held in place by friction until enough pressure forces movement.

Harry Fielding Reid's "elastic rebound" theory first explained how an earthquake released energy similarly to an elastic band breaking after being stretched. The rocks fracture first at the earthquake's focus, usually several miles below the surface. Fracturing can continue along the fault for many miles. Reid formulated his hypothesis after the San Andreas Fault ruptured in 1906, wreaking destruction on San Francisco. The fractures occurred a distance of about 430 km (270 miles), moving one side of the fault about 6 m (20 feet).

Faults can move in four different ways: strike-slip, normal, thrust, and reverse. In each of these faults, one mass of rock moves one way, while the other moves another way. When the rock fractures and slipage occurs, energy travels as seismic waves. There are four types of seismic waves. Primary (*P*) and Secondary (*S*) waves travel through Earth, while the third and fourth types, Love and Rayleigh waves, travel at the surface. They all move in different ways, at different speeds, and through different materials. Love and Rayleigh waves are slower than *P* and *S* waves; however, these surface waves are the ones that cause the most damage.

Seismologists use seismographs and other equipment, along with their knowledge of seismic waves to pinpoint the focus of an earthquake. Once they know the focus of the quake, they can better predict where other fault slips, called aftershocks, will occur following the initial event. There may be more than 1,000 aftershocks per day after an earthquake, and some may cause more damage than the initial event.

Earthquakes can cause massive loss of life. In underwater subduction zones, an earthquake is capable of displacing water, which may result in a tsunami. In 2004, more than 200,000 people were killed as a result of a tsunami occuring in the Indian Ocean near southeast Asia. Earthquakes can also cause other natural disasters, including landslides and avalanches. Many people have been hurt or have lost their lives when buildings and other structures collaps during earthquakes as well. In recent years, engineers have worked successfully with seismologists to build with materials "flexible" enough to withstand strong earthquakes.

This photo shows a tsunami hitting Marina beach in Madras, India, on December 26, 2004. More than 1000 people were killed in the Madras area alone. AFP/Getty Images

Plate tectonics is a relatively recent theory. In less than 100 years since Wegener proposed continental drift, scientists have designed underwater seismographs, harnessed geothermal volcanic energy for power, and explored the deepest trench in the world. Much more will be discovered over the next hundred years. Many more questions will likely be answered: How can we better prepare for earthquakes and volcanoes? How can we predict them? This book looks back at our planet's past, describing the processes that shape the Earth and its features. It attempts to explain the natural disasters that affect us today, and offers a glimpse into our planet's ever-changing future.

CHAPTER 1
EARTH'S DYNAMIC INTERIOR

Earth is a restless planet. The most easily observed evidence of this fact is revealed in the continuous movement of air and water. One should keep in mind, however, that the ground itself is also moving, albeit much more slowly. The hard crust of Earth's surface sits upon the weak, plastic rocks of the asthenosphere, and magma (molten or partially molten underground rock) continually rises from Earth's mantle toward the surface. These two factors cause continents to move and oceans to change shape; however, these changes are often imperceptible to the human eye. Occasionally, the ground moves suddenly and violently, when one section of the crust slides against another or when rising magma is delivered to Earth's surface or expelled into the atmosphere; such violent movements manifest themselves as earthquakes and volcanoes, respectively. This book considers the internal forces that act to change Earth's surface.

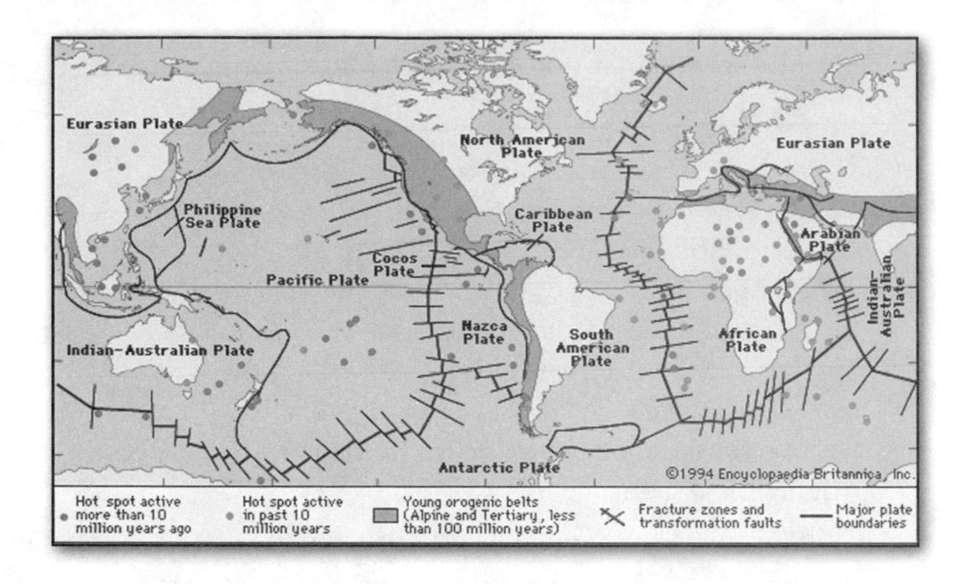

The principal tectonic plates that make up Earth's lithosphere. Also located are orogenic belts, or great mountain ranges, that have been produced comparatively recently at the boundaries of converging plates. The several dozen hot spots locate sites where plumes of hot mantle material are upwelling beneath the plates. Encyclopædia Britannica, Inc.

THE PROCESS OF PLATE TECTONICS

Plate tectonics is a theory dealing with the dynamics of Earth's outer shell, the lithosphere, that revolutionized earth sciences by providing a uniform context for understanding mountain-building processes, volcanoes, and earthquakes, as well as understanding the evolution of Earth's surface and reconstructing its past continental and oceanic configurations.

The concept of plate tectonics was formulated in the 1960s. According to the theory, Earth has a rigid outer layer, known as the lithosphere, which is about 100 km (60 miles) thick and overlies a plastic layer called the asthenosphere. The lithosphere is broken up into about a dozen large plates and several small ones. These plates

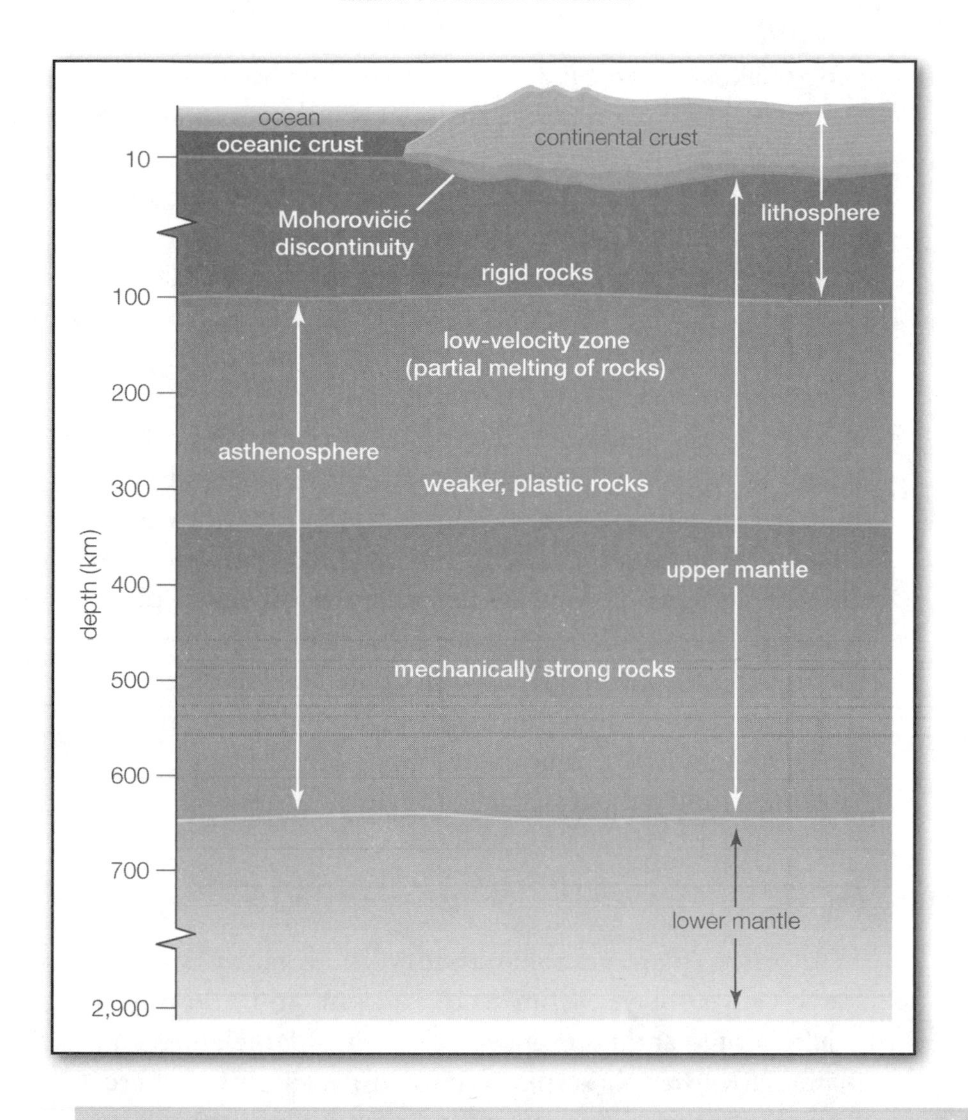

A cross section of Earth's outer layers, from the crust through the lower mantle. Encyclopædia Britannica, Inc.

move relative to each other, typically at rates of 5 to 10 cm (2 to 4 inches) per year, and interact at their boundaries, where they either converge, diverge, or slip past one another. Such interactions are thought to be responsible for most of Earth's seismic and volcanic activity, although earthquakes and volcanoes are not wholly absent in plate interiors. Plate motions cause mountains to rise where they push together or continents to fracture and oceans to form where they pull apart. The continents are embedded in the plates and drift passively with them, which over millions of years results in significant changes in Earth's geography.

The theory of plate tectonics is based on a broad synthesis of geologic and geophysical data. It is now almost universally accepted, and its adoption represents a true scientific revolution, analogous in its consequences to the Rutherford and Bohr atomic models in physics or the discovery of the genetic code in biology. Incorporating the much older idea of continental drift, the theory of plate tectonics has provided an overarching framework in which to describe the past geography of continents and oceans, processes controlling the creation and destruction of landforms, and the evolution of Earth's crust, atmosphere, biosphere, ancient oceans, and climates.

PRINCIPLES OF PLATE TECTONICS

In essence, plate tectonic theory is elegantly simple. Earth's surface layer, from 50 to 100 km (30 to 60 miles) thick, is rigid and is composed of a set of large and small plates. Together these plates constitute the lithosphere, from the Greek *lithos*, meaning "rock." The lithosphere rests on and slides over an underlying, weaker layer of plastic and partially molten rock known as the asthenosphere, from the Greek *asthenos*, meaning "weak." Plate movement is possible because the lithosphere-asthenosphere boundary is a zone of detachment. As the lithospheric plates move across Earth's surface, driven by forces as yet not fully understood, they interact along their boundaries, diverging, converging, or slipping past each other. While the interiors of the plates are presumed to remain essentially undeformed, plate boundaries are the sites of many of the principal processes that shape the terrestrial surface, including earthquakes, volcanism, and orogeny (that is, formation of mountain ranges).

Continental and Oceanic Crust

The lithosphere is subdivided on the basis of the presence of rock types with different chemical compositions. The outermost layer of the lithosphere is called the crust, of which there are two types, continental and oceanic, which differ in their composition and thickness. The distribution of these crustal types closely coincides with the division into continents and ocean basins. The continents have a crust that is broadly granitic in composition and, with a density of about 2.7 grams per cubic cm (0.098 pound per cubic inch), is somewhat lighter than oceanic crust, which is basaltic in composition and has a density of about 2.9 to 3 grams per cubic cm (0.1 to 0.11 pound per cubic inch). Continental crust is typically 40 km (25 miles) thick, while oceanic crust measures only 6 to 7 km (3.7 to 4.4 miles) in thickness.

These crustal rocks both sit on top of the mantle, which is ultramafic in composition (that is, rich in iron- and magnesium-bearing minerals). The boundary between the continental or oceanic crust and the underlying mantle, named the Mohorovičić discontinuity (also called Moho) for Andrija Mohorovičić, Croatian seismologist and its discoverer, has been clearly defined by seismic studies. The mantle is Earth's most voluminous layer, extending to a depth of 2,900 km (1,800 miles). However, increasing temperatures with depth cause mantle rocks to lose their rigidity at about 100 km (60 miles) below the surface. This change in rheology (a science examining the flow and deformation of materials) defines the base of the lithosphere and the top of the asthenosphere. This upper portion of the mantle, known as the lithospheric mantle, has an average density of about 3.3 grams per cubic cm (0.12 pound per cubic inch).

The effect of the different densities of lithospheric rock can be seen in the different average elevations of continental and oceanic crust. The less-dense continental crust has greater buoyancy, causing it to float much higher in the mantle. Its average elevation above sea level is 840 metres (2,750 feet), while the average depth of oceanic crust is 3,790 metres (12,400 feet). This density difference creates two principal levels of Earth's surface.

Plate Boundaries

Lithospheric plates are much thicker than oceanic or continental crust. Their boundaries do not usually coincide with those between oceans and continents, and their behaviour is only partly influenced by whether they carry oceans, continents, or both. The Pacific Plate, for example, is purely oceanic, whereas the North American Plate is capped by continental crust in the west (the North American continent) and by oceanic crust in the east—it extends under the Atlantic Ocean as far as the Mid-Atlantic Ridge.

Divergent Margins

As plates move apart at a divergent plate boundary, the release of pressure produces partial melting of the underlying mantle. This molten material, known as magma, is basaltic in composition and is buoyant. As a result, it wells up from below and cools close to the surface to generate new crust. Because new crust is formed, divergent margins are also called constructive margins.

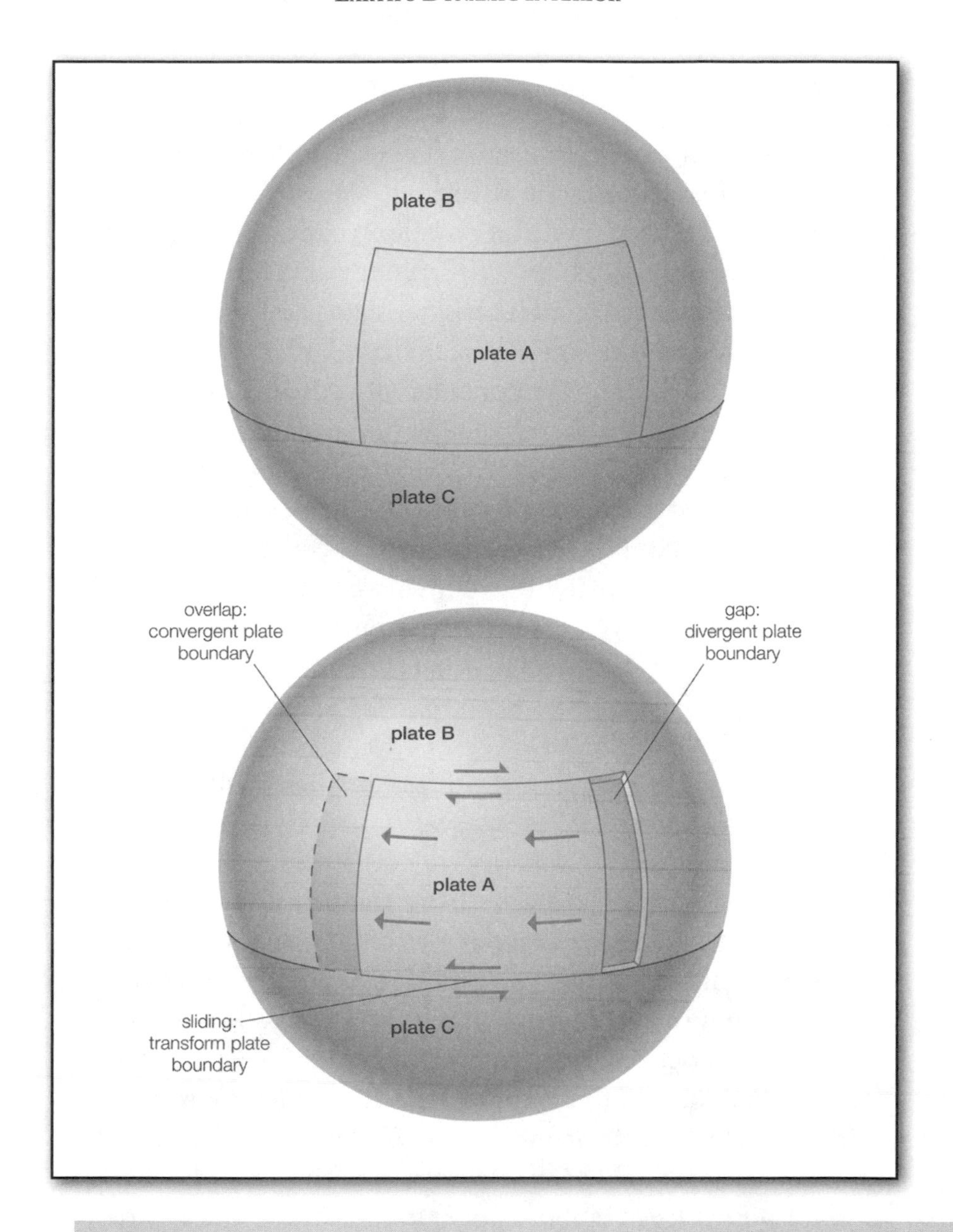

Theoretical diagram showing the effects of an advancing tectonic plate on other adjacent, but stationary, tectonic plates. At the advancing edge of plate A, the overlap with plate B creates a convergent boundary. In contrast, the gap left behind the trailing edge of plate A forms a divergent boundary with plate B. As plate A slides past portions of both plate B and plate C, transform boundaries develop. Encyclopædia Britannica, Inc.

Continental Rifting

Upwelling of magma causes the overlying lithosphere to uplift and stretch. If the diverging plates are capped by continental crust, fractures develop that are invaded by the ascending magma, prying the continents farther apart. Settling of the continental blocks creates a rift valley, such as the present-day East African Rift Valley. As the rift continues to widen, the continental crust becomes progressively thinner until separation of the plates is achieved and a new ocean is created. The ascending partial melt cools and crystallizes to form new crust. Because the partial melt is basaltic in composition, the new crust is oceanic. Consequently, diverging plate boundaries, even if they originate within continents, eventually come to lie in ocean basins of their own making.

Seafloor Spreading

As upwelling of magma continues, the plates continue to diverge, a process known as seafloor spreading. Samples collected from the ocean floor show that the age of oceanic crust increases with distance from the spreading centre—important evidence in favour of this process. These age data also allow the rate of seafloor spreading to be determined, and they show that rates vary from about 0.1 cm (0.04 inch) per year to 17 cm (6.7 inches) per year. Seafloor spreading rates in the Pacific Ocean are much more rapid than in the Atlantic or Indian oceans. At spreading rates of about 15 cm (6 inches) per year, the entire crust beneath the Pacific Ocean (about 15,000 km, or 9,300 miles, wide) could be produced in 100 million years.

Divergence and creation of oceanic crust are accompanied by much volcanic activity and by many shallow earthquakes as the crust repeatedly rifts, heals, and rifts again. These regions are swollen with heat and so are elevated by 2 to 3 km (1.2 to 1.9 miles) above the surrounding seafloor. Their summits are typically 1 to 5 km (0.6 to 3.1 miles) below the ocean surface. On a global scale, these features form an interconnected system of undersea mountains about 65,000 km (40,000 miles) in length and are called oceanic ridges.

Oceanic crust, once formed, cools as it ages and eventually becomes denser than the underlying asthenosphere, and so it has a tendency to subduct. The life span of this crust is prolonged by its rigidity, but eventually this resistance is overcome. The geologic record suggests that subduction commences when oceanic crust is about 200 million years old.

Convergent Margins

Given that Earth is constant in volume, the continuous formation of new crust produces an excess that must be balanced by destruction of crust elsewhere. This is accomplished at convergent plate boundaries, also known as destructive plate boundaries, where one plate descends at an angle—that is, is subducted—beneath the other. Where two oceanic plates meet, the older, denser plate is preferentially subducted beneath the younger, warmer one. Where one of the plate margins is oceanic and the other is continental, the greater buoyancy of continental crust prevents it from sinking, and the oceanic plate is preferentially subducted. Continents are preferentially preserved in this manner relative to oceanic crust, which is continuously recycled into the mantle; this explains why ocean floor rocks are generally less than 200 million years old whereas the oldest continental rocks are almost 4 billion years old. Where two plates carrying continental crust collide, neither is

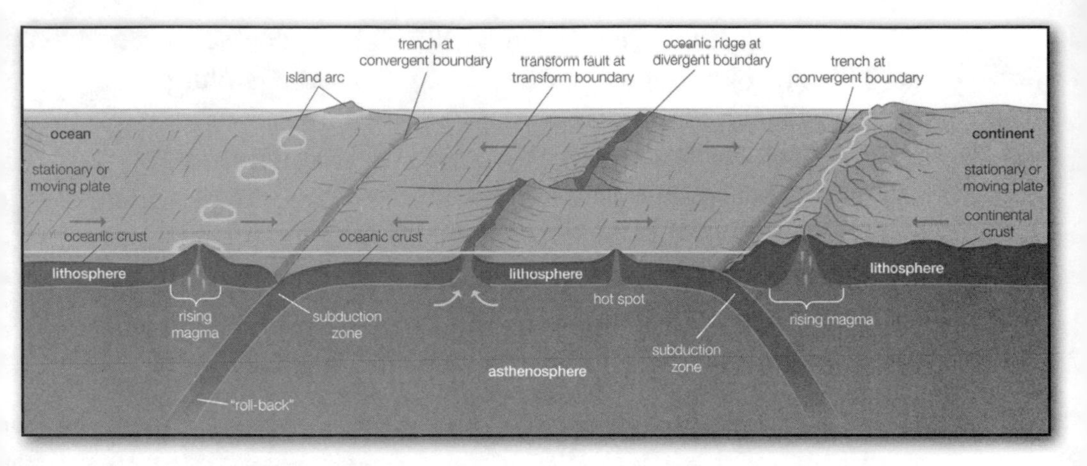

Three-dimensional diagram showing crustal generation and destruction according to the theory of plate tectonics; included are the three kinds of plate boundaries—divergent, convergent (or collision), and strike-slip (or transform). Encyclopædia Britannica, Inc.

subducted. Instead, towering mountain ranges, such as the Himalayas, are created.

Because the plates form an integrated system, it is not necessary that new crust formed at any given divergent boundary be completely compensated at the nearest subduction zone, as long as the total amount of crust generated equals that destroyed.

Subduction Zone Trenches

The subduction process involves the descent into the mantle of a slab of cold, hydrated oceanic lithosphere about 100 km (60 miles) thick that carries a relatively thin cap of oceanic sediments. The path of descent is defined by numerous earthquakes along a plane that is typically inclined between 30° and 60° into the mantle and is called the Benioff zone, for American seismologist Hugo Benioff, who pioneered its study. Most, but not all, earthquakes in this planar dipping zone result from compression, and the seismic activity extends 300 to 700 km (185 to 435 miles) below the surface. At greater depths, the subducted plate melts and is recycled into the mantle.

The site of subduction is marked by a deep trench between 5 and 11 km (3 and 7 miles) deep that is produced by frictional drag between the plates as the descending plate bends before it subducts. The overriding plate scrapes sediments and elevated portions of ocean floor off the upper crust of the lower plate, creating a zone of highly deformed rocks within the trench that becomes attached, or accreted, to the overriding plate. This chaotic mixture is known as an accretionary wedge.

The rocks in the subduction zone experience high pressures but relatively low temperatures, an effect of the descent of the cold oceanic slab. Under these conditions the rocks recrystallize, or metamorphose, to form a suite of rocks known as blueschists, named for the diagnostic blue mineral glaucophane, which is stable only at the high pressures and low temperatures found in subduction zones.

Island Arcs

When the downgoing slab reaches a depth of about 100 km (60 miles), it gets sufficiently warm to drive off its most volatile components, thereby stimulating partial melting of mantle in the plate above the subduction zone (known as the mantle wedge). Melting in the mantle wedge produces magma, which is predominantly basaltic in composition. This magma rises to the surface and gives birth to a line of volcanoes in the overriding plate, known as a volcanic arc, typically a few hundred kilometres behind the oceanic trench. The distance between the trench and the arc, known as the arc-trench gap, depends on the angle of subduction. Steeper subduction zones have relatively narrow arc-trench gaps. A basin may form within this region, known as a forearc basin, and may be filled with sediments derived from the volcanic arc or with remains of oceanic crust.

If both plates are oceanic, such as in the modern western Pacific Ocean, the volcanoes form a curved line of islands, known as an island arc, that is parallel to the trench. If one plate is continental, the volcanoes form inland, as they do in the Andes of western South America. Though the process of magma generation is similar, the ascending magma may change its composition as it rises through the thick lid of continental crust, or it may provide sufficient heat to melt the crust. In either case, the composition of the volcanic mountains formed tends to be more silicon-rich and iron- and magnesium-poor relative to the volcanic rocks produced by ocean-ocean convergence.

Back-Arc Basins

Where both converging plates are oceanic, the margin of the older oceanic crust will be subducted because older oceanic crust is colder and therefore more dense. As the dense slab collapses into the asthenosphere, however, it also may "roll back" oceanward and cause extension in the overlying plate. This results in a process known as back-arc spreading, in which a basin opens up behind the island arc. This style of subduction predominates in the western Pacific Ocean, in which a back-arc basin separates several island arcs from the Asian continent.

Continental Collision

If the rate of subduction in an ocean basin exceeds the rate at which the crust is formed at oceanic ridges, closure of the basin is inevitable, leading ultimately to terminal collision between the approaching continents. For example, the subduction of the Tethys Sea, a wedge-shaped body of water that was located between Gondwana and Laurasia, led to the accretion of terranes (crustal blocks or formations of related rocks) along the margins of Laurasia. These events were followed by continental collisions beginning about 30 million years ago between Africa and Europe and between India and Asia. These collisions culminated in the formation of the Alps and the Himalayas. Because continental lithosphere is too buoyant to be subducted, one continent overrides the other, producing crustal thickening and intense deformation that forces the crust skyward to form huge mountains.

Accretion and Obduction

As subduction leads to contraction of an ocean, elevated regions within the ocean basin such as linear island chains, oceanic ridges, and small crustal fragments (such as Madagascar or Japan), known as terranes, are transported toward the subduction zone, where they are scraped off the descending plate and added—accreted—to the continental margin. Since the Late Devonian and Early Carboniferous periods, some 360 million years ago, subduction beneath the western margin of North America has resulted in several collisions with terranes, each producing a mountain-building event. The piecemeal addition of these accreted terranes has added an average of 600 km (375 miles) in width along the western margin of the North American continent.

During these accretionary events, small sections of the oceanic crust may break away from the subducting slab as it descends. Instead of being subducted, these slices are thrust over the overriding plate and are said to be obducted. Where this occurs, rare slices of ocean crust, known as ophiolites, are preserved on land. They provide a valuable natural laboratory for studying the composition and character of the oceanic crust and the mechanisms of their emplacement and preservation on land. A classic example is the Coast Range ophiolite of California, which is one of the most extensive ophiolite terranes in North America. This oceanic crust likely formed during the middle Jurassic Period, roughly 170 million years ago, in an extensional regime within either a back-arc or a forearc basin. It was later accreted to the continental margin of Laurasia.

Mountain Building

Where the rate of seafloor spreading is outpaced by subduction, the oceanic crust eventually becomes completely destroyed, and collision between continental landmasses is inevitable. Because collision occurs between two buoyant plate margins, neither can be subducted. A complex sequence of events occurs, forcing one continent to override the other so that the thickness of the continental crust is effectively doubled. These collisions produce lofty landlocked mountain ranges such as the modern Himalayas. The buoyancy of continental crust eventually causes subduction to cease. Much later, after these ranges have been largely leveled by erosion, it is possible that the original contact, or suture, may be exposed.

The balance between creation and destruction is demonstrated by the expansion of the Atlantic Ocean by seafloor spreading over the past 200 million years, compensated by the contraction of the Pacific Ocean, and the consumption of an entire ocean between India and Asia (the Tethys Sea). The northward migration of India led to collision with Asia some 40 million years ago. Since that time, India has advanced a farther 2,000 km (1,250 miles) beneath Asia, pushing up the Himalayas and forming the Tibetan plateau. Pinned against stable Siberia, China and Indochina were pushed sideways, resulting in strong seismic activity thousands of kilometres from the site of the continental collision.

Section of the San Andreas Fault in the Carrizo Plain, western California. U.S. Geological Survey

Transform Faults

Along the third type of plate boundary, two plates move laterally and pass each other along giant fractures in Earth's crust, called transform faults, so called because they are linked to other types of plate boundaries. The majority of transform faults link the offset segments of oceanic ridges. However, transform faults also occur between plate margins with continental crust—for example, the San Andreas Fault in California and the North Anatolian fault system in Turkey. These boundaries are conservative because plate interaction occurs without creating or destroying crust. Because the only motion along these faults is the sliding of plates past each other, the horizontal direction along the fault surface must parallel the direction of plate motion. The fault surfaces are rarely smooth, and pressure may build up when the plates on either side temporarily lock. This build-up of stress may be suddenly released in the form of an earthquake.

Hot Spots

Although most of Earth's seismic and volcanic activity is concentrated along or adjacent to plate boundaries, there are some important exceptions in which this activity occurs within plates. Linear chains of islands, thousands of kilometres in length, that occur far from plate boundaries are the most notable examples. These island chains record a typical sequence of decreasing elevation along the chain from volcanic island to fringing reef, to atoll, and finally to a submerged seamount. An active volcano usually exists at one end of an island chain, with progressively older extinct volcanoes occurring along the rest of the chain. Canadian geophysicist J. Tuzo Wilson and American geophysicist W. Jason Morgan have explained such topographic features as the result of hot spots.

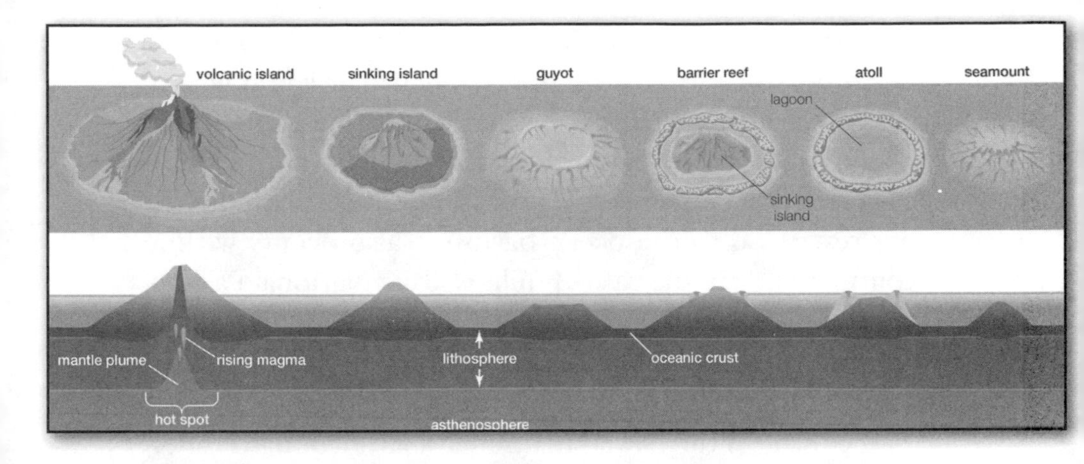

Diagram depicting the process of atoll formation. Atolls are formed from the remnant parts of sinking volcanic islands. Encyclopædia Britannica, Inc.

The number of these hot spots is uncertain (estimates range from 20 to 120), but most occur within a plate rather than at a plate boundary. Hot spots are thought to be the surface expression of giant plumes of heat, termed mantle plumes, that ascend from deep within the mantle, possibly from the core-mantle boundary, some 2,900 km (1,800 miles) below the surface. These plumes are thought to be stationary relative to the lithospheric plates that move over them. A volcano builds upon the surface of a plate directly above the plume. As the plate moves on, however, the volcano is separated from its underlying magma source and becomes extinct. Extinct volcanoes are eroded as they cool and subside to form fringing reefs and atolls, and eventually they sink below the surface of the sea to form a seamount. At the same time, a new active volcano forms directly above the mantle plume.

The best example of this process is preserved in the Hawaiian-Emperor seamount chain. The plume is presently situated beneath Hawaii, and a linear chain of islands, atolls, and seamounts extends 3,500 km (2,175 miles) northwest to Midway and a further 2,500 km (1,550 miles) north-northwest to the Aleutian trench. The age at which volcanism became extinct along this chain gets progressively older with increasing distance from Hawaii—critical evidence that supports this theory. Hot spot volcanism is not restricted to the ocean basins; it also occurs within continents, as in the case of Yellowstone National Park in western North America.

Plate Motion

In the 18th century, Swiss mathematician Leonhard Euler showed that the movement of a rigid body across the surface of a sphere can be described as a rotation around an axis that goes through the centre of the sphere, known as the axis of rotation. The location of this axis bears no relationship to Earth's spin axis. The point of emergence of the axis through the surface of the sphere is known as the pole of rotation. This theorem of spherical geometry provides an elegant way for defining the motion of the lithospheric plates across Earth's surface. Therefore, the relative motion of two rigid plates may be described as rotations around a common axis, known as the axis of spreading. Application of the theorem requires that the plates not be internally deformed—a requirement not absolutely adhered to but one that appears to be a reasonable approximation of what actually happens. Application of this theorem permits the mathematical reconstruction of past plate configurations.

Because all plates form a closed system, all movements can be defined by dealing with them two at a time. The joint pole of rotation of two plates can be determined from their transform boundaries, which are by definition parallel to the direction of motion. Thus, the plates move along transform faults, whose trace defines circles of latitude perpendicular to the axis of spreading, and so form

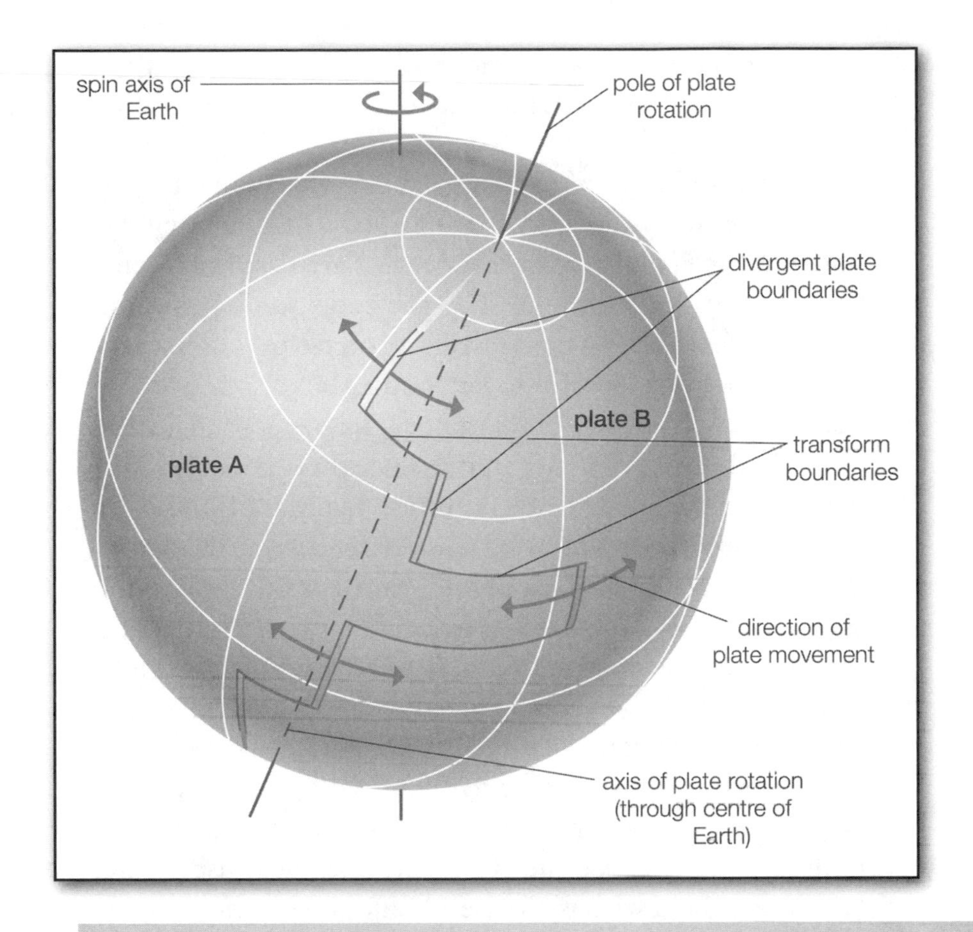

Theoretical depiction of the movement of tectonic plates across Earth's surface. Movement on a sphere of two plates, A and B, can be described as a rotation around a common pole. Circles around that pole correspond to the orientation of transform faults (that is, single lines in the horizontal that connect to divergent plate boundaries, marked by double lines, in the vertical). Encyclopædia Britannica, Inc.

small circles around the pole of rotation. A geometric necessity of this theorem—that lines perpendicular to the transform faults converge on the pole of rotation—is confirmed by measurements. According to this theorem, the rate of plate motion should be slowest near the pole of rotation and increase progressively to a maximum rate along fractures with a 90° angle to it. This relationship is also confirmed by accurate measurements of seafloor-spreading rates.

It is possible that the entire lithosphere might slide around over the asthenosphere like a loose skin, altering the positions of all plates with respect to Earth's spin axis and the Equator. To determine the true geographic positions of the plates in the past, investigators have to define their motions, not only relative to each other but also relative to this independent frame of reference. The plumes provide an example of such a reference frame, since they probably originate within the deep mantle and since many appear to have relatively fixed positions over time. As a result, the motion of the lithosphere above these plumes can be deduced. The hot spot island chains serve this purpose, their trends providing the direction of motion of a plate; the speed of the plate can be inferred from the increase in age of the volcanoes along the chain relative to the distance between the islands.

Earth scientists are able to accurately reconstruct the positions and movements of plates for the past 150 to 200 million years, because they have the oceanic crust record to provide them with plate speeds and direction of movement. However, since older oceanic crust is continuously consumed to make room for new crust, this kind of evidence is not available during earlier geologic time intervals, making it necessary for investigators to turn to other, less-precise techniques.

THE DEVELOPMENT OF TECTONIC THEORY

The modern theory of plate tectonics rests on the shoulders of past thinkers. One of the more influential thinkers was German meteorologist and geophysicist

Alfred Wegener, who formulated the continental drift hypothesis. Despite early challenges, the evidence of similarities between certain rocks on widely spaced continents, the observations of Earth's ancient magnetic field, the discovery of the oceanic ridge system, and the detection of magnetic anomalies in the seafloor all support Wegener's hypothesis. Such evidence, which mounted throughout the middle decades of the 20th century, allowed the greater part of the scientific community to accept continental drift and subsequently assemble the modern theory of plate tectonics.

The Precursors of Modern Thinking

The outlines of the continents flanking the Atlantic Ocean are so similar that many probably noticed the correspondence as soon as accurate maps became available. The earliest references to this similarity were made in 1620 by the English philosopher Francis Bacon, in his book *Novum Organum*, and by French naturalist Georges-Louis Leclerc, Count de Buffon, a century later. Toward the end of the 18th century, Alexander von Humboldt, a German naturalist, suggested that the lands bordering the Atlantic Ocean had once been joined.

In 1858, French geographer Antonio Snider-Pellegrini proposed that identical fossil plants in North American and European coal deposits could be explained if the two continents had formerly been connected. He suggested that the biblical flood was due to the fragmentation of this continent, which was torn apart to restore the balance of a lopsided Earth. In the late 19th century, the Austrian geologist Eduard Suess proposed that large ancient continents had been composed of several of the present-day smaller ones. According to this hypothesis, portions of a single enormous southern continent—designated

Gondwanaland, or Gondwana—foundered to become the Atlantic and Indian oceans. Such sunken lands, along with vanished land bridges, were frequently invoked in the late 1800s to explain sediment sources apparently present in the ocean and to account for floral and faunal connections between continents. These explanations remained popular until the 1950s and stimulated believers in the ancient submerged continent of Atlantis.

In 1908, American geologist Frank B. Taylor postulated that the arcuate mountain belts of Asia and Europe resulted from the equatorward creep of the continents. His analysis of tectonic features foreshadowed in many ways modern thought regarding plate collisions.

Alfred Wegener and the Concept of Continental Drift

In 1912, German meteorologist Alfred Wegener, impressed by the similarity of the geography of the Atlantic coastlines, explicitly presented the concept of continental drift. Though plate tectonics is by no means synonymous with continental drift, the term encompasses this idea and derives much of its impact from it.

Wegener came to consider the existence of a single supercontinent from about 350 to 245 million years ago, during the late Paleozoic Era, and named it Pangea, meaning "all lands." He searched the geologic and paleontological literature for evidence supporting the continuity of geologic features across the Indian and Atlantic oceans during that time period, which he assumed had formed during the Mesozoic Era (about 248 to 65 million years ago). He presented the idea of continental drift and some of the supporting evidence in a lecture in 1912, followed in 1915 by his major published work, *Die Entstehung der Kontinente und Ozeane* (*The Origin of Continents and Oceans*).

Isostasy

Wegener pointed out that the concept of isostasy, the balance of the forces supporting the crust with those that push down upon it, rendered large sunken continental blocks, as envisaged by Suess, geophysically impossible. He concluded that, if the continents had been once joined together, the consequence would have been drift of their fragments and not their foundering. The assumption of a former single continent could be tested geologically, and Wegener displayed a large array of data that supported his hypothesis, ranging from the continuity of fold belts across oceans, the presence of identical rocks and fossils on continents now separated by oceans, and the paleobiogeographic and paleoclimatological record that indicated otherwise unaccountable shifts in Earth's major climate belts. He further argued that, if continents could move up and down in the mantle as a result of buoyancy changes produced by erosion or deposition, they should be able to move horizontally as well.

The Driving Forces of Continental Drift

The main stumbling block to the acceptance of Wegener's hypothesis was the driving forces he proposed. Wegener described the drift of continents as a flight from the poles due to Earth's equatorial bulge. Although these forces do exist, Wegener's nemesis, British geophysicist Sir Harold Jeffreys, demonstrated that these forces are much too weak for the task. Another mechanism proposed by Wegener, tidal forces on Earth's crust produced by gravitational pull of the Moon, were also shown to be entirely inadequate.

Wegener's proposition was attentively received by many European geologists, and in England, Arthur Holmes pointed out that the lack of a driving force was insufficient grounds for rejecting the entire concept. In 1929, Holmes proposed an alternative mechanism—convection of the mantle—which remains today a serious candidate for the force driving the plates. Wegener's ideas also were well received by geologists in the Southern Hemisphere. One of them, the South African Alexander Du Toit, remained an ardent believer. After Wegener's death, Du Toit continued to amass further evidence in support of continental drift.

The Evidence Supporting Wegener's Hypothesis

The strikingly similar Paleozoic sedimentary sequences on all southern continents and also in India are an example of evidence that supports continental drift. This diagnostic sequence consists of glacial deposits called tillites, followed by sandstones and finally coal measures, typical of warm, moist climates. An attempt to explain this sequence in a world of fixed continents presents insurmountable problems. Placed on a reconstruction of Gondwana, however, the tillites mark two ice ages that occurred during the drift of this continent across the South Pole from its initial position north of Libya about 500 million years ago and its final departure from southern Australia 250 million years later. About this time, Gondwana collided with Laurentia (the precursor to the North American continent), which was one of the major collisional events that produced Panagea.

Both ice ages resulted in glacial deposits—in the southern Sahara during the Silurian Period (more than 400 million years ago) and in southern South America, South Africa, India, and Australia from 380 to 250 million years ago, spanning the latter part of the Devonian, the Carboniferous, and almost all of the Permian. At each location, the tillites were subsequently covered by desert sands of the subtropics, and these in turn by coal measures, indicating that the region had arrived near the paleoequator.

During the 1950s and 1960s, isotopic dating of rocks showed that the crystalline massifs of Precambrian age (from about 4 billion to 542 million years ago) found on opposite sides of the South Atlantic did indeed closely correspond in age and composition, as Wegener had surmised. It is now evident that they originated as a single assemblage of Precambrian continental nuclei later torn apart by the fragmentation of Pangea.

By the 1960s, although evidence supporting continental drift had strengthened substantially, many scientists were claiming that the shape of the coastlines should be more sensitive to coastal erosion and changes in sea level and are unlikely to maintain their shape over hundreds of millions of years. Therefore, they argued, the supposed fit of the continents flanking the Atlantic Ocean is fortuitous. In 1964, however, these arguments were laid to rest. A computer analysis by Sir Edward Bullard showed an impressive fit of these continents at the 1,000-metre (3,300-foot) depth contour. A match at this depth is highly significant and is a better approximation of the edge of the continents than the present shoreline. With this reconstruction of the continents, the structures and stratigraphic sequences of Paleozoic mountain ranges in eastern North America and northwestern Europe can be matched in detail in the manner envisaged by Wegener.

Disbelief and Opposition

Sir Harold Jeffreys was one of the strongest opponents of Wegener's hypothesis. He believed that continental drift is impossible because the strength of the underlying mantle should be far greater than any conceivable driving force. In North America, opposition to Wegener's ideas was most vigorous and very nearly unanimous. Wegener was attacked from virtually every possible vantage point—his paleontological evidence attributed to land bridges, the similarity of strata on both sides of the Atlantic called into question, and the fit of Atlantic shores declared inaccurate. This criticism is illustrated by reports from a symposium on continental drift organized in 1928 by the American Association of Petroleum Geologists. The mood that prevailed at the gathering was expressed by an unnamed attendant quoted with sympathy by the great American geologist Thomas C. Chamberlin: "If we are to believe Wegener's hypothesis, we must forget everything which has been learned in the last 70 years and start all over again." The same reluctance to start anew was again displayed some 40 years later by the same organization when its publications provided the principal forum for the opposition to plate tectonics.

The Renewed Interest in Continental Drift

Following World War II, paleomagnetic studies and the discovery of Earth's oceanic ridge system helped to validate Wegener's continental drift hypothesis.

Paleomagnetism, Polar Wandering, and Continental Drift

Ironically, the vindication of Wegener's hypothesis came from the field of geophysics, the subject used by Jeffreys to discredit the original concept. The ancient Greeks realized that some rocks are strongly magnetized, and the Chinese invented the magnetic compass in the 13th century. In the 19th century, geologists recognized that many rocks preserve the imprint of Earth's magnetic field as it was at the time of their formation. The study and measurement of Earth's ancient magnetic field is called paleomagnetism. Iron-rich volcanic rocks such as basalt contain minerals that are good recorders of paleomagnetism, and some sediments also align their magnetic particles with Earth's field at the time of deposition. These minerals behave like fossil compasses that indicate, like any magnet suspended in Earth's field, the direction to the magnetic pole and the latitude of their origin at the time the minerals were crystallized or deposited.

During the 1950s, paleomagnetic studies, notably those of Stanley K. Runcorn and his coworkers in England, showed that in the late Paleozoic the north magnetic pole—as reconstructed from European data—seems to have wandered from a Precambrian position near Hawaii to its present location by way of Japan. This could be explained either by the migration of the magnetic pole itself (that is, polar wandering) or by the migration of Europe relative to a fixed pole (that is, continental drift). The distinction between these two hypotheses came from paleomagnetic data from other continents. Each continent yielded different results, called apparent polar wandering paths. The possibility that they might reflect true wandering of the poles was discarded, because it would imply separate wanderings of many magnetic poles over the same period. However, these different paths could be reconciled by joining the continents in the manner and at the time suggested by Wegener.

Impressed by this result, Runcorn became the first of a new generation of geologists and geophysicists to accept continental drift as a proposition worthy of careful testing. Since then, more sophisticated paleomagnetic techniques have provided both strong supporting evidence for continental drift and a major tool for reconstructing the geography and geology of the past.

The Gestation and Birth of Plate Tectonic Theory

After World War II, rapid advances were made in the study of the relief, geology, and geophysics of the ocean basins. Owing in large part to the efforts of Bruce C. Heezen and Henry W. Menard of the United States, these features, which constitute more than two-thirds of Earth's surface, became well enough known to permit serious geologic analysis.

The Discovery of Ocean Basin Features

One of the most important discoveries was that of the oceanic ridge system. Oceanic ridges form an interconnected network about 65,000 km (40,000 miles) in length that nearly girdles the globe, has elevations that rise 2 to 3 km (1.2 to 1.9 miles) above the surrounding seafloor, and has widths that range from a few hundred to more than 1,000 km (600 miles). Their crests tend to be rugged and are often endowed with a rift valley at their summit where fresh lava, high heat flow, and shallow earthquakes of the extensional type are found.

Long, narrow depressions—oceanic trenches—were also discovered that contain the greatest depths of the ocean basins. Trenches virtually ring the Pacific Ocean; a few also occur in the northeastern part of the Indian Ocean, and some small ones are found in the central Atlantic Ocean. Elsewhere they are absent. Trenches have low heat flow, are often filled with thick sediments, and lie at the upper edge of the Benioff zone of compressive earthquakes. Trenches may border continents, as in the case of western Central and South America, or may occur in mid-ocean, as, for example, in the southwestern Pacific.

Offsets of up to several hundred kilometres along oceanic ridges and, more rarely, trenches were also recognized, and these fracture zones—later termed transform faults—were described as transverse features consisting of linear ridges and troughs. In oceanic domains, these faults were found to occur approximately perpendicular to the ridge crest, continue as fracture zones extending over long distances, and terminate abruptly against continental margins. They are not sites of volcanism, and their seismic activity is restricted to the area between offset ridge crests, where earthquakes indicating horizontal slip are common.

Hess's Seafloor-Spreading Model

The existence of these three types of large, striking seafloor features demanded a global rather than local tectonic explanation. The first comprehensive attempt at such an explanation was made by Harry H. Hess of the United States in a widely circulated manuscript written in 1960 but not formally published for several years. In this paper, Hess, drawing on Holmes's model of convective flow in the mantle, suggested that the oceanic ridges were the surface expressions of rising and diverging convective mantle flow, while trenches and Benioff zones, with their associated island arcs, marked descending limbs. At the ridge crests new oceanic crust would be generated and then carried away laterally to cool, subside, and finally be destroyed in the nearest trenches. Consequently, the age of the oceanic crust should increase with distance away from the ridge crests, and, because recycling was its ultimate fate, very old oceanic crust would not be preserved anywhere. This explained why rocks older than 200 million years had never been encountered in the oceans, whereas the continents preserve rocks up to 3.8 billion years old.

Hess's model was later dubbed seafloor spreading by the American oceanographer Robert S. Dietz. Confirmation of the production of oceanic crust at ridge crests and its subsequent lateral transfer came from an ingenious analysis of transform faults by Canadian geophysicist J. Tuzo Wilson. Wilson argued that the offset between two ridge crest segments is present at the outset of seafloor spreading. As each ridge segment generates new crust that moves laterally away from the ridge, the crustal slabs move in opposite directions along that part of the fracture zone that lies between the crests. In the fracture zones beyond the crests, adjacent portions of crust move in parallel (and are therefore aseismic—that is, do not have earthquakes) and are eventually absorbed in a trench. Wilson called this a transform fault and noted that on such a fault the seismicity should be confined to the part between ridge crests, a prediction that was subsequently confirmed by an American seismologist, Lynn R. Sykes.

The Vine-Matthews Hypothesis

Magnetic Anomalies

In 1961, a magnetic survey of the eastern Pacific Ocean floor off the coast of Oregon and California was published by two geophysicists, Arthur D. Raff and Ronald G. Mason. Unlike on the continents, where regional magnetic anomaly patterns tend to be confused and seemingly random, the seafloor possesses a remarkably regular set of magnetic bands of alternately higher and lower values than the average values of Earth's magnetic field. These positive and negative anomalies are strikingly linear and parallel with the oceanic ridge axis, show distinct offsets along fracture zones, and generally resemble the pattern of zebra skin. The axial anomaly tends to be higher and wider than the adjacent ones, and in most cases the sequence on one side is the approximate mirror image of that on the other.

Reversal of Earth's Magnetic Field

A key piece to resolving this pattern came with the discovery of magnetized samples from a sequence of basalt lavas. These lavas were extruded in rapid succession in a single locality on land and showed that the north and south poles had apparently repeatedly interchanged. This could be interpreted in one of two ways—either the rocks must have somehow reversed their magnetism, or the polarity of Earth's magnetic field must periodically reverse itself. Allan Cox of Stanford University and Brent Dalrymple of the United States Geological Survey collected magnetized samples and showed that these samples from around the world displayed the same reversal at the same time, implying that the polarity of Earth's magnetic field periodically reversed. These studies established a sequence of reversals dated by isotopic methods.

Assuming that the oceanic crust is indeed made of basalt intruded in an episodically reversing geomagnetic field, Drummond H. Matthews of the University of Cambridge and a research student, Frederick J. Vine, postulated in 1963 that the new crust would have a magnetization aligned with the field at the time of its formation. If the magnetic field was normal, as it is today, the magnetization of the crust would be added to that of Earth and produce a positive anomaly. If intrusion had taken place during a period of reverse magnetic polarity, it would subtract from the present field and appear as a negative anomaly. Subsequent to intrusion, each new block created at spreading centre would split and the halves, in moving aside, would generate the observed bilateral magnetic symmetry.

Given a constant rate of crustal generation, the widths of individual anomalies should correspond to the intervals between magnetic reversals. In 1966, correlation of magnetic traverses from different oceanic ridges demonstrated an excellent correspondence with the magnetic polarity-reversal time scale established by Cox and Dalrymple on land. This reversal time scale went back some three million years, but since then, further extrapolation based on marine magnetic anomalies (confirmed by deep-sea drilling) has extended the magnetic anomaly time scale far into the Cretaceous Period, which spans the interval from about 145 to 65 million years ago.

About the same time, Canadian geologist Laurence W. Morley, working independently of Vine and Matthews, came to the same explanation for the marine magnetic anomalies. Publication of his paper was delayed by unsympathetic referees and technical problems and occurred long after Vine's and Matthews's work had already firmly taken root.

Toward a Unifying Theory

With support of Hess's seafloor spreading model increasing, the scientific focus turned to explaining the driving forces of continental drift. The analysis work of Dan P. McKenzie, Robert L. Parker, and W. Jason Morgan produced conceptual models that described how tectonic plates moved around the globe. This work was validated by the computer modelling efforts of Xavier Le Pinchon. Other technological advances, including seismic tomography, continue to provide clues on how magma behaves underneath the lithosphere and its possible role as a driver of continental drift.

The Determination of Plate Thickness

After marine magnetic anomalies were explained, the cumulative evidence caused the concept of seafloor spreading to be widely accepted. However, the process responsible for continental drift remained enigmatic. Two important concerns remained. The spreading seafloor was generally seen as a thin-skin process, most likely having its base at the Mohorovičić discontinuity—that is, the boundary between the crust and mantle. If only oceanic crust was involved in seafloor spreading, as seemed to be the case in the Pacific Ocean, the thinness of the slab was not disturbing, even though the ever-increasing number of known fracture zones with their close spacing implied oddly narrow but very long convection cells. More troubling was the fact that the Atlantic Ocean had a well-developed oceanic ridge but lacked trenches adequate to dispose of the excess oceanic crust. This implied that the adjacent continents needed to travel with the spreading seafloor, a process that, given the thin but clearly undeformed slab, strained credulity.

Working independently but along very similar lines, McKenzie and Parker of Britain and Morgan of the United States resolved these issues. McKenzie and Parker showed with a geometric analysis that, if the moving slabs of crust were thick enough to be regarded as rigid and thus to remain undeformed, their motions on a sphere would lead precisely to those divergent, convergent, and transform boundaries that are indeed observed. Morgan demonstrated that the directions and rates of movement had been faithfully recorded by magnetic anomaly patterns and transform faults. He also proposed that the plates extended approximately 100 km (60 miles) to the base of a rigid lithosphere, which coincided with the top of the weaker asthenosphere. Seismologists had previously identified this boundary, which is marked by strong attenuation of earthquake waves, as a fundamental division in Earth's upper layers. Therefore, according to Morgan, this was the boundary above which the plates moved.

In 1968, a computer analysis by the French geophysicist Le Pichon proved that the plates did indeed form an integrated system where the sum of all crust generated at oceanic ridges is balanced by the cumulative amount destroyed in all subduction zones. That same year, the American geophysicists Bryan Isacks, Jack Oliver, and Lynn R. Sykes showed that the theory, which they enthusiastically labeled the "new global tectonics," was capable of accounting for the larger part of Earth's seismic activity. Almost immediately, others began to consider seriously the ability of the theory to explain mountain building and sea-level changes.

Plate-Driving Mechanisms and the Role of the Mantle

By the late 1960s, details of the processes of plate movement and of boundary interactions, along with much of the plate history of the Cenozoic Era (the past 65 million years), had been worked out. Yet the driving forces that bedeviled Wegener continue to remain enigmatic because there is little information about what happens beneath the plates.

The Convection of Earth's Mantle

Most agree that plate movement is the result of the convective circulation of Earth's heated interior, much as envisaged by Arthur Holmes in 1929. The heat source for convection is thought to be the decay of radioactive elements in the mantle. How this convection propels the plates is poorly understood. In the western Pacific Ocean, the subduction of old, dense oceanic crust may be self-propelled. The weight of the subducted slab may pull the rest of the plate toward the trench, a process known as slab pull. In the Atlantic Ocean, however, westward drift of North America and eastward drift of Europe and Africa may be due to push at the spreading ridge, known as ridge push. Hot mantle spreading out laterally beneath the ridges or hot spots may speed up or slow down the plates, a force known as mantle drag. However, the mantle flow pattern at depth does not appear to be reflected in the surface movements of the plates.

The relationship between the circulation within Earth's mantle and the movement of the lithospheric plates remains a first-order problem in the understanding of plate-driving mechanisms. Circulation in the mantle occurs by thermal convection, whereby warm, buoyant material rises, and cool, dense material sinks. Convection is possible even though the mantle is solid; it occurs by solid-state creep, similar to the slow downhill movement of valley glaciers. Materials can flow in this fashion if they are close to their melting temperatures. Several different models of mantle convection have been proposed. The simplest, called whole mantle convection, describes the presence of several large cells that rise from the core mantle boundary beneath oceanic ridges and begin their descent to that boundary at subduction zones. Some geophysicists argue for layered mantle convection, suggesting that more vigorous convection in the upper mantle is decoupled from that in the lower mantle. This model would be supported if it turned out that the boundary between the upper and lower mantle is coincident with a change in composition. A third model, known as the mantle plume model, suggests that upwelling is focused in plumes that ascend from the core-mantle boundary, whereas diffuse return flow is accomplished by subduction zones, which, according to this model, extend to the core-mantle boundary.

Seismic Tomography

A powerful technique, seismic tomography, is providing insights into this problem. This technique is similar in principle to that of the CT (computed tomography) scan and creates three-dimensional images of Earth's interior by combining information from many earthquakes. Seismic waves generated at the site, or focus, of an earthquake spread out in all directions, similar to light rays from a light source. As earthquakes occur in many parts of Earth's crust, information from many sources can be synthesized, mimicking the rotating X-ray beam of a CT scan. Because their speed depends on the density, temperature, pressure, rigidity, and phase of the material through which they pass, the velocity of seismic waves provides clues to the composition of Earth's interior. Seismic energy is absorbed by warm material, so that the waves are slowed down. As a result, anomalously warm areas in the mantle are seismically slow, clearly distinguishing them from colder, more rigid, anomalously fast regions.

Tomographic imaging shows a close correspondence between surface features such as ocean ridges and subduction zones to a depth of about 100 km (60 miles). Hot regions in the mantle occur beneath oceanic ridges, and cold regions occur beneath subduction zones. However, at greater depths, the pattern is more complex, suggesting that the simple whole mantle-convection model is not appropriate. On the other hand, subduction zones beneath Central America and Japan have been tracked close to the core-mantle boundary, suggesting that transition between the upper and lower mantle is not an impenetrable barrier to mantle flow. If so, convection is not decoupled across that boundary, again casting doubt upon the layered mantle model. Imaging the mantle directly beneath hot spots has identified anomalously warm mantle down to the core-mantle boundary, providing strong evidence for the existence of plumes and the possibility that the mantle plume hypothesis may indicate an important mechanism involved in mantle convection.

Dissenting Opinions and Unanswered Questions

While strongly supported by evidence from a variety of disciplines, the theory of plate tectonics had detractors throughout the middle of the 20th century. Several scientists who did not embrace the theory developed counterproposals. Although these counterproposals became discredited over time, the issues they raise continue to be debated.

The Dissenters

After decades of controversy, the concept of continental drift was finally accepted by the majority of Western scientists as a consequence of plate tectonics. Sir Harold Jeffreys continued his lifelong rejection of continental drift on grounds that his estimates of the properties of the mantle indicated the impossibility of plate movements. He did not, in general, consider the mounting geophysical and geologic arguments that supported the concept of Earth's having a mobile outer shell.

Russian scientists, most notably Vladimir Vladimirovich Belousov, continued to advocate a model of Earth with stationary continents dominated by vertical motions. The model, however, only vaguely defined the forces supposedly responsible for the motions. In later years, Russian geologists came to regard plate tectonics as an attractive theory and a viable alternative to the concepts of Belousov and his followers.

In 1958, the Australian geologist S. Warren Carey proposed a rival model, known as the expanding Earth model. Carey accepted the existence and early Mesozoic breakup of Pangea and the subsequent dispersal of its fragments and formation of new ocean basins, but he attributed it all to the expansion of Earth, the planet presumably having had a much smaller diameter in the late Paleozoic. In his view, the continents represented the preexpansion crust, and the enlarged surface was to be entirely accommodated within the oceans. This model accounted for a spreading ocean floor and for the young age of the oceanic crust; however, it failed to deal adequately with the evidence for subduction and compression. Carey's model also did not explain why the process should not have started until some four billion years after Earth was formed, and it lacked a reasonable mechanism for so large an expansion. Finally, it disregarded the evidence for continental drift before the existence of Pangea.

Unanswered Questions

In his famous book, *The Structure of Scientific Revolutions* (1962), the philosopher Thomas S. Kuhn pointed out that science does not always advance in the gradual and stately fashion commonly attributed to it. Most natural sciences begin with observations collected at random, without much regard to their significance or relationship between one another. As the numbers of observations increase, someone eventually synthesizes them into a comprehensive model, known as a paradigm. A paradigm is the framework, or context that is assumed to be correct, and so guides interpretations and other models. When a paradigm is accepted, advances are made by application of the paradigm. A crisis arises when the weight of observations points to the inadequacy of the old paradigm, and there is no comprehensive model that can explain these contradictions. Major breakthroughs often come from an intuitive leap that may be contrary to conventional wisdom and widely accepted evidence, while strict requirements for verification and proof are temporarily relaxed. If a new paradigm is to be created, it must explain most of the observations of the old paradigm and most of the contradictions.

This paradigm shift constitutes a scientific revolution; therefore, it often becomes widely accepted before the verdict from rigorous analysis of evidence is completely in. Such was certainly the case with the geologic revolution of plate tectonics, which also confirms Kuhn's view that a new paradigm is unlikely to supersede an existing one until there is little choice but to acknowledge that the conventional theory has failed. Thus, while Wegener did not manage to persuade the scientific world of continental drift, the successor theory, plate tectonics, was readily embraced 40 years later, even though it remained open to much of the same criticism that had caused the downfall of continental drift.

The greatest successes of plate tectonics have been achieved in the ocean basins, where additional decades of effort have confirmed its postulates and enabled investigators to construct a credible history of past plate movements. Inevitably in less-rigorous form, the reconstruction of early Mesozoic and Paleozoic continental configurations has provided a powerful tool with which to resolve many important questions.

There is further evidence, as held by the American geophysicist Thomas H. Jordan, that the base of the plates extends far deeper into the asthenosphere below the continents than below the oceans. How much of an impediment this might be for the free movement of plates and how it might affect their boundary interactions remain open questions. Others have postulated that the lower layer of the lithosphere peels off and sinks late in any collision sequence, producing high heat flow, volcanism, and an upper lithospheric zone vulnerable to contraction by thrusting.

It is understandable that any simple global tectonic model would work better in the oceans, which, being young, retain a record of only a brief and relatively uneventful history. On the continents, almost four billion years of growth and deformation, erosion, sedimentation, and igneous intrusion have produced a complex imprint that, with its intricate zones of varying strength, must directly affect the application of modern plate forces. Seismic reflection studies of the deep structure of the continents have demonstrated just how complex the events that form the continents and their margins may have been, and their findings sometimes are difficult to reconcile with the accretionary structures one would expect to see as a result of subduction and collision.

Notwithstanding these cautions and the continuing lack of an agreed-upon driving mechanism for the plates, one cannot help but conclude that the plate tectonics revolution has been fruitful and has immensely advanced the scientific understanding of Earth. Like all paradigms in science, it will most likely one day be replaced by a better one; yet there can be little doubt that, whatever the new theory may state, continental drift will be part of it.

PLATE TECTONICS AND THE GEOLOGIC PAST

The extent to which plate tectonics has influenced Earth's evolution through geologic time depends on when the process started. This is a matter of ongoing debate among geologists. The principal problem is that almost all oceanic crust older than about 200 million years has been obliterated by subduction. Although thick sequences of marine sedimentary rocks up to 3.5 billion years old imply that oceanic environments did exist early in Earth's history, virtually none of the oceanic crust that underlay these sediments has been preserved. Despite these disadvantages, there is enough fragmentary evidence to suggest that plate tectonic processes similar to those of today extend back in time at least as far as the Early Proterozoic Era, some 2.5 to 1.6 billion years ago.

The Wilson Cycle

The first step toward this conclusion was once again provided by J. Tuzo Wilson in 1966, when he proposed that the Appalachian-Caledonide mountain belt of western

Europe and eastern North America was formed by the destruction of an ocean that predated the Atlantic Ocean. Wilson was impressed with the similarity of thick sequences of Cambrian-Ordovician marine sediments to those of modern continental shelves. In a Pangea reconstruction, Wilson showed that these shelflike sediments extend along the entire length of the mountain chain from Scandinavia to the southeastern United States. However, these shelf sequences contain two distinct fossil assemblages on opposite sides of the mountain chain. The assemblage on the western side of the mountain chain he named the Pacific Realm, whereas the eastern side of the chain he named the Atlantic Realm. Both the Pacific and Atlantic realms could be traced for thousands of kilometres along the length of the mountain belt, but neither could be traced across it. Wilson concluded that these sediments with distinctive faunal realms represented two opposing flanks of an ancient ocean that was consumed by subduction to form the Appalachian-Caledonide mountain belt. According to this model, subduction in this ocean in Ordovician times led to the foundering of the continental shelves and the formation of volcanic arcs. The basaltic complexes of western Newfoundland were interpreted as ophiolitic complexes representing slivers of oceanic crust that escaped subduction as they were emplaced onto the continental margin. Continued subduction resulted in the closure of this ocean in the Devonian. Rocks representing each of these environments were found, lending strong support to this model. This ocean was subsequently named Iapetus, for the father of Atlantis in Greek mythology.

The concept that oceans may close and then reopen became known as the Wilson cycle, and with its acceptance came the application of plate tectonic principles to ancient orogenic belts. But how far back these principles may be extended is still an open question.

In the absence of the seafloor record, evidence of ancient oceans may be obtained from thick sedimentary sequences similar to those of modern continental shelves or from preserved features formed in or around subduction zones, such as accretionary wedges, glaucophane-bearing blueschists, volcanic rocks with compositions similar to modern island arcs, and remnants of oceanic crust preserved as ophiolites obducted onto continents. These features can be confidently identified in the Paleozoic Era (approximately 540 to 250 million years ago), and possibly the Neoproterozoic Era (the later part of the Proterozoic Eon, occurring approximately 1 billion to 540 million years ago), but their recognition is more problematic with increasing age. It is not known with any certainty whether this is because the dynamic nature of Earth's surface obliterates such evidence or because processes different from the modern form of plate tectonics existed at the time. Since the 1990s, however, most geoscientists have begun to accept that some form of plate tectonics occurred throughout the Proterozoic Eon, which commenced 2.5 billion years ago, and some extend these models back into the Archean, more than 2.5 billion years ago.

Some of the critical evidence supporting this assertion comes from a suite of rocks in the Canadian Shield known as the Trans-Hudson belt. This belt separates stable regions of continental crust, known as cratons. Marc St-Onge and colleagues from the Geological Survey of Canada provided strong evidence that the formation of the Trans-Hudson belt represents the oldest documented example of a Wilson cycle in which the cratonic areas, once separated by oceans, were brought together by subduction and continental collision. They found thick sedimentary sequences typical of modern continental rifts that are about 2 billion years old, and they found ophiolites of about the same age, which indicated that rifting resulted in continental drift and formation of an ocean. About 1.85 billion years ago, volcanic rocks typical of modern island arcs were deposited on top of this sequence, indicating that the continental margins had foundered and become subduction zones. Finally, they dated the time of continental collision at about 1.8 billion years. This collisional event is particularly important because welding the cratons together provided the core of the continent that was ultimately to become North America.

The Supercontinent Cycle

Although the Wilson cycle provided the means for recognizing the formation and destruction of ancient oceans, it did not provide a mechanism to explain why this occurred. In the early 1980s, a controversial concept known as the supercontinent cycle was developed to address this problem. When viewed in a global context, it is apparent that episodes of continental rifting and mountain building are not equally distributed throughout geologic time but instead are concentrated in relatively short time intervals approximately 350 to 500 million years apart. Mountain building associated with the formation of Pangea peaked at about 300 million years ago. This episode was preceded by other mountain-building events peaking at 650 million and at 1.1, 1.6, 2.1, and 2.6 billion years ago. Like Pangea, could these episodes represent times of supercontinent amalgamation? Similarly, the breakup of Pangea is documented by continental-rifting events that began about 200 million years ago. However, regionally extensive and thick sequences of similar deposits occur 550 million years ago and 1, 1.5, and 2 billion years ago. Could these represent times of supercontinent dispersal?

If indeed a supercontinent cycle exists, then there must be mechanisms responsible for breakup and amalgamation. The first step is to examine why a supercontinent like Pangea would break up. There are several theories, the most popular of which, proposed by American geophysicist Don Anderson, attributes breakup to the insulating properties of the supercontinent, which blocks the escape of mantle heat. As a result, the mantle beneath the supercontinent becomes anomalously hot, and vast volumes of basaltic magma pond beneath it, forcing it to arch up and crack. Magma invades the cracks, and the process of continental rifting, ultimately leading to seafloor spreading, begins. This model implies that supercontinents have in-built obsolescence and can exist only for so long before the buildup of heat beneath them results in their fragmentation. The dating of emplacement of vast suites of basaltic magma, known as basaltic dike swarms, is consistent with the ages of continental rifting, suggesting that mantle upwelling was an important contributor to the rifting process.

Continental Reconstructions

Magnetic anomalies, transform faults, hot spots, and apparent polar wandering paths permit rigorous geometric reconstructions of past plate positions, shapes, and movements. These reconstructions, known as paleogeographic reconstructions, show the changing geography of Earth's past and can be determined with excellent precision for the past 150 million years. Before that time, however, the absence of the ocean-floor record makes the process significantly more challenging. A variety of geologic data is used to help determine the proper fit of continents through time. Some of the methods used to test these reconstructions are based on matching patterns from one continental block to another and are similar to the approach of Wegener. However, modern geoscientists have more precise data that help constrain these reconstructions. Of the many advances, perhaps the most significant are the improved analytical techniques for radiometric dating, allowing the age of geologic events to be determined with much greater precision.

Since the 1990s, the database has improved so that reasonably constrained reconstructions can now be made as far back as 1 billion years. For example, the abundance of continental-collisional events about 1.1 billion years ago is one of the principal lines of evidence suggesting the presence of a supercontinent that is given the name of Rodinia. By about 760 million years ago, a number of continental-rift sequences had developed, suggesting that Rodinia had begun to break up. Between about 650 and 550 million years ago, however, a number of mountain belts formed by continental collision, which resulted in the amalgamation of Gondwana. The continental fragment that rifted away from Laurentia (the name given to ancestral North America) did not return to collide with North America as predicted by a simple Wilson cycle. Instead, it rotated counterclockwise away from Laurentia until it collided with eastern Africa.

THE INTERACTIONS OF TECTONICS WITH OTHER SYSTEMS

The forces that influence the movement of tectonic plates naturally affect the arrangement of the lithosphere; however, they also have the ability to change other aspects of the Earth system. In the hydrosphere, plate movement can alter the shape of the ocean basins as well as the chemistry of sea water. Tectonic activity can create, as well as destroy, habitats. In addition, modifications to the arrangement of continents may alter the path of ocean currents and thus bring about climatic changes.

Earth's Oceans

Sea Level

As plate tectonics changes the shape of ocean basins, it fundamentally affects long-term variations in global sea level. For example, the geologic record in which thick sequences of continental shelf sediments were deposited demonstrates that the breakup of Pangea resulted in the flooding of continental margins, indicating a rise in sea level. There are several contributing factors. First, the presence of new ocean ridges displaces seawater upward and outward across the continental margins. Second, the dispersing continental fragments subside as they cool. Third, the volcanism associated with breakup introduces greenhouse gases in the atmosphere, which results in global warming, causing continental glaciers to melt.

As the ocean widens, its crust becomes older and denser. It therefore subsides, eventually forming ocean trenches. As a result, ocean basins can hold more water, and sea level drops. This changes once again when subduction commences. Subduction preferentially consumes the oldest oceanic crust, so that the average age of oceanic crust becomes younger, and the material therefore becomes more buoyant. This increased buoyancy causes sea level to rise once more.

Composition of Ocean Water

Water's strong properties as a solvent mean that it is rarely pure. Ocean water contains about 96.5 percent by weight of pure water, with the remaining 3.5 percent predominantly consisting of ions such as chloride (1.9 percent), sodium, (1.1 percent), sulfate (0.3 percent), and magnesium (0.1 percent). The drainage of water from continents via the hydrologic cycle plays an important role in transporting chemicals from the land to the sea. The effect of this drainage is profoundly influenced by the presence of mountain belts. For example, the erosional power of the Ganges River, which drains from the Himalayas, carries 1.45 billion metric tons of sediment to the sea annually. This load is nine times that of the Mississippi River. The processes of weathering and erosion easily strip soluble elements such as sodium from their host minerals, and the relatively high concentration of sodium in ocean water is attributed to the effects of continental drainage.

Until the advent of plate tectonics, uncovering the source of chlorine was problematic because chlorine is present in only very minor amounts in the continental crust. Scientists hypothesized that the source of this element may lie in underwater volcanic activity. In the late 1970s, three scientists investigating the oceanic ridge off the coast of Peru from a submersible craft documented the occurrence of superheated jets of water, up to 350 °C (660 °F), continuously erupting from chimneys that stood 13 metres (43 feet) above the ocean floor. These hot springs were found to be rich in chlorine and metals, confirming that the source of chlorine in the oceans lay in the tectonic processes occurring at oceanic ridges.

Life

The continuous rearrangement over time of the size and shape of ocean basins and continents, accompanied by changes in ocean circulation and climate, has had a major impact on the development of life on Earth. One of the first studies of the potential effects of plate tectonics on life was published in 1970 by American geologists James W. Valentine and Eldridge M. Moores, who proposed that the diversity of life increased as continents fragmented and dispersed and diminished when they were joined together.

Deep Sea Vents

Plate tectonics has influenced the evolution and propagation of life in a variety of ways. The study of oceanic ridges revealed the presence of bizarre life adjacent to the chimneys of superheated water that together make up about 1 percent of the world's ecosystems. The existence of these life-forms in the deep ocean cannot be based on photosynthesis. Instead, they are nourished by minerals and heat. The energy released when hydrogen sulfide in the vent reacts with seawater is utilized by bacteria to convert inorganic carbon dioxide dissolved in seawater into organic compounds, a process known as chemosynthesis. Some scientists speculate that the cumulative effects of this process over time have had a significant effect on evolution. Others suggest that similar processes may ultimately be responsible for the origin of life on Earth.

Evolution

When Laurentia began to rift apart and the Atlantic Ocean started to open during the middle Mesozoic, the differences between the faunas of opposite shores gradually increased in an almost linear fashion—the greater the distance, the smaller the number of families in common. The difference increased more rapidly in the South Atlantic than in the North Atlantic, where a land connection between Europe and North America persisted until about 60 million years ago.

After the breakup of Pangea, no land animal could become dominant because the continents were disconnected. As a result, separate landmasses evolved highly specialized fauna. South America, for example, was rich in marsupial mammals, which had few predators. North America, on the other hand, was rich in placental mammals. However, about three million years ago, volcanic activity associated with subduction of the eastern Pacific Ocean formed a land bridge across the isthmus of Panama, reconnecting the separate landmasses.

The emergence of the isthmus made it possible for land animals to cross, forcing previously separated fauna to compete. Numerous placental mammals and herbivores migrated from north to south. They adapted well to the new environment and were more successful than the local fauna in competing for food. The invasion of highly adaptable carnivores from the north contributed to the extinction of at least four orders of South American land mammals. A few species, notably the armadillo and the opossum, managed to migrate in the opposite direction. Ironically, many of the invading northerners, such as the llama and tapir, subsequently became extinct in their country of origin and found their last refuge to the south.

Extinction

Perhaps the most dramatic example of the potential impact of plate tectonics on life occurred toward the end of the Permian Period (about 300 to 250 million years ago). During this time, several extinction events caused the permanent disappearance of half of Earth's known biological families. The marine realm was most affected, losing more than 90 percent of its species. This drop may be attributed in part to biogeographic changes associated with the formation of Pangea. Other factors, such as a sharp decrease in the area of shallow-water habitats, or a change in ocean fertility due to a lack of upwelling of nutrient-rich deep currents, have also been invoked.

The extinction had a complex history. High latitudes were affected first as a result of the waning of the Permian ice age when the southern edge of Pangea moved off the South Pole. The equatorial and subtropical zones appear to have been affected somewhat later by a global cooling. On the other hand, the extinctions were not felt as strongly on the continent itself. Instead, the vast semiarid and arid lands that emerged on so large a continent, the shortening of its moist coasts, and the many mountain ranges formed from the collisions that led to the formation of the supercontinent provided strong incentives for evolutionary adaptation to dry or high-altitude environments.

Earth's Climate

Climate changes associated with the supercontinent of Pangea and with its eventual breakup and dispersal provide an example of the effect of plate tectonics on paleoclimate. Pangea was completely surrounded by a world ocean (Panthalassa) extending from pole to pole and spanning 80 percent of the circumference of Earth at the paleoequator. The equatorial current system, driven by the trade winds, resided in warm latitudes much longer than today, and its waters were therefore warmer. The gyres that occupy most of the Southern and Northern hemispheres were also warmer, and consequently the temperature gradient from the paleoequator to the poles was less pronounced than it is at present.

Early in the Mesozoic, Gondwana split from its northern counterpart, Laurasia, to form the Tethys seaway, and the equatorial current became circumglobal. Equatorial surface waters were then able to circumnavigate the world and became even warmer. How this flow influenced circulation at higher latitudes is unclear. From about 100 to 70 million years ago, isotopic records show that Arctic and Antarctic surface water temperatures were at or above 10 °C (50 °F), and the polar regions were warm enough to support forests.

As the dispersal of continents following the breakup of Pangea continued, however, the surface circulation of the oceans began to approach the more complex circulation patterns of today. About 100 million years ago, the northward drift of Australia and South America created a new circumglobal seaway around Antarctica, which remained centred on the South Pole. A vigorous circum-Antarctic current developed, isolating the southern continent from the warmer waters to the north. At the same time, the equatorial current system became blocked, first in the Indo-Pacific region and next in the Middle East and eastern Mediterranean and, about 6 million years ago, by the emergence of the Isthmus of Panama. As a result, the equatorial waters were heated less and the mid-latitude ocean gyres were not as effective in keeping the high-latitude waters warm. Because of this, an ice cap began to form on Antarctica some 20 million years ago and grew to roughly its present size about 5 million years later. This ice cap cooled the waters of the adjacent ocean to such a low temperature that the waters sank and initiated the north-directed abyssal flow that marks the present deep circulation.

Also, at about six million years ago, the collision between Africa and Europe temporarily closed the Strait of Gibraltar, isolating the Mediterranean Sea and restricting its circulation. Evaporation, which produced thick salt deposits, virtually dried up this sea and lowered the salt content of the world's oceans, allowing seawater to freeze at higher temperatures. As a result, polar ice sheets grew, and sea level fell. About 500,000 years later, the barrier between the Mediterranean and the Atlantic Ocean was breached, and open circulation resumed.

The Quaternary Ice Age arrived in full when the first ice caps appeared in the Northern Hemisphere about two million years ago. It is highly unlikely that the changing configuration of continents and oceans can be held solely responsible for the onset of the Quaternary Ice Age, even if such factors as the drift of continents across the latitudes (with the associated changes in vegetation) and reflectivity for solar heat are included. There can be little doubt, however, that it was a contributing factor and that recognition of its role has profoundly altered concepts of paleoclimatology.

OTHER CONCEPTS RELATED TO PLATE TECTONICS

A number of other phenomena are naturally associated with the movements of Earth's tectonic plates. For example, as continents collide or rift apart, they may produce significant areas of diastrophism (crustal deformation) or initiate orogenies (mountain-building events). In addition, the elevation of various landmasses and even the seafloor itself may be responses to isostasy.

Continental Drift

This is the process that governs large-scale horizontal movements of continents relative to one another and to the ocean basins during one or more episodes of geologic time. This concept was an important precursor to the development of the theory of plate tectonics, which incorporates it.

The idea of a large-scale displacement of continents has a long history. Noting the apparent fit of the bulge of eastern South America into the bight of Africa, the German naturalist Alexander von Humboldt theorized about 1800 that the lands bordering the Atlantic Ocean had once been joined. Some 50 years later, Antonio Snider-Pellegrini, a French scientist, argued that the presence of identical fossil plants in both North American and European coal deposits could be explained if the two continents had formerly been connected, a relationship otherwise difficult to account for. In 1908 Frank B. Taylor of the United States invoked the notion of continental collision to explain the formation of some of the world's mountain ranges.

The first truly detailed and comprehensive theory of continental drift was proposed in 1912 by Alfred Wegener, a German meteorologist. Bringing together a large mass of geologic and paleontological data, Wegener postulated that throughout most of geologic time there was only one continent, which he called Pangea. Late in the Triassic Period (which lasted from approximately 250 to 200 million years ago), Pangea fragmented, and the parts began to move away from one another. Westward drift of the Americas opened the Atlantic Ocean, and the Indian block drifted across the Equator to merge with Asia. In 1937 Alexander L. Du Toit, a South African geologist, modified Wegener's hypothesis by suggesting two primordial continents: Laurasia in the north and Gondwana in the south.

Aside from the congruency of continental shelf margins across the Atlantic, modern proponents of continental drift have amassed impressive geologic evidence to support their views. Indications of widespread glaciation from 380 to 250 million years ago are evident in Antarctica, southern South America, southern Africa, India, and Australia. If these continents were once united around the south polar region, this glaciation would become explicable as a unified sequence of events in time and space. Also, fitting the Americas with the continents across the

Atlantic brings together similar kinds of rocks, fossils, and geologic structures. A belt of ancient rocks along the Brazilian coast, for example, matches one in West Africa. Moreover, the earliest marine deposits along the Atlantic coastlines of either South America or Africa are Jurassic in age (approximately 200 to 145 million years old), which suggests that the ocean did not exist before that time.

Interest in continental drift increased in the 1950s as knowledge of Earth's geomagnetic field during the geologic past developed from the studies of the British geophysicists Stanley K. Runcorn, Patrick M. S. Blackett, and others. Ferromagnetic minerals such as magnetite acquire a permanent magnetization when they crystallize as constituents of igneous rock. The direction of their magnetization is the same as the direction of Earth's magnetic field at the time and place of crystallization. Particles of magnetized minerals released from their parent igneous rocks by weathering may later realign themselves with the existing magnetic field at the time these particles are incorporated into sedimentary deposits. Studies by Runcorn of the remanent magnetism in suitable rocks of different ages from Europe produced a "polar wandering curve" indicating that the magnetic poles were in different places at different times. This could be explained either by the migration of the magnetic pole itself (that is, polar wandering) or by the migration of Europe relative to a fixed pole (that is, continental drift).

However, further work showed that the polar wandering curves are different for the various continents. The possibility that they might reflect true wander of the poles was discarded, because it implies separate wanderings of many magnetic poles over the same period. However, these different paths are reconciled by joining the continents in the manner proposed by Wegener. The curves for Europe and North America, for example, are reconciled by the assumption that the latter has drifted about 30° westward relative to Europe since the Triassic Period.

Increased knowledge about the configuration of the ocean floor and the subsequent formulation of the concepts of seafloor spreading and plate tectonics provided further support for continental drift. During the early 1960s, the American geophysicist Harry H. Hess proposed that new oceanic crust is continually generated by igneous activity at the crests of oceanic ridges—submarine mountains that follow a sinuous course of about 65,000 km (40,000 miles) along the bottom of the major ocean basins. Molten rock material from Earth's mantle rises upward to the crests, cools, and is later pushed aside by new intrusions. The ocean floor is thus pushed at right angles and in opposite directions away from the crests.

By the late 1960s, several American investigators, among them Jack E. Oliver and Bryan L. Isacks, had integrated this notion of seafloor spreading with that of drifting continents and formulated the basis of plate tectonic theory. According to the latter hypothesis, Earth's surface, or lithosphere, is composed of a number of large, rigid plates that float on a soft (presumably partially molten) layer of the mantle known as the asthenosphere. Oceanic ridges occur along some of the plate margins. Where this is the case, the lithospheric plates separate, and the upwelling mantle material forms new ocean floor along the trailing edges. As the plates move away from the flanks of the ridges, they carry the continents with them.

On the basis of all these factors, it may be assumed that the Americas were joined with Europe and Africa until approximately 190 million years ago, when a rift split them apart along what is now the crest of the Mid-Atlantic Ridge. Subsequent plate movements averaging about 2 cm (0.8 inch) per year have taken the continents to their present position. It seems likely, though it is still unproven, that this breakup of a single landmass and the drifting of its fragments is merely the latest in a series of similar occurrences throughout geologic time.

Diastrophism

Diastrophism, which is also called tectonism, is a large-scale deformation of Earth's crust by natural processes, which leads to the formation of continents and ocean basins, mountain systems, plateaus, rift valleys, and other features by mechanisms such as lithospheric plate movement (that is, plate tectonics), volcanic loading, or folding.

The study of diastrophism encompasses the varying responses of the crust to tectonic stresses. These responses include linear or torsional horizontal movements (such as continental drift) and vertical subsidence and uplift of the lithosphere (strain) in response to natural stresses on Earth's surface such as the weight of mountains, lakes, and glaciers. Subsurface conditions also cause subsidence or uplift, known as epeirogeny, over large areas of Earth's surface without deforming rock strata. Such changes include the thickening of the lithosphere by overthrusting, changes in rock density of the lithosphere caused by metamorphism or thermal expansion and contraction, increases in the volume of the asthenosphere (part of the upper mantle supporting the lithosphere) caused by hydration of olivine, and orogenic, or mountain-building, movements.

Isostasy

The ideal theoretical balance of all large portions of Earth's lithosphere as though they were floating on the denser underlying layer is called isostasy. This denser layer is called the asthenosphere, a section of the upper mantle composed of weak, plastic rock that is about 110 km (70 miles) below the surface. Isostasy controls the regional elevations of continents and ocean floors in accordance with the densities of their underlying rocks. Imaginary columns of equal cross-sectional area that rise from the asthenosphere to the surface are assumed to have equal weights everywhere on Earth, even though their constituents and the elevations of their upper surfaces are significantly different. This means that an excess of mass seen as material above sea level, as in a mountain system, is due to a deficit of mass, or low-density roots, below sea level. Therefore, high mountains have low-density roots that extend deep into the underlying mantle. The concept of isostasy played an important role in the development of the theory of plate tectonics.

In 1735, expeditions over the Andes led by Pierre Bouguer, a French photometrist and the first to measure the horizontal gravitational pull of mountains, noted that the Andes could not represent a protuberance of rock sitting on a solid platform. If it did, then a plumb-line should be deflected from the true vertical by an amount proportional to the gravitational attraction of the mountain range. The deflection was less than that which was anticipated. About a century later, similar discrepancies were observed by Sir George Everest, surveyor general of India, in surveys south of the Himalayas, indicating a lack of compensating mass beneath the visible mountain ranges.

In the theory of isostasy, a mass above sea level is supported below sea level, and there is thus a certain depth at which the total weight per unit area is equal all around the Earth; this is known as the depth of compensation. The depth of compensation was taken to be 113 km (70 miles) according to the Hayford-Bowie concept, named for American geodesists John Fillmore Hayford and William Bowie. Owing to changing tectonic environments, however, perfect isostasy is approached but rarely attained, and some regions, such as oceanic trenches and high plateaus, are not isostatically compensated.

The Airy hypothesis says that Earth's crust is a more rigid shell floating on a more liquid substratum of greater density. Sir George Biddell Airy, an English mathematician and astronomer, assumed that the crust has a uniform density throughout. The thickness of the crustal layer is not uniform, however, and so this theory supposes that the thicker parts of the crust sink deeper into the substratum, while the thinner parts are buoyed up by it. According to this hypothesis, mountains have roots below the surface that are much larger than their surface expression. This is analogous to an iceberg floating on water, in which the greater part of the iceberg is underwater.

The Pratt hypothesis, developed by John Henry Pratt, English mathematician and Anglican missionary, supposes that Earth's crust has a uniform thickness below sea level with its base everywhere supporting an equal weight per unit area at a depth of compensation. In essence, this says that areas of Earth of lesser density, such as mountain ranges, project higher above sea level than do those of greater density. The explanation for this was that the mountains resulted from the upward expansion of locally heated crustal material, which had a larger volume but a lower density after it had cooled.

The Heiskanen hypothesis, developed by Finnish geodesist Weikko Aleksanteri Heiskanen, is an intermediate, or compromise, hypothesis between Airy's and Pratt's. This hypothesis says that approximately two-thirds of the topography is compensated by the root formation (the Airy model) and one-third by Earth's crust above the boundary between the crust and the substratum (the Pratt model).

Orogeny

An orogeny is a mountain-building event, generally one that occurs in geosynclinal areas. In contrast to epeirogeny, an orogeny tends to occur during a relatively short time in linear belts and results in intensive deformation. Orogeny is usually accompanied by folding and faulting of strata, development of angular unconformities (interruptions in the normal deposition of sedimentary rock), and the deposition of clastic wedges of sediments in areas adjacent to the orogenic belt. Regional metamorphism and magmatic activity are often associated with an orogenic event as well. Orogenies may result from subduction, terrane accretion (landmass expansion due to its collision with other landmasses), the underthrusting of continents by oceanic plates, continental collisions, the overriding of oceanic ridges by continents, and other causes.

Tectonics

Tectonics is the scientific study of the deformation of the rocks that make up Earth's crust and the forces that produce such deformation. It deals with the folding and faulting associated with mountain building; the large-scale, gradual upward and downward movements of the crust (epeirogenic movements); and sudden horizontal displacements along faults. Other phenomena studied include igneous processes and metamorphism. Tectonics embraces as its chief working principle the concept of plate tectonics, a theory that was formulated in the late 1960s by American, Canadian, and British geophysicists to broaden and synthesize the notion of continental drift and the seafloor spreading hypothesis.

CHAPTER 2
VOLCANOES AND VOLCANISM

A volcano is a vent in the crust of the Earth or another planet or satellite, from which issue eruptions of molten rock, hot rock fragments, and hot gases. A volcanic eruption is an awesome display of Earth's power. Yet while eruptions are spectacular to watch, they can cause disastrous loss of life and property, especially in densely populated regions of the world. Sometimes beginning with an accumulation of gas-rich magma in reservoirs near the surface of Earth, they can be preceded by emissions of steam and gas from small vents in the ground and by a swarm of small earthquakes. In some cases, magma rises in conduits to the surface as a thin and fluid lava, either flowing out continuously or shooting straight up in glowing fountains or curtains. In other cases, entrapped gases tear the magma into shreds and hurl viscous clots of lava into the air. In more violent eruptions, the magma conduit is cored out by an explosive blast, and solid fragments are ejected in a great cloud of ash-laden gas that

Mount St. Helens volcano, viewed from the south during its eruption on May 18, 1980. © Getty Images

rises tens of thousands of metres into the air. One feared phenomenon accompanying some explosive eruptions is the nuée ardente, or pyroclastic flow, a fluidized mixture of hot gas and incandescent particles that sweeps down a volcano's flanks, incinerating everything in its path. Great destruction also can result when ash collects on a high snowfield or glacier, melting large quantities of ice into a flood that can rush down a volcano's slopes as an unstoppable mudflow.

Strictly speaking, the term *volcano* means the vent from which magma and other substances erupt to the surface, but it can also refer to the landform created by the accumulation of solidified lava and volcanic debris near the vent. One can say, for example, that large lava flows erupt from Mauna Loa volcano in Hawaii, referring here to the vent; but one can also say that Mauna Loa is a gently sloping volcano of great size, the reference in this case being to the landform. Volcanic landforms have evolved over time as a result of repeated volcanic activity. Mauna Loa typifies a shield volcano, which is a huge, gently sloping landform built up of many eruptions of fluid lava. Mount Fuji in Japan is an entirely different formation. With its striking steep slopes built up of layers of ash and lava, Mount Fuji is a classic stratovolcano. Iceland provides fine examples of volcanic plateaus, while the seafloor around Iceland provides excellent examples of submarine volcanic structures.

Volcanoes figure prominently in the mythology of many peoples who have learned to live with eruptions, but science was late in recognizing the important role of volcanism in the evolution of the Earth. As late as 1768, the first edition of *Encyclopædia Britannica* gave voice to a common misconception by defining volcanoes as "burning mountains, which probably are made up of sulphur and some other matter proper to ferment with it, and take fire." Today geologists agree that volcanism is a profound process resulting from the thermal evolution of planetary bodies. Heat does not easily escape from large bodies such as the Earth by the processes of conduction or radiation. Instead, heat is transferred from Earth's interior largely by convection—that is, the partial melting of Earth's crust and mantle and the buoyant rise of magma to the surface. Volcanoes are the surface sign of this thermal process. Their roots reach deep inside Earth, and their fruits are hurled high into the atmosphere.

Volcanoes are closely associated with plate tectonic activity. Most volcanoes, such as those of Japan and Iceland, occur on the margins of the enormous solid rocky

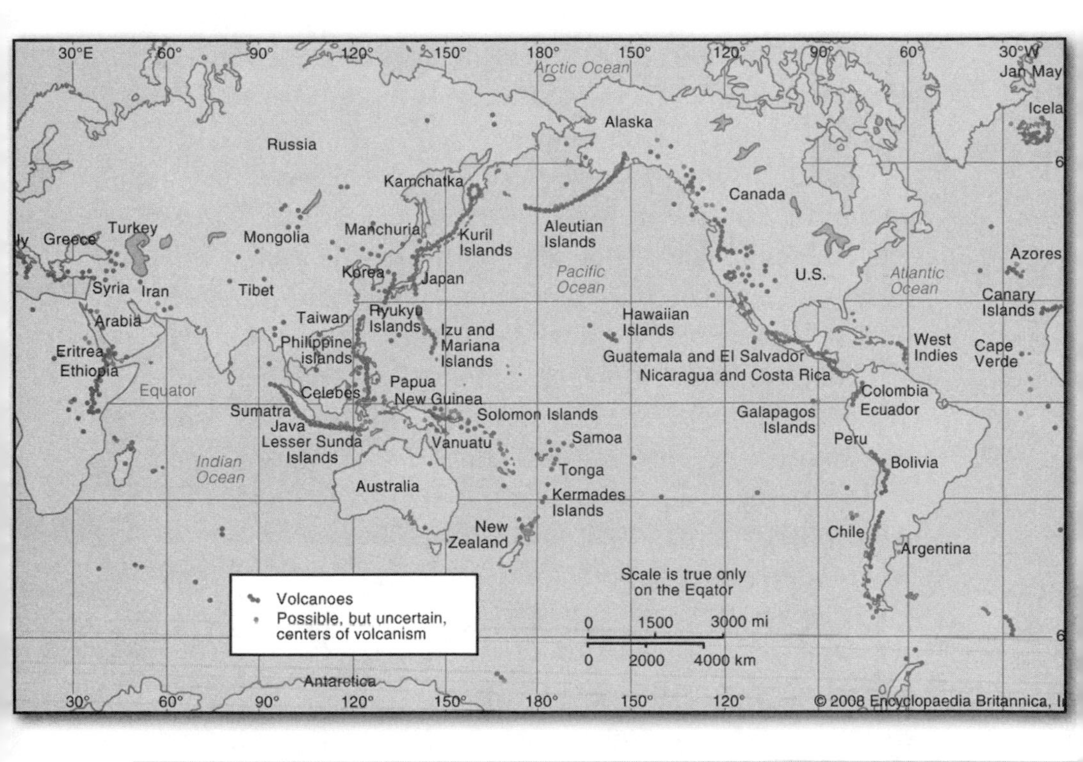

Volcanoes and thermal fields that have been active during the past 10,000 years. Encyclopædia Britannica, Inc.

plates that make up Earth's surface. Other volcanoes, such as those of the Hawaiian Islands, occur in the middle of a plate, providing important evidence as to the direction and rate of plate motion.

The study of volcanoes and their products is known as volcanology, but these phenomena are not the realm of any single scientific discipline. Rather, they are studied by many scientists from several specialties: geophysicists and geochemists, who probe the deep roots of volcanoes and monitor signs of future eruptions; geologists, who decipher prehistoric volcanic activity and infer the likely nature of future eruptions; biologists, who learn how plants and animals colonize recently erupted volcanic rocks; and meteorologists, who determine the effects of volcanic dust and gases on the atmosphere, weather, and climate.

Clearly the destructive potential of volcanoes is tremendous. But the risk to people living nearby can be reduced significantly by assessing volcanic hazards, monitoring volcanic activity and forecasting eruptions, and instituting procedures for evacuating populations. In addition, volcanism affects humankind in beneficial ways. Volcanism provides beautiful scenery, fertile soils, valuable mineral deposits, and geothermal energy. Over geologic time, volcanoes recycle Earth's hydrosphere and atmosphere.

VOLCANIC ERUPTIONS

The hazards associated with a volcanic eruption do not end with the sudden venting of rocks and other material. Lava and pyroclastic material traveling down the mountainside, suffocating gas clouds, sudden mudflows and tsunamis, and other hazards are capable of causing widespread death and devastation. In contrast, over the long term, these phenomena may promote life by replenishing the soil. Certain types of eruptions can also alter Earth's climate. Beyond the hazards associated with volcanic eruptions, the remainder of this chapter considers the various types of volcanic events, two archetypal 20th-century eruptions, the four worst eruptions in human history, and recent advances in volcanic forecasting and warning.

Lava, Gas, and Other Hazards

The list of hazards associated with volcanic eruptions is long and varied: lava flows, explosions, toxic gas clouds, ash falls, pyroclastic flows, avalanches, tsunamis, and mudflows. In addition to these immediate dangers, volcanic activity produces secondary effects such as property damage, crop loss, and perhaps changes to weather and climate. These hazards and long-term effects are described in this section.

Lava Flows

The root zone of volcanoes is found some 70 to 200 km (40 to 120 miles) below the surface of Earth. There, in Earth's upper mantle, temperatures are high enough to melt rock and form magma. At these depths, magma is generally less dense than the solid rocks surrounding and overlying it, and so it rises toward the surface by the buoyant force of gravity. In some cases, as in the undersea zones where the tectonic plates of Earth's crust are separating, magma may move directly up to the surface through fissures that reach as deep as the mantle. In other cases, it collects in large underground reservoirs known as magma chambers before erupting to the surface. Molten rock that reaches the surface is called lava.

The term *lava* is also used for the solidified rock formed by the cooling of a molten lava flow. The temperatures of molten lava range from about 700 to 1,200 °C (1,300 to 2,200 °F). The material can be very fluid, flowing almost like syrup, or it can be extremely stiff, scarcely flowing at all. The higher the lava's silica content, the higher its viscosity.

Mafic (ferromagnesian, dark-coloured) lavas such as basalt characteristically form flows known by the Hawaiian names *pahoehoe* and *aa* (or *a'a*). Pahoehoe lava flows are characterized by smooth, gently undulating, or broadly hummocky surfaces. The liquid lava flowing beneath a thin, still-plastic crust drags and wrinkles it into tapestry-like folds and rolls resembling twisted rope. Pahoehoe lava flows are fed almost wholly internally by streams of liquid lava flowing beneath a solidified or partly solidified surface. Typically, the margin of a pahoehoe flow advances by protruding one small toe or lobe after another.

In contrast to pahoehoe, the surface of aa lava is exceedingly rough, covered with a layer of partly loose, very irregular fragments commonly called clinkers. Aa lava flows are fed principally by rivers of liquid lava flowing in open channels. Typically, such a feeding river forms a narrow band that is 8 to 15 metres (25 to 50 feet) wide along the centre line of the flow, with broad fields of less actively moving clinkers on each side of it. At the front of the flow, clinkers from the top roll down and are overridden by the pasty centre layer, like a tread on an advancing bulldozer.

Pahoehoe and aa flows from the same erupting vent are usually identical in chemical composition. In fact, it is common for a flow that leaves the vent as pahoehoe to change to aa as it progresses downslope. The greater the viscosity and the greater the stirring of the liquid (as by rapid flow down a steep slope), the greater the tendency for the material to change from pahoehoe to aa. The reverse change rarely occurs.

Lavas of andesitic or intermediate composition commonly form a somewhat different type of flow, known as a block lava flow. These resemble aa in having tops consisting largely of loose rubble, but the fragments are more regular in shape, most of them polygons with fairly smooth sides. Flows of more siliceous lava tend to be even more fragmental than block flows.

Thin basaltic lava flows generally contain many holes, or vesicles, left by bubbles of gas frozen into the congealing liquid. Thick flows, which remain hot for long periods, may lose most of their gas before the lava congeals, and the resulting rock may be dense with few vesicles.

If the vast, unseen undersea lava flows of the oceanic ridge system are considered, lava flows are the most common products of Earth's volcanoes. As much as 99

Pahoehoe lava flow, Kilauea volcano, Hawaii, November 1985. J. D. Griggs U. S. Geological Survey

percent of the island of Hawaii is composed of aa and pahoehoe flows.

Explosions

Massive volcanic explosions are caused by the rapid expansion of gases, which in turn can be triggered by the sudden depressurization of a shallow hydrothermal system or gas-charged magma body or by the rapid mixing of magma with groundwater. The ash, cinders, hot fragments, and bombs thrown out in these explosions are the major products observed in volcanic eruptions around the world. These solid products are classified by size. Volcanic dust is the finest, usually about the consistency of flour. Volcanic

A cloud of ash and pumice rises into the air on July 22, 1980, following an explosive eruption of Mount St. Helens, Washington State, U.S. Mike Doukas/U.S. Geological Survey

ash is also fine but more gritty, with particles up to the size of grains of rice. Cinders, sometimes called scoriae, are next in size; these coarse fragments can range from 2 mm (0.08 inch) up to about 64 mm (2.5 inches). Fragments larger than 64 mm are called either blocks or bombs. Volcanic blocks are usually older rock broken by the explosive opening of a new vent. Large blocks ejected in such explosions have been hurled as far as 20 km (12 miles) from the vent. Volcanic bombs, in contrast, are generally incandescent and soft during their flight. Some bombs take on strange, twisted shapes as they spin through the air. Others have a cracked and separated crust that has cooled and hardened in flight; they are called "breadcrust bombs."

A directed blast in which one side of a volcanic cone fails, as happened at Mount St. Helens in the United States in 1980, can cause destruction over several hundred square kilometres on the failed flank of the volcano. This is especially true if the blast cloud is heavily laden with fragmental debris and becomes dense and fluidized. It then takes on characteristics similar to a pyroclastic flow.

Pyroclastic Flows

Pyroclastic flows are the most dangerous and destructive aspect of explosive volcanism. Variously called nuées ardentes ("glowing clouds"), glowing avalanches, or ash flows, they occur in many sizes and types. During a volcanic eruption, this fluidized mixture of hot rock fragments, hot gases, and entrapped air moves at high speed in thick, gray-to-black, turbulent clouds that hug the ground. The temperature of the volcanic gases can reach about 600 to 700 °C (1,100 to 1,300 °F). The velocity of a flow often exceeds 100 km (60 miles) per hour and may attain speeds as great as 160 km (100 miles) per hour. A pyroclastic flow can pour over the lip of an erupting vent, or it may form when an ash column becomes too dense to continue rising and falls back to the ground. In major caldera collapses associated with explosive volcanoes, huge pyroclastic flows may issue from the ring fractures as the caldera block subsides.

Flows may even travel some distance uphill when they have sufficient velocity, which they achieve either through the simple effects of gravity or from the force of a lateral blast out of the side of an exploding volcano. Reaching such temperatures and velocities, pyroclastic flows can be extremely dangerous.

They sweep away and incinerate nearly everything in their path. Smaller pyroclastic flows are often confined to valleys. Large pyroclastic flows may spread out as a blanket deposit across many hundreds or even thousands of square kilometres around a major caldera collapse. During the past two million years, the area around Yellowstone National Park in the western United States has undergone three major caldera collapses involving pyroclastic eruptions of 280 to 2,500 cubic km (67 to 600 cubic miles) of ash flows and ash falls.

Perhaps the most famous flow of this type occurred in 1902 on the French Caribbean island of Martinique, when a huge nuée ardente ("glowing cloud") swept down the slopes of Mount Pelée and incinerated the small port city of Saint-Pierre, killing all but two of its 29,000 residents.

Pyroclastic flows have their origin in explosive volcanic eruptions, when a violent expansion of gas shreds escaping magma into small particles, creating what are known as pyroclastic fragments. (The term *pyroclastic* derives from the Greek pyro, meaning "fire,"and clastic, meaning "broken.") Pyroclastic materials are classified according to their size, measured in millimetres: dust (less than 0.6 mm), ash (fragments between 0.6 and 2 mm), cinders (fragments between 2 and 64 mm, also known as lapilli), blocks (angular fragments greater than 64 mm), and bombs (rounded fragments greater than 64 mm). The fluid nature of a pyroclastic flow is maintained by the turbulence of its internal gases. Both the incandescent pyroclastic particles and the rolling clouds of dust that rise above them actively liberate more gas. The expansion of these gases accounts for the nearly frictionless character of the flow as well as its great mobility and destructive power.

The nomenclature of pyroclastic flows is complex for two main reasons. Varieties of pyroclastic flows have been named by volcanologists using several different languages, resulting in a multiplicity of terms. Also, the danger from pyroclastic flows is so great that they have seldom been observed during their formation. Therefore, the nature of the flows must be inferred from their deposits rather than from direct evidence, leaving ample room for interpretation. Ignimbrites (from the Latin for "fire rain rocks") are deposited by pumice flows, creating thick formations of various-sized fragments of very porous, frothlike volcanic glass. Ignimbrites are generally produced by large eruptions that form calderas. Nuées ardentes deposit ash- to block-sized fragments that are denser than pumice. Pyroclastic surges are low-density flows that leave thin but extensive deposits with cross-bedded layering. Ash flows leave deposits known as tuff, which are made up mainly of ash-sized fragments. Nuée ardente deposits are confined mainly in valleys, while ignimbrites form plateaulike deposits that bury the previous topography. Thick ignimbrites that were very hot when erupted may compact and consolidate into hard, welded tuffs.

The term *tephra* as originally defined was a synonym for pyroclastic materials, but it is now used in the more-restricted sense of pyroclastic materials deposited by falling through the air rather than those settling out of pyroclastic flows. For example, ash particles that fall from a high eruption cloud to form widespread layers downwind from a volcanic eruption are referred to as tephra and not as a pyroclastic flow deposit.

Many newspaper accounts of explosive volcanic eruptions incorrectly refer to pyroclastic flows as lava flows. Moving lava flows are composed of viscous, molten rock. Unlike pyroclastic flows, lavas move slowly, and on cooling they harden into solid rock.

Gas Clouds

Even beyond the limit of explosive destruction, the hot, ash-laden gas clouds associated with an explosive eruption can scorch vegetation and kill animals and people by suffocation. Gas clouds emitted from fumaroles (volcanic gas vents) or from the sudden overturn of a crater lake may contain suffocating or poisonous gases such as carbon dioxide, carbon monoxide, hydrogen sulfide, and sulfur dioxide. At Lake Nyos, a crater lake in Cameroon, West Africa, more than 1,700 people were killed by a sudden release of carbon dioxide in August 1986. Scientists theorize that carbon dioxide of volcanic origin had been seeping into the lake, perhaps for centuries, and had accumulated in its deep layers. It is thought that some disturbance, such as a large landslide into the lake, could have triggered the outburst of gas, creating an effervescence that stirred the lake and started the degassing.

The most common volcanic gases are water vapour, carbon dioxide, sulfur dioxide, and hydrogen sulfide. Small quantities of other volatile elements and compounds also are present, such as hydrogen, helium, nitrogen, hydrogen chloride, hydrogen fluoride, and mercury. The specific gaseous compounds released from magma depend on the temperature, pressure, and overall composition of the volatile elements present. The amount of available oxygen is of critical importance in determining which volatile gases are present. When oxygen is lacking, methane, hydrogen, and hydrogen sulfide are chemically stable, but when hot volcanic gases mix with atmospheric gases, water vapour, carbon dioxide, and sulfur dioxide are stable.

Some volcanic gases are less soluble in magma than others and therefore separate at higher pressures. Studies at Kilauea in Hawaii indicate that carbon dioxide begins to separate from its parent magma at depths of about 40 km (25 miles), whereas most of the sulfur gases and water are not released until the magma has nearly reached the surface. Fumaroles near Halemaumau Crater at Kilauea's summit are rich in carbon dioxide that leaks from the magma chamber located 3 to 4 km (1.9 to 2.5 miles) beneath the surface. Fumaroles on the rift zones of Kilauea, however, are richer in water vapour and sulfur because much of the carbon dioxide leaks away at the summit before the magma is intruded into the rift zones.

Ash Falls

Ash falls from continued explosive jetting of fine volcanic particles into high ash clouds generally do not cause any direct fatalities. However, where the ash accumulates more than a few centimetres, collapsing roofs and failure of crops are major secondary hazards. Crop failure can occur over large areas downwind from major ash eruptions, and widespread famine and disease may result, especially in poorly developed countries. In the long run, however, the decomposition of nutrient-rich volcanic fallout is responsible for some of the world's best soils.

Avalanches, Tsunamis, and Mudflows

Avalanches of rock and ice also are common on active volcanoes. They may occur with or without an eruption. Those without an eruption are often triggered by earthquakes, by weakening of rock into clay by hydrothermal activity, or by heavy rainfall or snowfall. Those associated with eruptions are sometimes caused by oversteepening of a volcano's flank by intrusion of a shallow body of magma within or just beneath the volcanic cone, as happened at Mount St. Helens.

A caldera collapse that is in part or entirely submarine usually generates a tsunami. The larger and more rapid the collapse, the larger the tsunami. Tsunamis also can be caused by avalanches or large pyroclastic flows rapidly entering the sea on the flank of a volcano.

Mudflows, or lahars, are common hazards associated with stratovolcanoes and can happen even without an eruption. They occur whenever floods of water mixed with ash, loose soil, or hydrothermal clay sweep down valleys that drain the sides of large stratovolcanoes. The huge mudflows generated by meltwater from the ice cap of Mount Ruiz, Colombia, in 1985 are classic examples of mudflows associated with eruptions. Heavy rainfall or earthquake-induced avalanches of ice or hydrothermal clay also can cause mudflows on steep volcanoes during periods of repose between eruptions.

Secondary Damage

Property damage from volcanic eruptions is difficult to estimate because of differing value systems and changes in land use. One study estimates an average of $1 billion per year in property damage worldwide from volcanic eruptions. As with casualties, a few eruptions cause staggering damage, while most are much less destructive. The

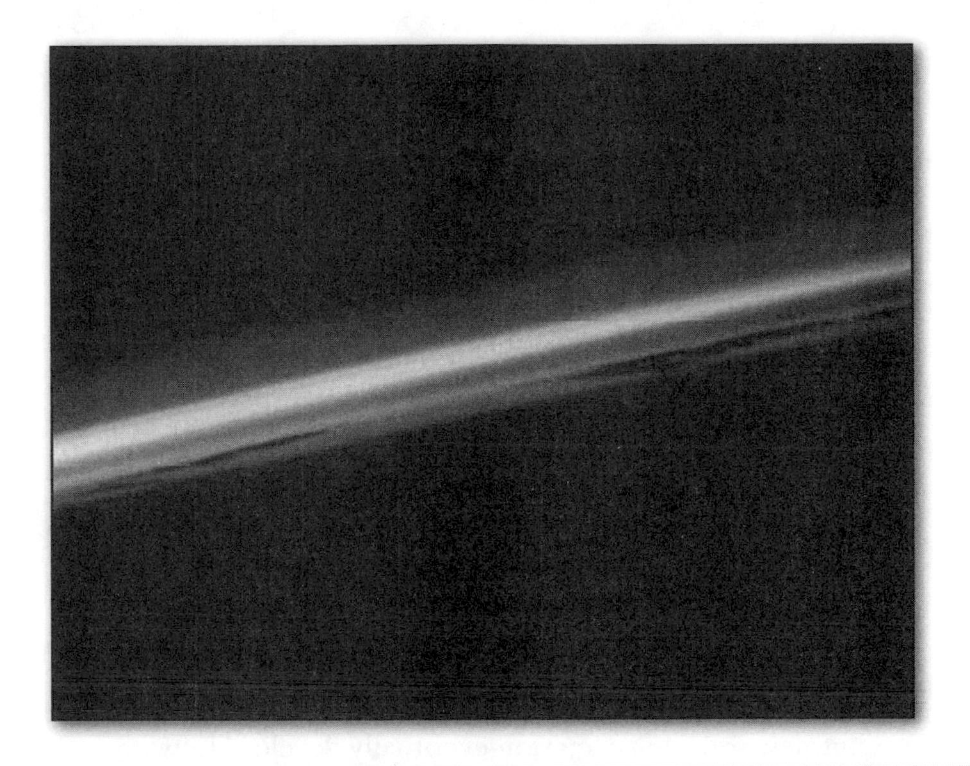

Earth's atmosphere showing the Mount Pinatubo dust layer, photographed from the U.S. space shuttle Atlantis, 1992. NASA/Johnson Space Center

Mount St. Helens eruption in 1980 caused more than $1 billion worth of damage, mainly to the timber industry. The economic cost of the 1991 eruption of Mount Pinatubo in the Philippines was estimated at $7 billion, though it is likely that losses continued to mount for years afterward because of the inundation of much arable land by mudflows.

A new danger that has emerged with the increase in air travel is the serious threat posed to jet aircraft by high clouds of volcanic ash and aerosols. These clouds cannot be detected by weather radar, and they are difficult for pilots to distinguish from meteorological clouds. In a small number of documented cases, jet engines have stopped operating after airliners have flown through volcanic clouds. Catastrophe was avoided only at the last minute when the pilots were able to restart the engines as their planes descended below the clouds. The engines had to be replaced and major abrasive damage to the planes repaired. During the Pinatubo eruption, aircraft had 16 damaging encounters with ash clouds, one as far away as 1,700 km (1,050 miles) west of the volcano. In response to these hazards, a worldwide system has been established to alert pilots by radio of volcanic eruption clouds and their probable extent.

Long-Term Environmental Effects

Not all volcanic phenomena are destructive. The oceans, atmosphere, and continents owe their origin and evolution in large measure to volcanic processes throughout geologic time. A lava flow may engulf and bury the land, but new soil and vegetation eventually develop. In warm, humid climates the recovery is rapid; a few decades will suffice to hide the rocky surface of solidified lava flows. In desert or Arctic climates, on the other hand, recovery is slower; flows more than 1,000 years old may still retain their barren appearance. Volcanic ash slowly weathers to form rich, loamy soils. On the volcanic island of Java, terraced rice paddies support a dense population. Across the Java Sea is Borneo, an island with a similar climate but no volcanoes. The jungles of Borneo provide only temporary slash-and-burn agriculture and support a much smaller population.

Climate, too, is subject to the effects of volcanic activity. High ash clouds, especially if they are rich in sulfur dioxide, can inject much fine dust and aerosol droplets of sulfuric acid into the stratosphere, above tropospheric rain clouds. Their height greatly increases the residence time of these fine particles in the atmosphere—they are not washed quickly back to Earth but spread slowly into haze layers that can blanket a hemisphere or even the entire Earth.

World climate seems to have been affected by the eruptions of Krakatoa (Krakatau) near Java in 1883, Mount Agung in Bali in 1963, and Pinatubo in 1991. The high ash clouds thrown up by these volcanoes apparently lowered average world temperature by about 0.5 °C (0.9 °F) over one to three years following their eruptions. Although world temperature data was poorly recorded in the early 1800s, the eruption of Mount Tambora on the island of Sumbawa in 1815 was followed in 1816 in North America and Europe by what was called "the year without a summer." On the other hand, other large eruptions, such as Novarupta near Mount Katmai in Alaska in 1912, appear to have produced no cooling effect. Records of average world temperature over the past several decades often show changes of 0.1 to 0.3 °C (0.2 to 0.5 °F) from year to year unrelated to any known volcanic eruptions, so it is difficult to establish with certainty whether volcanoes have a major impact on climate.

Direct sampling of the stratosphere has shown that the major haze-forming agent from volcanic eruptions is not fine dust but an aerosol of tiny sulfuric acid droplets. This indicates that the composition of high volcanic ash clouds may be as important as their volume in affecting climate. Atmospheric chemists are interested in atmospheric perturbations that may be caused not only by volcanic eruptions but also by man-made aerosols of chlorofluorocarbons, exhaust from high-altitude jet aircraft, and a general increase in carbon dioxide and other greenhouse gases from the burning of fossil fuels. Earth has many buffers that maintain its environment, but their interactions are not clearly understood. Many questions as to how volcanic and human activity affect climate remain largely unanswered, and they are important problems of ongoing research.

Six Types of Eruptions

Volcanoes are frequently classified by their size and shape, but they can also be classified by their eruptive habits. Indeed, the type of volcanic eruption that occurs plays an important role in the evolution of a volcanic landform, thus forming a significant link between eruptive habit and volcanic structure. In general, eruptions can be categorized as either effusive or explosive. Effusive eruptions involve the outpouring of basaltic magma that is relatively low in viscosity and in gas content. Explosive eruptions generally involve magma that is more viscous and has a higher gas content. Such magma is often shattered into pyroclastic fragments by explosive gas expansion during an eruption.

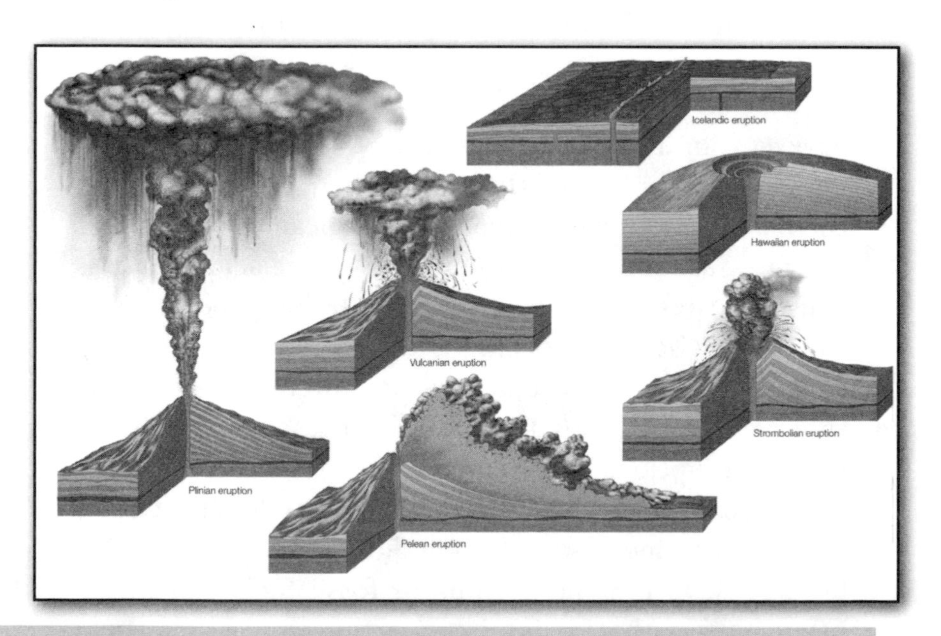

The major types of volcanic eruptions. Encyclopædia Britannica, Inc.

In more-detailed classification schemes based on character of eruption, volcanic activity and volcanic areas are commonly divided into six major types. They are listed as follows in order of increasing degree of explosiveness:

- Icelandic
- Hawaiian
- Strombolian
- Vulcanian
- Pelean
- Plinian

The Icelandic type is characterized by effusions of molten basaltic lava that flow from long, parallel fissures. Such outpourings often build lava plateaus.

The Hawaiian type is similar to the Icelandic variety. In this case, however, fluid lava flows from a volcano's summit and radial fissures to form shield volcanoes, which are quite large and have gentle slopes.

Strombolian eruptions involve moderate bursts of expanding gases that eject clots of incandescent lava in cyclical or nearly continuous small eruptions. Because of such small frequent outbursts, Stromboli volcano, located on Stromboli Island off the northeast coast of Italy, has been called the "lighthouse of the Mediterranean."

The Vulcanian type, named for Vulcano Island near Stromboli, generally involves moderate explosions of gas laden with volcanic ash. This mixture forms dark, turbulent eruption clouds that rapidly ascend and expand in convoluted shapes.

A Pelean eruption is associated with explosive outbursts that generate pyroclastic flows, dense mixtures of hot volcanic fragments and gas. Pelean eruptions are named for the destructive eruption of Mount Pelée on the

Eruption of Mount St. Helens on May 18, 1980. U.S. Geological Survey

Caribbean island of Martinique in 1902. The fluidized slurries produced by these eruptions are heavier than air but are of low viscosity and pour down valleys and slopes at great velocities. As a result, they are extremely destructive.

The Plinian type is an intensely violent kind of volcanic eruption exemplified by the outburst of Mount Vesuvius in Italy in 79 CE that killed the famous Roman scholar Pliny the Elder and was described in an eyewitness account by his nephew, the historian Pliny the Younger. In this type of eruption, gases boiling out of gas-rich magma generate enormous and nearly continuous jetting blasts that core out the magma conduit and rip it apart. The uprushing gases and volcanic fragments resemble a gigantic rocket blast directed vertically upward. Plinian eruption clouds can rise into the stratosphere and are sometimes continuously produced for several hours. Lightning strikes caused by a buildup of static electricity are common close to Plinian ash clouds, adding one more element of terror to the eruption.

Why are some volcanic eruptions so explosive while others are so spectacular but relatively harmless? The answer involves at least four factors: the amount of gas dissolved in the magma, the viscosity of the magma, the rate of decompression of the magma as it rises toward the surface, and the number of nucleation sites on which the gases can begin to form bubbles. Volcanoes related to converging plate margins generally have a high gas content, and their magma is very viscous. This combination is explosive because the gases cannot easily boil out; rather, they remain pent up until they reach the pressure at which they blow the viscous magma into fragments. The rate at which pressure is reduced also controls the explosiveness. If magma moves slowly toward the surface, its dissolved gases will be released slowly and can escape. During the

1991 Plinian-type eruption of Mount Pinatubo, magma moved quite rapidly toward the surface, resulting in retention of most of the dissolved gases. Finally, the speed at which gases are released from magma is affected by the number of small crystals, which can act as nucleation sites where gas bubbles begin to form. At Pinatubo the magma was more than 40 percent small crystals before the eruption, while at the Hawaiian volcanoes Kilauea and Mauna Loa the percentage of small crystals in the magma is very low (less than 5 percent).

Two 20th-Century Eruptions

There are many gradations among—and exceptions to—the idealized eruption types listed in the previous section, and it is not unusual for an eruption sequence to involve more than one type of activity. For example, the eruptions of Mount St. Helens from 1980 to 1986 followed a sequence of small Vulcanian-type explosions, large Pelean and Plinian explosions, and finally extrusions of viscous lava into a lava dome that capped the vent. The different types of volcanic activity can best be understood by making comparisons, and in this section two specific eruptions are compared—the 1991 eruption of Mount Pinatubo (a classic example of explosive volcanism) and the 1984 eruption of Mauna Loa (illustrative of effusive volcanism).

The Eruption of Mount Pinatubo in the Philippines in 1991

Earthquakes and steam explosions announced the reawakening of Mount Pinatubo in 1991, surprising many geologists because Pinatubo was not even listed in catalogs of world volcanoes. This mountain (at that time having an elevation of 1,745 metres, or 5,725 feet) lacked the classic conical shape of a volcano because erosion had carved its summit into a ragged ridge with steep

A column of gas and ash rising from Mount Pinatubo in the Philippines on June 12, 1991, just days before the volcano's climactic explosion on June 15. David H. Harlow/U.S. Geological Survey

jungle-covered slopes, and there was no written record of any eruptions. Nevertheless, scientists at the Philippine Institute of Volcanology and Seismology (PHIVOLCS) took the awakening of Pinatubo very seriously, knowing that the longer the repose between eruptions, the more dangerous a volcano may be. The area surrounding the volcano included densely populated regions. Clark Air Base, a major U.S. Air Force base in the Philippines, also abutted the volcano.

The eruption developed in several stages. On March 15, 1991, a swarm of small, locally discernible earthquakes began on the northwest side of Pinatubo. On April 2, steam explosions opened up three large steam and sulfur-gas vents, or fumaroles, along a fissure 3 km (1.9 mile) in length located high on the north flank of the volcano. Evacuation of residents living within a 10-km (6-mile) radius of the summit was recommended. Through April and May, a network of seismometers set up by PHIVOLCS recorded between 30 and 180 small earthquakes per day. In late April the seismic network was expanded in conjunction with the U.S. Geological Survey to provide better determination of the ongoing earthquakes' epicentres and depths. Airborne measurements of sulfur dioxide (SO_2) gas from the fumaroles were started on May 13, and the measurements showed the SO_2 emissions increasing from 500 metric tons per day to more than 5,000 tons per day by May 28.

On June 1 a new swarm of earthquakes began at shallow depths about 1 km (0.6 mile) northwest of the summit, indicating that magma was creating fractures as it forced open a conduit toward the surface from the magma chamber beneath the volcano. On June 3 a small explosion signaled the beginning of a new stage of activity. Minor, intermittent eruptions of ash began at the summit area, and a tiltmeter high on the volcano's east side began to lean outward. On June 7 an eruption of steam and ash reached a height of 7 to 8 km (4.3 to 5 miles), and the next morning an observer in a helicopter confirmed that magma had indeed reached the surface. From June 8 to June 12, ash eruptions and shallow earthquakes increased. The alert level was raised to "eruption in progress," and the evacuation radius was extended to 20 km (12 miles) from the summit. About 25,000 residents left, and Clark Air Base evacuated 14,500 people.

The first major explosive eruption occurred the morning of June 12; it lasted about an hour and generated a column of volcanic gas and ash 20 km (12 miles) high. The danger radius was increased to 30 km (19 miles), and the total number of evacuees increased to about 60,000 people. Another major explosion occurred during the night on June 12, followed by five more over the next two days. The character of the eruptions changed on June 14, with

Buildings and vegetation at Clark Air Base, Philippines, are destroyed by a thick, wet layer of ash following the gigantic explosion of Mount Pinatubo on June 15, 1991. Willie Scott/U.S. Geological Survey

increasing production of pyroclastic flows. Observation of the volcano was greatly hindered by the arrival of a major typhoon on June 15. Ten closely spaced explosive eruptions occurred during the night and morning of that day, but little could be seen.

The climactic eruption began in the early afternoon of June 15. Visible observations were impossible because of winds and rain brought by the typhoon, but seismograph, barograph, and satellite observations recorded the second largest eruption of the 20th century—exceeded only by the giant 1912 eruption of Novarupta near Mount Katmai in Alaska. The huge Plinian-type eruption of Pinatubo lasted about nine hours. By mid-afternoon, conditions around the volcano included pitch-darkness, falling ash and pumice lumps as large as 4 cm (1.6 inches) in diameter, high winds and heavy rain, lightning flashes, and earthquakes. Major ground tremors were felt about every 10 to 15 minutes. Satellite images showed that a giant, umbrella-shaped eruption cloud had formed that was 400 km (250 miles) in diameter and 34 km (21 miles) high at its apex. The ash fall from this cloud covered an area of 7,500 square km (2,900 square miles) to a depth of 1 cm (0.4 inch) or more with wet, gray ash and pumice; the maximum thickness was about 50 cm (20 inches) a few kilometres southwest of the vent area. The volume of ash was about 5 cubic km (1.2 cubic miles). Most of the 300 deaths caused directly by the eruption were the result of roofs and buildings collapsing from the weight of wet ash.

During the giant eruption, huge pyroclastic flows—mixtures of hot ash and gases denser than air—swept down the flanks of Pinatubo as far as 16 km (10 miles) from its old summit. These intensely hot ash flows sterilized 400 square km (154 square miles) of land around the volcano, filling valleys with high-temperature deposits as much as 200 metres (660 feet) thick. Floods from the typhoon rains churned up the loose volcanic ash and pyroclastic deposits and poured thick mudflows down all the streams and river valleys around the mountain. For years after the eruption, as heavy rainfall and flooding eroded the thick pyroclastic deposits, recurring mudflows buried towns and farm fields, destroyed roads and bridges, and displaced more than 100,000 people.

An estimated 17 million tons of SO_2 gas were injected into the stratosphere by Pinatubo's high eruption cloud. This formed an aerosol of tiny sulfate droplets that, with the extremely fine volcanic dust, circled the globe in about three weeks and reduced solar radiation reaching Earth's surface. This stratospheric haze layer diminished during the next three years and apparently caused an average cooling of 0.4 °C (0.7 °F) of Earth's climate during 1992–93.

The Eruption of Mauna Loa in Hawaii in 1984

On average, Mauna Loa, located on the island of Hawaii in the Pacific Ocean, erupts every three and a half years with fountains and streams of incandescent lava. Following a year of increased seismicity, Mauna Loa began erupting at 1:25 AM on March 25, 1984. The outbreak began along a fissure that split the long axis of the summit caldera, an oval, cliff-bounded basin approximately 3 to 5 km (1.9 to 3.1 miles) from rim to rim that had been formed by prehistoric subsidence. Lava fountains along the fissure formed a curtain of fire that illuminated the clouds and volcanic fumes into a red glow backlighting the black profile of the volcano's huge but gently sloping summit. Lava from the summit fissure ponded in the caldera, and the first observers in the air reported that much of the caldera floor was covered by a lake of orange-red molten rock, which quickly cooled to a black crust with zigzag-shaped fractures that were still incandescent.

At dawn the summit fissure began to propagate down the northeast rift zone, and a new line of lava fountains formed at an elevation of 3,800 metres (12,500 feet). Two hours later the fracture extended an additional 6 km (3.7 miles) down the northeast rift, forming another curtain of fire about 2 km (1.2 miles) long and 50 metres (164 feet) high at an elevation of 3,450 metres (11,300 feet). As new vents opened at lower elevations, the higher vents stopped erupting. The vents at 3,450 metres continued to erupt throughout the early afternoon, sending a small lava flow down the high southeast flank of Mauna Loa. At about 4:00 PM the lava fountains dwindled, and a swarm of new earthquakes indicated that the fissure was propagating even farther down the rift. It stopped opening some 7 km (4.3 miles) down the ridge at an elevation of 2,900 metres (9,500 feet), where new and final vents opened at 4:40 PM.

The output of lava from these final vents was vigorous. Although the fountains were only about 20 metres (66 feet) high, the volume of lava produced amounted to approximately 500,000 cubic metres (about 17.6 million cubic feet) per hour. In 24 hours the river of lava flowed 12 km (7.5 miles) northeast toward the city of Hilo. The vents erupted steadily for the next 10 days. Even though the eruption rate remained high, the advance of the front of the lava flow slowed, traveling 6 km (3.7 miles) on the second day, 4 km (2.5 miles) on the third day, and 3 km (1.9 miles) on the fourth day. This progressive slowing of the lava front had several causes. The lava supply was increasingly starved at lower altitudes by a slow widening of flows at higher elevations, by thickening of flows at higher elevations through overplating (that is, accumulation of new layers on top of layers only a few hours or days old), and by branching of the flows upstream into new lobes that robbed the lower flows of their lava. An additional cause was the thickening and widening of flows at lower elevations where the slope of the land is more gradual.

By April 5, output from the vents at 2,900 metres (9,500 feet) had begun to wane, and the eruption was over by April 15. The longest flows had traveled 27 km (16.8 miles), stopping at an elevation of 900 metres (3,000 feet)—10 km (6 miles) from the outskirts of Hilo. The total volume of the eruption was 220 million cubic metres (7.7 billion cubic feet), and new lava flows covered 48 square km (18.5 square miles). No one was hurt, and the only significant damage was the cutting of power lines and the blocking of a few jeep roads.

The temperature of the erupting lava was 1,140 °C (2,084 °F) and its viscosity was about 10^3 poise (dyne-second per cm^2), which is roughly equivalent to the viscosity of liquid honey at 20 °C (68 °F). A household analog of a Hawaiian lava flow in miniature is the slow and erratic advance of molten wax as it adds new lobes to a pile of candle drippings.

Mauna Loa's massive outpourings of lava have made it the world's largest volcano. Its summit rises 4,170 metres (13,680 feet) above sea level and more than 9,000 metres (29,500 feet) above the seafloor surrounding the Hawaiian Ridge. The volume above its base, which has subsided well below the adjacent seafloor, is estimated to be about 75,000 cubic km (18,000 cubic miles).

The Four Worst Eruptions in History

Since the late 1700s, volcanoes have caused more than 250,000 deaths. Most of these occurred during four disastrous eruptions.

The largest of the four occurred on April 10–11, 1815, at Mount Tambora on Sumbawa Island, now a part of Indonesia. Fifty cubic km (12 cubic miles) of magma were expelled in Plinian ash clouds and pyroclastic flows. Ash layers greater than 1 cm (0.4 inch) thick fell on more than 500,000 square km (193,000 square miles) of Indonesia and the Java Sea. Before the eruption Tambora was a stratovolcano some 4,300 metres (14,100 feet) high; following the eruption, approximately 1,400 metres (4,600 feet) of the summit cone were missing, and in its place was a collapsed caldera 6 by 7 km (3.7 by 4.4 miles) wide and 1 km (0.6 mile) deep. About 10,000 people were killed by the explosive eruption and the tsunamis caused by massive pyroclastic flows entering the sea. Agricultural losses from the thick ash deposits resulted in famine and disease, leading to an additional 82,000 deaths.

The second largest eruption of the 19th century also occurred in Indonesia. Krakatoa (Krakatau), a composite volcano on a small uninhabited island between Sumatra and Java, erupted explosively on Aug. 26–27, 1883. The eruption was similar to the Tambora outburst but smaller, involving about 18 cubic km (4.3 cubic miles) of magma erupted in Plinian ash clouds and pyroclastic flows. Krakatoa was a smaller volcano than Tambora, and, when the eruption had emptied part of its magma chamber, it collapsed to form a caldera that was partly below sea level. Twenty-three square km (8.9 square miles) of the island disappeared, and where a volcanic peak 450 metres (1,475 feet) high once stood was water as deep as 275 metres (900 feet). The largest explosion on the morning of August 27 produced an ash cloud that was reported to have reached a height of 80 km (50 miles), and the detonation was heard as far away as Australia. A tsunami over 30 metres (100 feet) high followed the explosion and apparent caldera collapse, killing about 36,000 people on the adjacent shores of Java and Sumatra.

On May 8, 1902, there occurred a violent eruption of Mount Pelée, a stratovolcano on the island of Martinique in the Caribbean Sea. Although less than 1 cubic km (0.24 cubic mile) of magma was erupted, much of it formed a high-velocity pyroclastic flow that swept down a steep valley to the port of Saint-Pierre. Within minutes the town and virtually all of its inhabitants (some 29,000 people) were incinerated.

The second worst volcanic disaster of the 20th century occurred on Nov. 13, 1985, when a relatively small eruption of Mount Ruiz, a stratovolcano in the Andes Mountains of Colombia, killed 25,000 people. This volcano is tall enough, at an elevation of 5,400 metres (17,700 feet), to have a glacial ice cap. When a brief explosive eruption dumped several million cubic metres of hot pyroclastic fragments onto the ice surrounding the summit crater, a sudden surge of meltwater sent massive mudflows down canyons on both the east and west sides of the volcano. Much of the town of Armero, built on a low plain beside the Lagunilla River 50 km (30 miles) east of and nearly 5 km (3 miles) in elevation below the summit of Ruiz, was buried by the mudflows. Twenty-two thousand of its inhabitants were killed.

About 70 percent of the people who died from volcanic eruptions in the past 200 years perished in those four outbursts. The remaining 30 percent were killed in many other less-devastating eruptions. As world population increases, however, so does the risk of greater loss of life from volcanic eruptions. This was made all too clear by the tragedy at Armero. In 1845 a mudflow from Mount Ruiz killed approximately 1,000 people on farms near the site where the town of Armero was later built. In the 1985 mudflow, which was smaller in volume than the 1845 mudflow, more than 20 times as many people were killed.

Volcano Forecasting and Warning

The greatest hazard at potentially active volcanoes is human complacency. The physical hazards can be reliably estimated by studying past eruptive activity as recorded in history or in the prehistoric deposits around a volcano. Volcano observatories can monitor local earthquake activity and the surface deformation of a potentially active volcano and make useful, if not yet precise, forecasts of eruptions. For instance, the measurement of increased earthquake activity beneath Mauna Loa in 1983 led to a forecast of an increase in probability of an eruption for 1984 or 1985; an eruption occurred in March 1984. The major eruption of Mount St. Helens on May 18, 1980, was much larger than anticipated, but a high number of local earthquakes and a visible bulge forming on the north flank of the mountain provided enough warning to encourage a partial evacuation of the surrounding area. Lives were lost, but the toll would have been much higher if access to the area had not been restricted by local authorities. A major problem in reducing volcanic risk is that most explosive volcanoes have such long repose periods that people living nearby consider them extinct rather than dormant.

The correct forecast and evacuation of residents before the 1991 eruption of Mount Pinatubo saved thousands of lives, but the science of eruption forecasting is only beginning and is still fraught with uncertainty. Evacuation of large numbers of people is difficult and expensive. A major evacuation not followed by any major eruption would be a serious mistake, but not evacuating people from a threatening volcano that then erupts catastrophically would be a much worse mistake. It is not a simple problem.

MAJOR VOLCANOES OF THE WORLD

REGION	ELEVATION*		FIRST RECORDED ERUPTION	COMMENTS
	FEET	METRES		
Mediterranean				
Etna, Sicily, Italy	10,991	3,350	1500 BCE	The tallest active volcano in Europe, Etna has had recorded eruptions for millennia, including a huge blast in 1669 that left 20,000 people dead.
Vesuvius, Campania, Italy	4,203	1,281	217 BCE	This storied volcano, which in 79 ADE destroyed the city of Pompeii, is still active and is surrounded by several million people living in the area of Naples.
Stromboli, Eolie Islands, Italy	3,038	926	350 BCE	Nearly continuous small eruptions of incandescent lava have given this volcano, located on an island north of Sicily, the nickname "lighthouse of the Mediterranean."

MAJOR VOLCANOES OF THE WORLD				
REGION	ELEVATION*		FIRST RECORDED ERUPTION	COMMENTS
	FEET	METRES		
Vulcano, Eolie Islands, Italy	1,640	500	*360 BCE	Vulcano, the ancient archetype of the term *volcano*, has not erupted since the late 19th century.
Thera (Santoríni), Cyclades, Greece	1,204	367	*197 BCE	The scenic island of Thera is actually the remains of a volcano that exploded about 1500 BC in one of the largest eruptions of historic times.
Atlantic Ocean				
Teide, Tenerife, Canary Islands	12,188	3,715	1396	The highest peak in the Atlantic Ocean, Teide was observed in eruption by Christopher Columbus and still emits hot gas from vents on its slopes.
Fogo, Cape Verde Islands	9,281	2,829	1500	The highest peak in the Cape Verde Islands, Fogo rises from a caldera created by an ancient volcanic collapse.
Beerenberg, Jan Mayen, Norway	7,470	2,277	1732	Located on an island in the Arctic Circle, Beerenberg is the northernmost active volcano on Earth.
Tristan da Cunha, South Atlantic	6,758	2,060	1961	The only recorded eruption of this remote island-volcano occurred in 1961, forcing the evacuation of its small population for two years.

MAJOR VOLCANOES OF THE WORLD				
REGION	ELEVATION*		FIRST RECORDED ERUPTION	COMMENTS
	FEET	METRES		
Askja, Iceland	4,974	1,516	1875	Askja's three large calderas are dotted by volcanically active fissures and cones.
Hekla, Iceland	4,892	1,491	1104	One of Iceland's most active volcanoes, it has an elongated profile caused by frequent eruptions of lava from a long fissure running parallel to the Mid-Atlantic Ridge.
Deception Island, South Shetland Islands	1,890	576	1800	This ring-shaped island-volcano off the Antarctic Peninsula has a natural inner harbour formed from a huge caldera.
Surtsey, Iceland	554	169	1963	This volcanic island emerged from the Atlantic Ocean in a fiery eruption in 1963.
North America				
Citlaltépetl, Veracruz-Puebla, Mexico	18,619	5,675	1545	This volcano has been dormant since 1846; its snowcapped cone is the third highest peak in North America.
Popocatépetl, México-Puebla, Mexico	17,802	5,426	1345	Popocatépetl (Aztec for "smoking mountain") still spreads ash on occasion over the surrounding region.
Rainier, Washington, U.S.	14,409	4,392	1825	This dormant volcano is one of the premier mountain-climbing destinations in the United States.

MAJOR VOLCANOES OF THE WORLD

REGION	ELEVATION*		FIRST RECORDED ERUPTION	COMMENTS
	FEET	METRES		
Colima, Colima, Mexico	12,631	3,850	1519	This active volcano frequently ejects ash plumes and lava bombs.
Hood, Oregon, U.S.	11,240	3,426	1859	The highest peak in Oregon and visible from Portland, this dormant volcano is the focal point of Mount Hood National Forest.
Lassen, California, U.S.	10,456	3,187	1914	A series of eruptions from 1914 to 1917 marked the southernmost volcanic activity recorded in the Cascade Range.
Redoubt, Alaska, U.S.	10,197	3,108	1902	Lava domes on this volcano occasionally collapse, melting glaciers and sending mudflows streaming down nearby river valleys.
Shishaldin, Alaska, U.S.	9,373	2,857	1824	The snow-covered, beautifully symmetrical cone of this Aleutian volcano frequently spouts ash and lava.
Parícutin, Michoacán, Mexico	9,210	2,807	1943	One of the youngest volcanoes on Earth, it was born of a continuous eruption of lava and ash that lasted from 1943 to 1952.
St. Helens, Washington, U.S.	8,363	2,549	1831	A gigantic eruption in 1980 devastated 550 square km (210 square miles) of mountain terrain and spread ash over Washington, Idaho, and Montana.

MAJOR VOLCANOES OF THE WORLD				
REGION	ELEVATION*		FIRST RECORDED ERUPTION	COMMENTS
	FEET	METRES		
Pavlof, Alaska, U.S.	8,264	2,519	1790	This active volcano forms a striking landform with its nearby twin peak, Pavlof Sister.
Veniaminof, Alaska, U.S.	8,225	2,507	1838	Two cones rise from a huge glacier-filled caldera at the top of this volcano.
Katmai, Alaska, U.S.	6,716	2,047	1912	The summit of this volcano collapsed in 1912 following the gigantic explosion of nearby Novarupta Volcano—the largest eruption recorded in the 20th century.
El Chichón, Chiapas, Mexico	3,773	1,150	1982	A powerful blast in 1982 destroyed most villages within 8 km (5 miles) and left behind a crater that is now filled with an acidic lake.
Central America and Caribbean				
Tajumulco, Guatemala	13,845	4,220	1821(?)	The highest volcano in Central America, its twin peaks rise almost from sea level near the city of San Marcos.
Acatenango, Guatemala	13,044	3,976	1924	This peak and its twin, Fuego, rise above the old colonial city of Antigua Guatemala.
Fuego, Guatemala	12,346	3,763	1524	This twin of Acatenango is one of Central America's most active volcanoes, frequently erupting ash and lava.

MAJOR VOLCANOES OF THE WORLD

REGION	ELEVATION*		FIRST RECORDED ERUPTION	COMMENTS
	FEET	METRES		
Irazú, Costa Rica	11,260	3,432	1723	The highest volcano in Costa Rica, it is a popular tourist spot that offers views of the country's Pacific and Atlantic coasts.
Poás, Costa Rica	8,884	2,708	1828	Two of the three craters at the summit contain lakes that regularly attract tourists and observers.
Pacaya, Guatemala	8,373	2,552	1565	Lava explosions are visible from Guatemala City, 30 km (18 miles) away.
Santa Ana, El Salvador	7,812	2,381	1521	El Salvador's highest volcano.
San Miguel, El Salvador	6,988	2,130	1510	The slopes of this active volcano are home to coffee plantations and to the important city of San Miguel.
Izalco, El Salvador	6,398	1,950	1770	Born of a series of eruptions in 1770; its frequent glowing activity caused it to be called the "lighthouse of the Pacific."
San Cristóbal, Nicaragua	5,725	1,745	1528	The highest volcano in Nicaragua.
Concepción, Nicaragua	5,577	1,700	1883	This active volcano rises from the northern half of Ometepe Island in Lake Nicaragua.

MAJOR VOLCANOES OF THE WORLD				
REGION	ELEVATION*		FIRST RECORDED ERUPTION	COMMENTS
	FEET	METRES		
Arenal, Costa Rica	5,436	1,657	1922	Frequent explosions and effusions of lava have made this volcano a popular destination for sightseers.
Pelée, Martinique	4,583	1,397	1792	An eruption of hot gas and ash in 1902 killed 26,000 people in the port city of Saint-Pierre.
Momotombo, Nicaragua	4,255	1,297	1524	The cone of this volcano, rising on the northern shore of Lake Managua, is a prominent landmark.
Soufrière, Saint Vincent and the Grenadines	4,003	1,220	1718	An eruption in 1902 killed 2,000 people and ruined half the island of Saint Vincent.
South America				
Guallatiri, Chile	19,918	6,071	1825	This volcano is occasionally observed venting steam and gas.
Cotopaxi, Ecuador	19,393	5,911	1534	Though Cotopaxi is Ecuador's best-known volcano, it has not erupted since the first half of the 20th century.
El Misti, Peru	19,101	5,822	1542	This volcano, its symmetrical cone towering over the city of Arequipa, holds an important place in Peruvian culture.
Lascar, Chile	18,346	5,592	1848	This active volcano frequently ejects clouds of ash and pumice.

MAJOR VOLCANOES OF THE WORLD				
REGION	ELEVATION*		FIRST RECORDED ERUPTION	COMMENTS
	FEET	METRES		
Ruiz, Colombia	17,457	5,321	1570	In 1985 a relatively mild eruption melted a glacier on this volcano, triggering mudflows that buried several villages and killed more than 25,000 people.
Sangay, Ecuador	17,159	5,230	1628	This steep-sided, glacier-covered volcano is almost constantly erupting.
Tungurahua, Ecuador	16,479	5,023	1640	Lava and mixtures of hot ash and gas frequently flow down the sides of this steep and active volcano.
Guagua Pichincha, Ecuador	15,695	4,784	1566	Rising just west of the capital city of Quito, this volcano regularly has small eruptions.
Llaima, Chile	10,253	3,125	1640	Ash columns and lava flows frequently issue from this glacier-clad volcano, which, like Villarrica, is a popular ski area.
Villarrica, Chile	9,340	2,847	1558	Ash columns and lava flows frequently issue from this glacier-clad volcano, which, like Llaima, is a popular ski area.
Hudson, Chile	6,250	1,905	1891	This southernmost volcano in the Chilean Andes exploded violently in 1991.
Pacific Ocean				
Mauna Kea, Hawaii, U.S.	13,796	4,205	. . .	This dormant volcano, often snowcapped because of its great height, is home to an astronomical observatory.

MAJOR VOLCANOES OF THE WORLD				
REGION	ELEVATION*		FIRST RECORDED ERUPTION	COMMENTS
	FEET	METRES		
Mauna Loa, Hawaii, U.S.	13,681	4,170	1832	Every three to four years, this huge shield volcano erupts with fountains and streams of incandescent lava.
Erebus, Ross Island	12,447	3,794	1841	The southernmost active volcano in the world, Erebus ejects lava almost constantly.
Kilauea, Hawaii, U.S.	4,009	1,222	1790	Since 1983 Kilauea has been in almost continual eruption, producing rivers of lava that flow to the sea 50 km (30 miles) away.
Loihi, Hawaii, U.S.	-3,199	-975	1996	Frequent effusions of lava from this submarine volcano will bring it to the surface between 10,000 and 100,000 years from now.
East Asia				
Klyuchevskaya, Kamchatka, Russia	15,863	4,835	1697	The highest and most active volcano on the Kamchatka Peninsula.
Fuji, Honshu, Japan	12,388	3,776	781	Dormant since 1707, this volcano has a graceful conical form and is a sacred symbol of Japan.
Tolbachik, Kamchatka, Russia	12,080	3,682	1739	Tolbachik is enormous, composed of a rounded shield volcano and a conical stratovolcano.

MAJOR VOLCANOES OF THE WORLD

REGION	ELEVATION*		FIRST RECORDED ERUPTION	COMMENTS
	FEET	METRES		
Shiveluch, Kamchatka, Russia	10,771	3,283	1854	Rising dramatically from a plain north of Klyuchevskaya Volcano, Shiveluch occasionally spouts plumes of ash.
Ontake, Honshu, Japan	10,049	3,063	1919	Ontake is an object of worship for pilgrims who climb it each year
Bezymianny, Kamchatka, Russia	9,455	2,882	1955	This volcano was considered dormant until 1955-56; in the latter year a gigantic blast created a large crater that has since been filled by a growing lava dome.
Alaid, Kuril Islands, Russia	7,674	2,339	1790	The largest volcano in the Kuril Islands, Alaid has been observed ejecting huge plumes of ash.
Aso, Kyushu, Japan	5,223	1,592	864	The gigantic caldera of this volcano is occupied by many peaks, including Naka-dake, one of Japan's most active volcanoes.
Unzen, Kyushu, Japan	4,921	1,500	1663	A 1792 eruption caused a debris avalanche and tsunami that killed more than 10,000 people.
Southeast Asia and Oceania				
Kerinci, Sumatra, Indonesia	12,467	3,800	1838	Located in a national park in central Sumatra, Kerinci is the highest volcano in Indonesia.

MAJOR VOLCANOES OF THE WORLD

REGION	ELEVATION*		FIRST RECORDED ERUPTION	COMMENTS
	FEET	METRES		
Rinjani, Lombok, Indonesia	12,224	3,726	1847	The caldera at the summit of this volcano is the site of a lake and of an active cone that frequently issues lava.
Semeru, Java, Indonesia	12,060	3,676	1818	The highest volcano on Java, Semeru is almost continuously erupting lava or ash.
Slamet, Java, Indonesia	11,247	3,428	1772	Slamet periodically ejects plumes of ash, often in conjunction with mild ground tremors.
Raung, Java, Indonesia	10,932	3,332	1593	Explosive eruptions frequently originate in vents located within a broad caldera at the peak of this volcano.
Agung, Bali, Indonesia	10,308	3,142	1808	The highest and most sacred point in Bali, it is traditionally considered to be a throne of the gods and the centre of the world.
Merapi, Java, Indonesia	9,737	2,968	1548	Located in a densely populated region, Merapi ("Mountain of Fire") is known for ejecting dangerous mixtures of hot gas and ash.
Apo, Mindanao, Philippines	9,691	2,954	...	The highest peak in the Philippines, Apo is the site of a national park.
Marapi, Sumatra, Indonesia	9,485	2,891	1770	Sumatra's most active volcano, Marapi has had more than 50 reported eruptions, most of them small or moderate explosions.

MAJOR VOLCANOES OF THE WORLD				
REGION	ELEVATION*		FIRST RECORDED ERUPTION	COMMENTS
	FEET	METRES		
Tambora, Sumbawa, Indonesia	9,350	2,850	1812	In 1815 Tambora blew 1,400 metres (4,600 feet) off its top in the largest explosive eruption ever recorded.
Ruapehu, North Island, New Zealand	9,176	2,797	1861	Permanently snow-covered above the tree line, this volcano is in a popular ski area.
Papandayan, Java, Indonesia	8,743	2,665	1772	The collapsed summit of this volcano contains a famous area of sulfurous vents known as Kawah Mas ("Golden Crater").
Mayon, Luzon, Philippines	8,077	2,462	1616	The Philippines' most active volcano, Mayon frequently ejects plumes of ash and streams of lava.
Canlaon, Negros, Philippines	7,989	2,435	1866	The highest point in the Visayan Islands, Canlaon is located in a national park that includes craters, hot springs, and a variety of wildlife.
Ulawun, New Britain, Papua New Guinea	7,657	2,334	1700	The highest peak on the island of New Britain, Ulawun ("North Son") forms a pair with its nearby twin, Bamus ("South Son").
Kelud, Java, Indonesia	5,679	1,731	1000	The summit crater contains a lake that caused devastating mudflows in previous eruptions but is now controlled by drainage tunnels.

MAJOR VOLCANOES OF THE WORLD				
REGION	ELEVATION*		FIRST RECORDED ERUPTION	COMMENTS
	FEET	METRES		
Lamington, New Guinea, Papua New Guinea	5,512	1,680	1951	Lamington was not known to be a volcano until 1951, when a powerful blast swept the area with hot gas and ash, killing 3,000 people.
Pinatubo, Luzon, Philippines	4,875	1,486	1991	A gigantic explosion in 1991 may have produced more ash and smoke than any other volcanic eruption of the 20th century.
Krakatoa (Krakatau), Sunda Strait, Indonesia	2,667	813	1680	In 1883 a series of tremendous explosions collapsed the island of Krakatoa; since 1927 a new cone, Anak Krakatau ("Son of Krakatoa"), has risen from the submerged caldera of the old volcano.
Taal, Luzon, Philippines	1,312	400	1572	Taal Volcano, also called Volcano Island, rises from Taal Lake, which fills the caldera of an ancient volcano.
Africa and Indian Ocean				
Cameroon, Cameroon	13,435	4,095	1650	Lava frequently flows down the flanks of this volcano, located near the Gulf of Guinea in West Africa.
Nyiragongo, Congo (Kinshasa)	11,384	3,470	1884	Lava flowing from its crater in 1977 and 2002 killed thousands of people and damaged the city of Goma.

MAJOR VOLCANOES OF THE WORLD				
REGION	ELEVATION*		FIRST RECORDED ERUPTION	COMMENTS
	FEET	METRES		
Nyamulagira, Congo (Kinshasa)	10,033	3,058	1865	The most active volcano in Africa, it often emits lava and ash, though fatalities are rare.
Ol Doinyo Lengai, Tanzania	9,482	2,890	1880	Masai for "Mountain of God," Ol Doinyo Lengai still issues lava from its summit crater.
Fournaise, Réunion	8,632	2,631	1640	One of the world's most active volcanoes, it regularly issues flows of lava and is the site of a French volcanic observatory.
Karthala, Comoros	7,746	2,361	1808	Lava flowing from the summit and flanks of this shield volcano frequently reaches the sea.
Erta-Ale, Ethiopia	2,011	613	1906	Ethiopia's most active volcano; its summit caldera frequently overflows with lava.
Barren Island, Andaman Islands, India	1,161	354	1787	Located in the Andaman Sea some 1,300 km (800 miles) east of the Indian mainland, Barren Island is the only historically active volcano on Indian territory.

*Elevation figures may differ from other sources.

Source: Lee Siebert and Tom Simkin, *Volcanoes of the World: An Illustrated Catalog of Holocene Volcanoes and Their Eruptions* (2002-), Smithsonian Institution, Global Volcanism Program Digital Information Series, GVP-3, http://www.volcano.si.edu/world.

Significant Volcanoes of the World

Throughout human history, people have witnessed the awesome power of volcanic eruptions. Although many have been able to observe them from a safe distance, too often humans, their crops and domesticated animals, and their dwellings fall victims to the ashfall, mudslides, tsunamis, or other phenomena that accompany volcanic events. Some of the more notable eruptions are described below.

Mount Agung

Located in northeastern Bali, Indonesia, Mount Agung is the highest point in Bali and the object of traditional veneration. It rises to a height of 9,888 feet (3,014 m). In 1963 it erupted after being dormant for 120 years; some 1,600 people were killed and 86,000 left homeless.

According to one Balinese myth, the deities made mountains for their thrones and placed the highest, Mount Agung, in Bali. According to another myth, the deities found the island of Bali unstable and wobbling and, to still it, set down upon it the holy mountain of Hinduism, Mahameru, renamed Gunung Agung. To the Balinese the mountain became the "Navel of the World," and in every Balinese temple a shrine is dedicated to its spirit. Such religious items as temple offerings and cremation mounds are shaped in the form of mountains out of reverence for the volcano. The mother temple of Bali, Pura Besakih, lies on the slopes of Mount Agung.

Askja

The largest caldera (volcanic crater) in the Dyngjufjöll volcanic massif in east-central Iceland, Askja lies 20 miles (32 km) north of Vatnajökull, the island's largest ice field. Its rugged peaks, up to 4,954 feet (1,510 m) above sea level, encircle a 4.25-square-mile (11-square-kilometre) lake that

Askja caldera (volcanic crater), east-central Iceland. U.S. Geological Survey

occupies the caldera. Askja (Icelandic: "Box") is the highest peak in the Dyngjufjöll; surrounding it is the Ódádhahraun, an extensive lava field covering 1,422 square miles (3,681 square km). The volcano erupted in 1875 and again in 1961.

Mount Aso

Mount Aso (Japanese: Aso-san), in Kumamoto *ken* (prefecture), Kyushu, Japan, rises to an elevation of 5,223 feet (1,592 m). It has the largest active crater in the world, measuring 71 miles (114 km) in circumference, 17 miles (27 km) from north to south, and 10 miles (16 km) from east to west. Its caldera (bowl-shaped volcanic depression) marks the original crater and contains the active volcano of Naka-dake and numerous hot springs. The crater is inhabited and is crossed by roads and railways. Its mountain pastures are used for cattle raising and dairy farming. The volcano is the central feature of Aso-Kuju National Park.

The caldera of Mount Aso in central Kyushu, Japan. Kazumi Yahagi—Bon. Encyclopædia Britannica, Inc.

Mount Cameroon

Mount Cameroon (French: Mont Cameroun) is a volcanic massif located in southwestern Cameroon that rises to a height of 13,435 feet (4,095 metres) and extends 14 miles (23 km) inland from the Gulf of Guinea. It is the highest peak in sub-Saharan western and central Africa and the westernmost extension of a series of hills and mountains that form a natural boundary between northern Cameroon and Nigeria. The Englishman Sir Richard Burton (1821–90) climbed its summit in 1861. The volcano is still active.

The town of Buea lies on the southeastern slope of the mountain, and the port of Limbe (formerly Victoria) lies at its southern foot. The side of the mountain facing the sea has a mean annual precipitation level of more than

400 inches (10,000 mm) and is one of the wettest places in the world. The mountain's rich volcanic soils support bananas, rubber, oil palms, tea, and cacao; valleys are used as pasture.

Cotopaxi

A volcanic peak located in the Cordillera Central of the Andes, central Ecuador, Cotopaxi is 19,347 feet (5,897 m) tall and has the distinction of being the world's highest continuously active volcano. Cotopaxi has an almost perfectly symmetrical cone, interrupted only by one minor cone—the Cabeza del Inca ("Inca's Head"). The mountain has a long record of violent eruption and has seldom remained quiescent for more than 15 years. The terrain around the mountain's base has many times been devastated by earthquakes or been buried in pumice and ash

Cotopaxi volcano, Ecuador. Shostal Associates

blown out of the crater. Lava that boils constantly in its crater emits plumes of steam. The mountain itself is built up of alternating flows of dark-coloured trachytic lava and falls of lighter-coloured ash. The crater at the top is 2,300 feet (700 m) in diameter from north to south and 1,650 feet (500 m) from east to west. Its depth is 1,200 feet (366 m). The base of the volcano stands on open mountain grassland, but the whole upper part of the mountain is covered with permanent snow.

The first European to attempt an ascent of Cotopaxi was Alexander von Humboldt in 1802. He failed to reach the top and pronounced the mountain unclimbable. Other failures in 1831 and 1858 seemed to confirm this verdict. But in 1872 the German scientist and traveler Wilhelm Reiss succeeded in reaching the top on November 28, and in May of the following year A. Stübel was also successful. Cotopaxi and its surrounding grasslands are protected in Cotopaxi National Park, a major tourist attraction.

Mount Etna

Mount Etna (Latin: Aetna; Sicilian: Mongibello) is an active volcano on the east coast of Sicily. The name comes from the Greek *Aitne*, from *aithō* "I burn." Mount Etna is the highest active volcano in Europe, its topmost elevation being more than 10,000 ft (3,200 m). Like other active volcanoes, its height varies: in 1865, for example, the volcanic summit was 170 ft higher than it was in the late 20th century. Etna covers an area of 600 sq mi (1,600 sq km); its base has a circumference of about 93 mi (150 km).

Its geological characteristics indicate that Etna has been active since the end of the Tertiary Period, somewhat more than 2,500,000 years ago. The volcano has had more than one active centre. A number of subsidiary cones have been formed on lateral fissures extending out from the centre and down the sides. The present structure of the mountain is the result of the activity of at least two main eruptive centres.

The Greeks created legends about the volcano, saying that it was the workshop of Hephaestus and the Cyclops or that underneath it the giant Typhon lay, making Earth tremble when he turned. The ancient poet Hesiod spoke of Etna's eruptions, and the Greeks Pindar and Aeschylus referred to a famous eruption of 475 BCE. From 1500 BCEto 1669 CE there are records of 71 eruptions, of which 14 occurred before the Christian Era. The most violent historical eruption was in 1669 (March 11–July 15), when about 990,000,000 cu yd (830,000,000 cu m) of lava were thrown out. The eruption took place along a fissure that opened above the town of Nicolosi, widening into a chasm from which lava flowed and solid fragments, sand, and ashes were hurled. The latter formed a double cone more than 150 ft high, named Monti Rossi. The lava flow destroyed a dozen villages on the lower slope and submerged the western part of the town of Catania. Efforts to divert the lava stream away from Catania were made by workers who dug a trench above the village. Historically, this seems to have been the first attempt to divert a lava stream. Between 1669 and 1900, 26 more eruptions were reported. During the 20th century there were eruptions in 1908, 1910, 1911, 1918, 1923, 1928, 1942, 1947, 1949, 1950, 1955, and 1971. Activity was almost continuous in the decade following 1971, and in 1983 an eruption that lasted four months prompted authorities to explode dynamite in an attempt to divert lava flows.

Among Etna's better known ancient eruptions was that of 396 BCE, which kept the Carthaginian army from reaching Catania. An eruption of 1381 sent a lava flow as far as the sea. The eruption of 1852 took many lives. That of 1928 cut off the railway that runs around the base of the mountain and buried the village of Mascali. That of 1971 threatened several villages with its lava flow and destroyed some orchards and vineyards.

The mountain has three ecological zones, one above the other, each exhibiting its own characteristic vegetation. The lowest zone, sloping gradually upward to perhaps 3,000 feet (915 m), is fertile and rich in vineyards, olive groves, citrus plantations, and orchards. Several densely populated settlements, notably the city of Catania, are found on the lower slopes, but they become less frequent as the height increases. Above, the mountain grows steeper and is covered with forests of chestnut, beech, oak, pine, and birch. At heights of more than 6,500 feet (1,980 m), the mountain is covered with ashes, sand, and fragments of lava and slag; there are a few scattered plants such as *Astragalus aetnensis* (local name: spino santo), which forms typical bushes almost 1 yard (about 0.9 m) high, while some alpine plants manage to survive even near the top. Algae have been found near the steam outlets at 9,800 feet (2,990 m).

Etna has been studied systematically since the middle of the 19th century, and three observatories have been set up on its slopes; they are located at Catania, Casa Etnea, and Cantoniera.

Mount Fuji

Mount Fuji (Japanese: Fuji-san) is the highest mountain in Japan, rising to 12,388 feet (3,776 metres) near the Pacific coast in Yamanashi and Shizuoka *ken* (prefectures), central Honshu, about 60 miles (100 km) west of Tokyo. It is a volcano that has been dormant since its last eruption in 1707 but is still generally classified as active by geologists. The mountain's name, of Ainu origin, means "everlasting life," and it is also called Fujiyama or Fuji No Yama. Mount Fuji, with its graceful conical form, has become famous throughout the world and is considered the sacred symbol of Japan. Among Japanese there is a sense of personal identification with the mountain, and thousands of Japanese climb to the shrine on its peak every summer. The mountain is the major feature of Fuji-Hakone-Izu National Park (1936).

According to tradition, the volcano was formed in 286 BCE by an earthquake. The truth is somewhat more complex. The age of Fuji is disputed, but it seems to be a Quaternary formation on a Tertiary base, the first eruptions and the first peaks probably occurring some 600,000 years ago. Although Mount Fuji appears to be a simple cone-type volcano, it is in fact three separate volcanoes, Komitake, Ko Fuji, and Shin Fuji. The most recent, Shin Fuji ("New Fuji"), first became active about 10,000 years ago and has continued ever since to smolder or erupt occasionally. Over the millennia, the lava and other effusions from Shin Fuji have covered over the two older volcanoes, enlarged the slopes to their present expansive girth, and otherwise given the mountain its current tapered form. The mountain is part of the Fuji Volcanic Zone, a volcanic chain that extends from the Mariana Islands and the Izu Islands through Izu Peninsula on up to northern Honshu.

The base of the volcano is about 78 miles (125 km) in circumference and has a diameter of some 25 to 30 miles (40 to 50 km). At the summit of Mount Fuji the crater spans about 1,600 feet (500 metres) in surface diameter and sinks to a depth of about 820 feet (250 metres). Around the jagged edges of the crater are eight peaks—Oshaidake, Izudake, Jojudake, Komagatake, Mushimatake, Kengamme, Hukusandake, and Kukushidake.

On the northern slopes of Mount Fuji lie the Fuji Five Lakes (Fuji Goko), comprising, east to west, Lake Yamanaka, Lake Kawaguchi, Lake Sai, Lake Shoji, and Lake Motosu, all formed by the damming effects of lava flows. The lowest, Lake Kawaguchi, at 2,726 feet (831 metres), is noted for the inverted reflection of Mount Fuji on its still waters. Tourism in the area is highly developed, with Lake Yamanaka, the largest of the lakes (at 2.5 square miles [6.4 square km]), being the focus of the most popular resort area. Southeast of Mount Fuji is the wooded volcanic Hakone region, well-known for its hot-springs resorts at Yumoto and Gōra.

The area's abundant groundwater and streams facilitate the operation of paper and chemical industries and farming. Cultivation of rainbow trout and dairy farming are other activities.

A sacred mountain (one sect, the Fujikō, accords it virtually a soul), Mount Fuji is surrounded by temples and shrines, there being shrines even at the edge and the bottom of the crater. Climbing the mountain has long been a

Hekla volcano, Iceland. Courtesy of the Iceland Tourist Bureau

religious practice (though until the Meiji Restoration women were not allowed to climb it). The ascent in early times was usually made in the white robes of a pilgrim. Today great crowds flock there, mostly during the climbing season from July 1 to August 26.

Mount Hekla

An active volcano located in southern Iceland, Hekla is the country's best-known volcano. Hekla stands 4,892 ft (1,491 m) above sea level 70 mi (110 km) east of Reykjavík, the capital, at the eastern end of the island's most extensive farming region. Known in early times as the Mountain of Hell, it erupted 18 times between 1104 and 2000, with major eruptions occurring in 1300, 1766, and 1947; the 1766 explosion caused great loss of life. In the late 20th century, Hekla had three minor eruptions: in 1970, 1980, and 1991. An eruption in 2000 lasted four days but caused no significant damage.

Mount Hood

Mount Hood is the highest peak (11,239 feet [3,425 metres]) in Oregon, U.S., and the fourth highest peak in the Cascade Range, 45 miles (70 km) east-southeast of Portland. It is a dormant volcano that last erupted about 1865, with minor steam and ash (tephra) emissions in 1903; debris flows, glacial flooding, and earthquakes regularly occur there. First sighted in 1792 by the English navigator William Broughton, and named for the British admiral Lord Hood, the snowcapped peak was used as a landmark by early settlers. Twelve glaciers and snowfields cover approximately 80 percent of Mount Hood's cone above the 6,890-foot (2,100-metre) level.

Mount Hood is the focal point of Mount Hood National Forest, a popular tourist and recreation area that extends along the Cascade Range from the Columbia River.

Mount Hood, with Lost Lake in the foreground, Oregon. Scenics of America/PhotoLink/Getty Images

Irazú Volcano

An active volcano in the Cordillera Central of east-central Costa Rica, Irazú (Spanish: Volcán Irazú) is named for the indigenous word for "thunder." The highest mountain in the Cordillera Central, it reaches an elevation of 11,260 feet (3,432 metres). It is a popular ascent for tourists, as its cone offers (on rare clear days) views of both the Atlantic and Pacific coasts of Costa Rica. The active crater is 980 feet (300 metres) deep. Irazú Volcano National Park is linked by paved road to Cartago. The volcano's eruptions of 1963–65 produced ash that dammed a nearby small river, flooding the city of Cartago and causing serious damage to coffee crops. The ashfall created considerable inconvenience for residents of San José, 34 miles (54 km) away.

Izalco Volcano

Located in western El Salvador on the southern slope of Santa Ana, Izalco (Spanish: Volcán Izalco) is the most active volcano in Central America, having erupted more than 50 times since 1770. Its black symmetrical cone, which was formed by a number of eruptions over a period of 200 years, is devoid of vegetation and reaches a height of 6,004 feet (1,830 metres). During the 19th century, oceangoing sailors set their course by the continuous glow from Izalco's summit, nicknaming it the "Lighthouse of the Pacific." The volcano derives its name from the Izalco Indians. The town of Izalco is located at the southwestern foot of the volcano.

Kilauea

One of the world's most active volcanic masses, Kilauea is located on the southeastern part of the island of Hawaii, Hawaii State, U.S. The central feature of Hawaii Volcanoes National Park, Kilauea ("Much Spreading" in Hawaiian), is an elongated dome built of lava eruptions from a central crater and from lines of craters extending along east and southwest rifts, or fissures. The volcano's 4,090-foot (1,250-metre) summit has collapsed to form a caldera, a broad shallow depression nearly 3 miles (5 km) long and 2 miles (3.2 km) wide with an area of more than 4 square miles (10 square km). Kilauea's slopes merge with those of the nearby volcano Mauna Loa on the west and north.

During the 19th century the main floor of Kilauea's caldera went through several periods of lava filling and collapse. By 1919 it assumed its present depth of 500 feet (150 metres). The floor, paved with recent lava flows, contains the Halema'uma'u ("Fern House") Crater, an inner crater that is Kilauea's most active vent. Halema'uma'u is the legendary home of Pele, the Hawaiian fire goddess.

The Hawaiian Volcano Observatory is at Uwēkahuna Bluff on the western rim of Kilauea, near Halema'uma'u.

Kilauea's frequent eruptions are usually nonexplosive and are contained within Halema'uma'u as a boiling lake of active lava, which sometimes rises and overflows along the floor and flanks of the caldera proper. In 1790, however, a paroxysmal steam explosion killed part of a Hawaiian army marching near the caldera. A less violent eruption in 1924 enlarged Halema'uma'u Crater to a depth of 1,300 feet (400 metres). In 1955 an eruption in the east rift, accompanied by a series of violent quakes, was one of the most destructive in the island's history, with lava pouring from fissures over a period of 88 days, destroying more than 6 square miles (15 square km) of valuable sugarcane fields and orchards. A similar but shorter-lived occurrence in 1975 was followed by a destructive tsunami. In a series of eruptions that began in 1983 and continued into the early 21st century, Kilauea produced a river of flowing lava that reached the sea 10 miles (16 km) south of the volcano.

Kilauea Iki, a crater directly east of Kilauea, erupted spectacularly in 1959, creating a 400-foot- (120-metre-) deep lake of molten lava and Pu'u Pua'i ("Gushing Hill"), a cinder cone near its southern rim. The east rift zone supports numerous pit craters ending in Makaopuhi, with a depth of 1,000 feet (300 metres). Mauna Iki (elevation 3,032 feet [924 metres]), situated 6 miles (9.5 km) from Kilauea on the southwest rift zone, is a low volcanic dome in a desert area.

Kilauea is bordered by Mauna Loa volcano (west and north), the Ka'ū Desert (southwest), Āinahou Ranch (south), and a tropical fern jungle (north-northeast). The littoral Ka'ū Desert consists of barren lava, crusted volcanic ash, and moving dunes of windblown ash and pumice

Basaltic lava erupting from the Pu'u 'O'o spatter and cinder cone on Kilauea volcano, Hawaii, Jan. 31, 1984. J. D. Griggs/U.S. Geological Survey

10 to 30 feet (3 to 9 metres) high. The Thurston Lava Tube, a 450-foot (135-metre) tunnel east of the caldera, was formed when a lava stream's outer crust hardened while the molten lava continued its flow.

Klyuchevskaya Volcano

This active volcano sits on the Kamchatka Peninsula in far eastern Russia. Klyuchevskaya Volcano (Russian: Klyuchevskaya Sopka) is one of the highest active volcanoes in the world, rising to a height of 15,584 feet (4,750 m), the highest point on the peninsula. The volcano consists of a truncated cone with a central crater, with some 70 lateral craters and cones on the lower slopes. The

Eruption of Krakatoa in 1960. Geological Survey of Indonesia; photograph, D. Hadikusumo

volcano, which has erupted more than 50 times since 1700, is characterized by smoke continuously billowing above its summit. The Kamchatka Volcanological Station, established in 1935, is located at its base.

Krakatoa

Krakatoa (Indonesian: Krakatau) was a volcano located on Rakata Island in the Sunda Strait between Java and Sumatra, Indonesia. Its explosive eruption in 1883 was one of the most catastrophic in history.

Krakatoa lies along the convergence of the Indian-Australian and Eurasian tectonic plates, a zone of high volcanic and seismic activity. Sometime within the past million years, the volcano built a cone-shaped mountain composed of flows of volcanic rock alternating with layers of cinder and ash. From its base, 1,000 feet (300 metres) below sea level, the cone projected about 6,000 feet (1,800 metres) above the sea. Later (possibly in 416 CE), the mountain's top was destroyed, forming a caldera, or bowl-shaped depression, 4 miles (6 km) across. Portions of the caldera projected above the water as four small islands: Sertung (Verlaten) on the northwest, Lang and Polish Hat on the northeast, and Rakata on the south. Over the years, three new cones were formed, merging into a single island. The highest of the three cones rose to 2,667 feet (813 metres) above sea level.

The only confirmed eruption prior to 1883 was a moderate one in 1680. On May 20, 1883, one of the cones again became active; ash-laden clouds reached a height of 6 miles (10 km), and explosions were heard in Batavia (Jakarta), 100 miles (160 km) away, but by the end of May the activity had died down. It resumed on June 19 and became paroxysmal by August 26. At 1:00 PM of that day the first of a series of increasingly violent explosions occurred, and at 2:00 PM a black cloud of ash rose 17 miles (27 km) above Krakatoa.

The climax was reached at 10:00 AM on August 27, with tremendous explosions that were heard 2,200 miles (3,500 km) away in Australia and propelled ash to a height of 50 miles (80 km). Pressure waves in the atmosphere were recorded around Earth. Explosions diminished throughout the day, and by the morning of August 28, the volcano was quiet. Small eruptions continued in the following months and in February 1884.

The discharge of Krakatoa threw into the air nearly 5 cubic miles (21 cubic km) of rock fragments, and large quantities of ash fell over an area of some 300,000 square miles (800,000 square km). Near the volcano, masses of floating pumice were so thick as to halt ships. The surrounding region was plunged into darkness for two and a half days because of ash in the air. The fine dust drifted several times around Earth, causing spectacular red and orange sunsets throughout the following year.

After the explosion, only a small islet remained in a basin covered by 900 feet (250 metres) of ocean water; its highest point reached about 2,560 feet (780 metres) above the surface. As much as 200 feet (60 metres) of ash and pumice fragments had accumulated on Verlaten and Lang islands and on the remaining southern part of Rakata. Analysis of this material revealed that little of it consisted of debris from the former central cones: the fragments of old rock in it represented less than 10 percent of the volume of the missing part of the island. Most of the material was new magma brought up from the depths of Earth, most of it distended into pumice or completely blown apart to form ash as the gas it contained expanded. Thus, the former volcanic cones were not blown into the air, as was first believed, but sank out of sight, the top of the volcano collapsing as a large volume of magma was removed from the underlying reservoir.

Krakatoa was apparently uninhabited, and few people died outright from the eruptions. However, the volcano's collapse triggered a series of tsunamis, or seismic sea waves, recorded as far away as South America and Hawaii. The greatest wave, which reached a height of 120 feet (37 metres) and took some 36,000 lives in nearby coastal towns of Java and Sumatra, occurred just after the climactic explosion. All life on the Krakatoa island group was buried under a thick layer of sterile ash, and plant and animal life did not begin to reestablish itself for five years.

Krakatoa was quiet until December 1927, when a new eruption began on the seafloor along the same line as the previous cones. In early 1928 a rising cone reached sea level, and by 1930 it had become a small island called Anak Krakatau ("Child of Krakatoa"). The volcano has been active sporadically since that time, and the cone has continued to grow to an elevation of about 1,000 feet (300 metres) above the sea.

Lassen Peak

This volcanic peak in northern California, U.S., which is also called Mount Lassen, is the principal attraction of Lassen Volcanic National Park. Lassen Peak stands at the southern end of the Cascade Range, some 50 miles (80 km) east of Redding, and rises above the surrounding area to an elevation of 10,457 feet (3,187 metres). It is classified as a volcanic dome, formed when lava is too viscous to flow away and accumulates around its vent.

The volcano lies on the northern edge of an ancient caldera created when the top of Mount Tehama exploded and collapsed about 350,000 years ago. Lassen Peak was thought to be extinct when it erupted without warning on May 30, 1914. Minor eruptions continued for the following year, until May 19, 1915, when larger and more spectacular explosions propelled a stream of molten lava 1,000 feet (300 metres) down the mountain, melting snow and causing mudflows. Three days later a blast of hot gases felled many trees and produced a mushroom-shaped cloud that rose some 7 miles (11 km) above the summit. The eruptions ceased in 1921, but evidence has suggested the possibility of a periodic cycle for volcanic activity in the area.

Luis Argüello, a Spanish officer, was the first European to sight the peak, in 1821. He named it San José, which subsequently became St. Joseph and then Mount St. Joseph. It was renamed for Peter Lassen, a Danish-born explorer and homesteader in the region who guided settlers through the surrounding area in the mid-19th century.

Mauna Loa

Mauna Loa is the world's largest volcano. It is located on the south-central part of the island of Hawaii, Hawaii

Lava fountains during the 1984 eruption of Mauna Loa, Hawaii Volcanoes National Park, Hawaii. J. D. Griggs/U.S. Geological Survey

State, U.S., and a part of Hawaii Volcanoes National Park. One of the largest single mountain masses in the world, Mauna Loa (meaning "Long Mountain" in Hawaiian) rises to 13,677 feet (4,169 metres) above sea level and constitutes half of the island's area. Its dome is 75 miles (120 km) long and 64 miles (103 km) wide. Moku'āweoweo, its summit caldera, has an area of nearly 6 square miles (15 square km) and a depth of 600 feet (180 metres). Frequently snowcapped in winter, Mauna Loa is a shield volcano that has erupted some three dozen times since its first well-documented eruption in 1843. Many of its eruptions are confined within Moku'āweoweo Caldera; others are lower flank eruptions along northeast or southwest fissure

Mayon Volcano, Luzon, Philippines. Ted Spiegel—Rapho/Photo Researchers

zones. During eruptions in 1935 and 1942, U.S. military planes dropped bombs in attempts (that were partially successful) to divert the path of lava flows that threatened the city of Hilo. In June 1950 a 23-day flow from a 13-mile (21-km) fissure in the southwest rift destroyed a small village. Substantial eruptions at the summit occurred in 1975 and 1984.

MAYON VOLCANO

Located in southeastern Luzon, Philippines, dominating the city of Legaspi, the Mayon Volcano is called the world's most perfect cone, it has a base 80 miles (130 km) in circumference and rises to 8,077 feet (2,462 metres) from the shores of Albay Gulf. Popular with climbers and campers, it is the centre of Mayon Volcano National Park (21 square miles [55 square km]). There are large abaca plantations on its lower slopes. There have been more than 30 eruptions recorded since 1616; an eruption in 1993 caused 75 deaths. Its most destructive eruption was in 1814, when the town of Cagsawa was buried.

MOUNT UNZEN

Mount Unzen is a volcano located in western Kyushu, Japan. Its strong eruption in 1792 led to a destructive landslide and a tsunami. The death toll from the disaster is estimated at some 15,000 people, making it the most deadly volcanic eruption in Japan's history.

Mount Unzen actually consists of a group of composite volcanoes located on Japan's Shimabara Peninsula east of Nagasaki. The area was the site of a major volcanic eruption in 1792. After an initial eruption, a large earthquake triggered a landslide from the Mayuyama peak, a 4,000-year-old lava dome rising above the city of Shimabara. The massive landslide swept through the city and eventually reached the Ariake Sea, where it set off a

Mount Unzen, Japan. U.S. Geological Survey

tsunami. The wave surge devastated nearby areas, causing further widespread damage and death. Most of the estimated 15,000 deaths caused by the event are believed to have resulted from the landslide and the tsunami. The scar created from the Mayuyama landslide remains visible today.

The 1792 eruption served as a reminder to the Japanese people of Earth's unpredictability. A series of earthquakes and small eruptions at Mount Unzen in the early 1990s escalated fears of another disaster, but that catastrophe never materialized. Still, anxiety has remained over the Mount Unzen volcano because of the dense population nearby and its history of catastrophic events.

Mount Nyamulagira

Mount Nyamulagira (also spelled Nyamlagiri or Nyamuragira) is a volcano located in the Virunga Mountains of east-central Africa, 15 miles (24 km) northeast of Sake, in the volcano region of Virunga National Park, Congo (Kinshasa). It is about 10,023 feet (3,055 metres) high. The most active volcano in Africa, Nyamulagira often emits lava and ash, though fatalities are rare. Since 1882 there have been more than 35 eruptions, including a major one in 1938, when the southwest slope opened, and the lava reached Lake Kivu to the south. In 1998 lava from the volcano flowed some 6 miles (10 km) into the surrounding forest and forced the closure of several refugee camps. In January 2000 a series of eruptions occurred, but the presence of Congolese rebels in the surrounding area has hampered geological research.

Mount Nyiragongo

An active volcano in the Virunga Mountains of east-central Africa, Mount Nyiragongo lies in the volcano region of Virunga National Park, Congo (Kinshasa), near the border with Rwanda, 12 miles (19 km) north of Goma. It is 11,385 feet (3,470 metres) high, with a main crater 1.3 miles (2 km) wide and 820 feet (250 metres) deep containing a liquid lava pool. Some older craters on the mountain are noted for their plant life. Nyiragongo is known for its devastating eruptions. In 1977 some 2,000 people were killed, and in 2002 Goma was largely destroyed by lava, creating a refugee crisis.

Ol Doinyo Lengai

This active volcano, northern Tanzania, East Africa, sits at the southern end of Lake Natron. It rises to an elevation of 9,442 ft (2,878 m) and is one of the many volcanoes situated along the East African rift system. Ol Doinyo Lengai ("Mountain of God") contains basalts rich in sodium and potassium, and is so alkaline that its lavas resemble washing soda. Eruptions have been recorded from 1880 to 1967.

The volcano has more than one active centre and most of the recent eruptions were from its northern crater. Subsidiary cones extend out from the centre and down its sides. The fertile lower levels of the Ol Doinyo Lengai are planted in vineyards and citrus. The steep higher slopes are covered with oak, birch, and beech. Above 6,500 ft a few plants are found scattered among ashes, sand, and fragments of lava and slag.

Paricutín

Paricutín resides in western Michoacán state, west-central Mexico, just north of the Tancítaro Peak and 20 miles (32 km) west-northwest of Uruapan. It is one of the youngest volcanoes on Earth.

On Feb. 20, 1943, Paricutín began to erupt in an open field. The fire, lava, and ashes destroyed and buried two villages and hundreds of homes. In the first year, the volcano's cone had risen 1,475 feet (450 metres) from the base (at 7,480 feet [2,280 metres] above sea level) and had buried the village of Paricutín. Its peak had reached an elevation of 9,210 feet (2,808 metres) in 1952, when the eruptions finally ended. The partially buried church of San Juan Parangaricutiro at the edge of the village of Paricutín is a local tourist attraction.

Pavlof Volcano

A volcanic peak of the Aleutian Range, southwestern Alaska, U.S., Pavlof Volcano is situated about 580 miles (930 km) southwest of Anchorage, on the west side of Pavlof Bay near the southwestern tip of the Alaska Peninsula. Rising to more than 8,260 feet (2,518 metres), Pavlof is one of the tallest volcanoes in Alaska. It is also one of the most consistently active, having had about 40 eruptions recorded since 1790. Just northeast of Pavlof

Pavlof Volcano, southwestern Alaska. T. Miller/U.S. Geological Survey

Volcano stands its "twin," a volcano known as Pavlof Sister (7,028 feet [2,142 metres]). Pavlof Sister is also active, but no eruptions have been reported there since 1762. Built high on a base of older volcanic rock, the two symmetrical, cone-shaped peaks are a prominent feature of the landscape.

Mount Pelée

An active volcanic mountain on the Caribbean island of Martinique, Mount Pelée (French: Montagne Pelée) is situated 15 miles (24 km) northwest of Fort-de-France and reaches an elevation of 4,583 feet (1,397 metres). Pelée, whose name is a French term meaning "bald," consists of layers of volcanic ash and lavas. Its gently sloping cone is scored with ravines and supports luxuriant forests. Minor eruptions occurred in 1792 and 1851, but on May 8, 1902, it violently destroyed the port of Saint-Pierre, killing approximately 30,000 people, 15 percent of the island's population. So dramatic was this event that the name of the mountain has been adopted (as in the term *pelean*) to describe that particular kind of eruption of ash, gas, and deadly nuée ardente ("fiery cloud"). A minor eruption occurred in 1929.

Volcano Pico de Orizaba

Pico de Orizaba (also called Citlaltépetl Volcano) straddles the border of Veracruz and Puebla states in south-central Mexico. Its name comes from the Nahuatl for "Star Mountain," and it rises on the southern edge of the Mexican Plateau, 60 miles (100 km) east of the city of Puebla. At 18,406 feet (5,610 metres) above sea level, the Pico de Orizaba's symmetrical, snowcapped cone is the third highest peak in North America after Mount

Volcano Pico de Orizaba, Veracruz and Puebla, Mexico. © Digital Vision/ Getty Images

McKinley, Alaska, and Mount Logan, Canada. The volcano has been dormant since 1687. Pico de Orizaba was first climbed in 1848.

Mount Pinatubo

This volcano, located in western Luzon, Philippines, erupted in 1991 (for the first time in 600 years) and caused widespread devastation. Mount Pinatubo is located about 55 miles (90 km) northwest of Manila and rose to a height of about 4,800 feet (1,460 m) prior to its eruption. After two months of emissions and small explosions, a series of major explosions began on June 12. These explosions reached a peak on June 14–16, producing a column of ash and smoke more than 19 miles (30 km) high, with rock debris falling the same distance from the volcano. The resulting heavy ashfalls left about 100,000 people homeless, forced thousands more to flee the area, and caused 300 deaths. The ashfalls forced the evacuation and eventual closing of U.S.-leased Clark Air Force Base, 10 miles (16 km) east of the volcano.

The ash and smoke cloud ejected by Mount Pinatubo in 1991 contained about twice as much matter as that thrown up by the El Chichón volcano (1982), making Pinatubo perhaps the largest eruption of the 20th century. Pinatubo erupted again in late August 1992, killing more than 72 people.

Popocatépetl

A volcano residing on the border of the states of México and Puebla, central Mexico. Its name in Nahuatl means "Smoking Mountain." Popocatépetl lies along Mexico's Cordillera Neo-Volcánica at the southern edge of the Mexican Plateau, 10 miles (16 km) south of its twin, Iztaccíhuatl, and 45 miles (72 km) southeast of Mexico City. The perpetually snowcapped, symmetrical cone of

Popocatépetl rises to an elevation of 17,930 feet (5,465 metres), surpassed only by Mexico's tallest volcano, Pico de Orizaba (18,406 feet [5,610 metres]).

The first Spanish ascent of Popocatépetl is thought to have been made in 1522 by Hernán Cortés's men, who needed to acquire sulfur for the manufacture of gunpowder. After lying inactive for more than 70 years, Popocatépetl erupted in December 1994, causing an ashfall over Puebla. Volcanic activity recurred in March and October 1996, as well as in April 1997, and in December 2000 thousands of villagers were forced to evacuate after another eruption.

Mount Rainier

Mount Rainier is the highest mountain (14,410 feet [4,392 metres]) in the state of Washington, U.S., and in the

Mount Rainier, Washington. © Michael Hynes

Summit of Mount Rainier, Washington. Glen Allison/Getty Images

Cascade Range. It lies about 40 miles (64 km) southeast of the city of Tacoma, within Mount Rainier National Park. The mountain, geologically young, was formed by successive lava flows from eruptions that began about one million years ago. The dormant volcano last erupted 150 to 175 years ago. Covering 100 square miles (260 square km), Rainier is surrounded by the largest single-mountain glacier system in the United States outside Alaska, with 41 glaciers radiating from the broad summit, including Nisqually Glacier, whose retreat and advance over the last 150 years has allowed scientists to determine patterns in Earth's climate. The mountain contains three major peaks—Liberty Cap, Point Success, and Columbia Crest (the latter being the summit)—and is noted for dense stands of coniferous trees on lower slopes, scenic alpine meadows, waterfalls and lakes, and an abundance of wildlife and flowers.

The English explorer George Vancouver sighted the summit on May 8, 1792, and named it for fellow navigator Peter Rainier. The first well-documented ascent was completed by Hazard Stevens and Philemon Van Trump on Aug. 17, 1870. The mountain is now one of the country's premier destinations for climbers and is among the top venues for mountaineering training and instruction. Each year several thousand people attempt the climb to the summit, many of them on a guided two-day trip. Rainier is sometimes referred to by its Native American name, Mount Tacoma, or Tahoma.

Mount Ruapehu

An active volcano and the highest peak (9,176 feet [2,797 m]) on North Island, New Zealand, in Tongariro National Park, Mount Ruapehu is situated on the Taupo Plateau, which rises 2,000 to 3,000 feet (about 600 to 900 m) above sea level. Ruapehu erupted in 1945–46 and again in 1995–96.

Christine Falls, near the base of Mount Rainier, Washington.
© Michael Hynes

The volcano is forested below its line of permanent snow cover. Above the line, glaciers flow from the peak. Within the crater lies a lake, which is drained by the Whangaehu River. Ruapehu is the most southerly of the large volcanic cones within the park, the others being Ngauruhoe (7,503 feet [2,287 m]) and Tongariro (6,453 feet [1,967 m]). These mountains form the centre of one of New Zealand's major ski resorts. Ruapehu was first climbed to its highest point by J. Park, C. Dalin, and W. H. Dunnage in 1886.

Mount Ruiz

A volcano in the Cordillera Central of the Andes in west-central Colombia, Mount Ruiz (Spanish: Nevado del Ruiz) is noted for its two eruptions on Nov. 13, 1985, which were among the most destructive in recorded history. Located about 80 miles (130 km) west of Bogotá, it is the northernmost of some two dozen active volcanoes scattered along the Cordillera Central and reaches an elevation of 17,717 feet (5,400 m). Although eruptions of Mount Ruiz have not been frequent, geological evidence suggests that a major eruption in 1595 damaged an area extending from central Colombia north to the southern border of Panama. An eruption in 1845 caused mud slides and flooding in which 1,000 people were killed.

The 1985 disaster was preceded by a buildup of highly viscous magma within the volcano's neck. Two explosions occurred on the northeast side of the mountain, and magma, blasting outward, melted the mountain's cap of ice and snow. A mixture of mud, ash, and water with a crest of 15 to 50 feet (4.5 to 15 m) raced down the volcano's eastern slope through the Azufrado and Lagunilla river channels. Torrents of mud almost totally buried the town of Armero on the Lagunilla River, 30 miles (48 km) from the volcano, killing an estimated 25,000 people. Mud also swelled the nearby Gualí River to overflowing, and on the western side of the mountain another mud slide killed about 1,000 people in the town of Chinchiná on the Claro River.

Mount Saint Helens

Mount Saint Helens is a volcanic peak in the Cascade Range, southwestern Washington, U.S. Its eruption on

May 18, 1980, was one of the greatest volcanic explosions ever recorded in North America.

Mount St. Helens, named by the English navigator George Vancouver for a British ambassador, had been dormant since 1857. An explosive steam eruption on March 27, 1980, was followed by alternating periods of quiescence and minor eruption. Pressure from rising magma within the volcano caused extensive fissures and the growth of a bulge on the north flank of the peak. On the morning of May 18, an earthquake with a magnitude of 5.1 on the Richter scale triggered a gigantic landslide on the mountain's north face. The north slope fell away in an avalanche that was followed and overtaken by a lateral air blast, which carried a high-velocity cloud of superheated ash and stone outward some 15 miles (25 km) from the

The north face of Mount St. Helens in June 1970. R. W. Decker

Statue of a man planting trees, dedicated to those who replanted the area around Mount St. Helens, Washington. © Michael Hynes

volcano's summit; the blast reached temperatures of 660 °F (350 °C) and speeds of at least 300 miles (500 km) per hour. The avalanche and lateral blast were followed by mudflows, pyroclastic flows, and floods that buried the river valleys around Mount St. Helens in deep layers of mud and debris as far as 17 miles (27 km) away. Meanwhile, simultaneously with the blast, a vertical eruption of gas and ash formed a column some 16 miles (26 km) high that produced ash falls as far east as central Montana. Complete darkness occurred in Spokane, Washington, about 250 miles (400 km) northeast of the volcano.

A total of 57 people and thousands of animals were killed in the May 18 event, and trees over an area of some 200 square miles (500 square km) were blown down by the lateral air blast. At the event's end, Mount St. Helens's volcanic cone had been completely blasted away; in place of its 9,677-foot (2,950-metre) peak was a horseshoe-shaped crater with a rim reaching an elevation of 8,363 feet (2,549 metres). Further eruptions occurred until 1986, and a dome of lava grew intermittently in the crater. Seismic activity occurred again between 1989 and 1991 (including some small explosions) as well as in 1995 and 1998.

In 1982, 172 square miles (445 square km) of land surrounding the volcano was designated Mount St. Helens National Volcanic Monument, administered by the U.S. Forest Service as part of Gifford Pinchot National Forest. The monument provides a unique opportunity for scientific study of the dynamics of an active composite volcano and for research on how ecosystems respond to cataclysmic disturbances. The monument also presents many recreational and educational opportunities. Visitors can view the crater, lava dome, pumice plain, and effects of the landslide from Johnston Ridge Observatory on the monument's west side, less than 5 miles (8 km) from the volcano. The west side also provides opportunities to observe

Mount St. Helens, Washington. © Michael Hynes

animals and plants that have recolonized the blast zone and lakes that have formed as a result of the eruption. The edge of the blast zone, marked by standing dead trees, lies in the eastern part of the monument where old-growth forests, undamaged by the blast, still stand. On the south side are lava formations of various ages, including the longest continuous lava tube in the 48 conterminous U.S. states, which formed during an eruption about 2,000 years ago. Mount Rainier National Park is to the northeast.

Tajumulco Volcano

A mountain peak in southwestern Guatemala, Tajumulco Volcano (Spanish: Volcán Tajumulco) is the highest peak in Central America, rising essentially from sea level to an elevation of 13,845 feet (4,220 metres). The peak is part of the Sierra Madre de Chiapas, a mountain range that extends into Guatemala from Chiapas state in southern Mexico. Tajumulco is thought to sit atop the remains of an older volcano and has two peaks. The extinct volcano can be reached from the city of San Marcos, which is situated 9 miles (14 km) to the southeast.

Mount Tambora

Mount Tambora (Indonesian: Gunung Tambora) is a dormant volcanic mountain on the northern coast of Sumbawa island, Indonesia. It is now 2,851 metres (9,354 feet) high. It erupted violently in April 1815, when it lost much of its top. The blast, pyroclastic flow, and moderate tsunamis that followed caused the death of at least 10,000 islanders and destroyed the homes of 35,000 more. Some 80,000 people in the region eventually died from starvation and disease related to the event. Before that eruption Mount Tambora was about 4,300 metres (14,000 feet) high.

Many volcanologists regard the eruption as the largest in recorded history; it expelled roughly 100 cubic km (24 cubic miles) of ash, pumice, and aerosols into the atmosphere. As this material mixed with atmospheric gases, it prevented substantial amounts of sunlight from reaching Earth's surface, eventually reducing the average global temperature by about 3 °C (5.4 °F). The immediate effects were most profound on Sumbawa and surrounding islands; many tens of thousands of people perished from disease and famine since crops could not grow. In 1816, parts of the world as far away as western Europe and eastern North America experienced sporadic periods of heavy snow and killing frost through June, July, and August. Such cold weather events led to crop failures and starvation in these regions, and the year 1816 was called the "year without a summer."

Teide Peak

Teide Peak (Spanish: Pico del Teide) is a volcano that sits in the centre of the island of Tenerife in the Santa Cruz de Tenerife provincia (province) of the Canary Islands comunidad autónoma (autonomous community), Spain. At 12,198 feet (3,718 metres), it is the highest point on Spanish soil. Teide is the peak atop El Pilón, a 492-foot- (150-metre-) high volcanic cone that rises from a crater on the upper reaches of the mountain El Teide, which is itself a conglomeration of several volcanoes rising within a 10-mile- (16-km-) wide caldera called Las Cañadas. Snow covers the summit only in winter. Teide Peak has a crater about 260 feet (80 metres) in diameter. Hot gases are ejected from vents within the crater and on the slopes. The last eruption of the mountain El Teide was in 1909, on the northwestern flank of the volcano. El Teide dominates Teide National Park (established 1954), in which it is located. The park was designated a UNESCO World Heritage site in 2007. An international

Teide Peak at the summit of El Pilón on Tenerife in the Canary Islands, Spain. K. Scholz/Shostal Assoc.

solar observatory is located at Izaña, about 4 miles (6 km) northeast of the park.

Vesuvius

An active volcano that rises above the Bay of Naples on the plain of Campania in southern Italy, the western base of Vesuvius (Italian: Vesuvio) rests almost upon the bay. The height of the cone in 1980 was 4,198 ft (1,280 m), but it varies considerably after each major eruption. At about 1,968 ft a high semicircular ridge, called Mt. Somma, begins, girding the cone on the north and rising to 3,714 ft. Between

Mt. Somma and the cone is the Valle del Gigante (Giant's Valley). At the summit of the cone is a large crater about 1,000 ft deep and 2,000 ft across; it was formed in the eruption of 1944. More than 2,000,000 people live in the area of Vesuvius and on its lower slopes. There are industrial towns along the coast of the Bay of Naples and small agricultural centres on the northern slopes.

Vesuvius originated during the late Pleistocene Epoch, probably somewhat less than 200,000 years ago. Although a relatively young volcano, Vesuvius had been dormant for centuries before the great eruption of 79 CE that buried the cities of Pompeii and Stabiae under ashes and lapilli and the city of Herculaneum under a mud flow. The writer Pliny the Younger, who was staying at a place west of Naples, gave an excellent account of the catastrophe in two letters to the historian Tacitus. Between the years 79 and 1631, several eruptions were reported. Confirmed eruptions occurred in 203, 472, 512, 787, 968, 991, 999, 1007, and 1036. The explosions of 512 were so severe that Theodoric the Goth released the people living on the slopes of Vesuvius from payment of taxes.

After some centuries of quiescence, a series of earthquakes, lasting for six months and gradually increasing in violence, preceded a major eruption that took place on Dec. 16, 1631. Many villages on the slopes of the volcano were destroyed; about 3,000 people were killed; the lava flow reached the sea; and the skies were darkened for days. After 1631 there was a change in the eruptive character of the volcano and activity became continuous. Two stages could be observed: quiescent and eruptive. During the quiescent stage the volcano's mouth would be obstructed, whereas in the eruptive stage it would be almost continually open.

Between 1660 and 1944 some 19 of these cycles were observed. Severe paroxysmal eruptions, concluding an eruptive stage, occurred in the years 1660, 1682, 1694, 1698, 1707, 1737, 1760, 1767, 1779, 1794, 1822, 1834, 1839, 1850, 1855, 1861, 1868, 1872, 1906, and 1944. The eruptive stages varied in length from 6 months to 30 3/4 years. The quiescent stages have varied from 18 months to 7 1/2 years.

Scientific study of the volcano did not begin until late in the 18th century. An observatory was opened in 1845 at 1,995 ft, and, in the 20th century, numerous stations were set up at various heights for making volcanologic measurements. A large laboratory and a deep tunnel for seismo-gravimetric measurements were also built.

The slopes of Vesuvius are covered with vineyards and orchards, and the wine grown there is known as Lacrima Christi; in ancient Pompeii the wine jars were frequently marked with the name Vesuvinum. Higher up, the mountain is covered with copses of oak and chestnut, and on the northern side along the slopes of Mt. Somma the woods proceed to the very summit. On the western side the chestnut groves give way above 2,000 ft to undulating plateaus covered with broom, where the crater left by the great eruption of the year 79 has been filled in. Still higher, on the slopes of the great cone and on the inner slope of Mt. Somma, the surface is almost barren; during quiescent periods it is covered by tufts of meadow plants.

The soil is very fertile, and in the long period of inactivity before the eruption of 1631 there were forests in the crater and three lakes from which pasturing herds drank. Vegetation on the slope dies off during eruptive periods because of the volcanic gases. After the eruption of 1906, forests were planted on the slopes in order to protect inhabited places from the flows of mud that usually occur after violent eruptions, and in the fertile soil the trees grew rapidly. In 73 BCE the gladiator Spartacus was besieged by the praetor Publius Claudius Pulcher on the barren summit of Mt. Somma, which was then a wide, flat depression walled by rugged rocks festooned with wild vines. He escaped by twisting ropes of vine branches and descending through unguarded fissures in the crater rim. Some paintings excavated in Pompeii and Herculaneum represent the mountain as it looked before the eruption of 79 CE, when it had only one peak.

VOLCANIC LANDFORMS

The Major Types of Volcanic Landforms

The common mental image of a volcano is that of a steep symmetrical cone sweeping upward in a concave curve to a sharp summit peak. Mount Fuji in Japan is the archetype of this image, but in reality only a few volcanoes attain this ideal shape. Each of the more than 1,500 potentially active volcanoes or volcanic areas around the world has a distinct form, though most can be generalized into nine categories. These categories are described below in order of their numerical importance

Stratovolcanoes

Stratovolcanoes such as Mayon Volcano in the Philippines, Mount Momotombo in Nicaragua, and Ol Doinyo Lengai in Tanzania are steep cones built by both pyroclastic and lava-flow eruptions. The cone-shaped form slopes up gradually and becomes steeper (up to 35°) toward the summit, which generally contains a crater. Stratovolcanoes are composed of volcanic rock types that vary from basalt to rhyolite, but their composition is generally andesite. They may erupt many thousands of times over life spans of millions of years. A typical eruption begins with ash explosions and ends with extrusion of thick, viscous lava

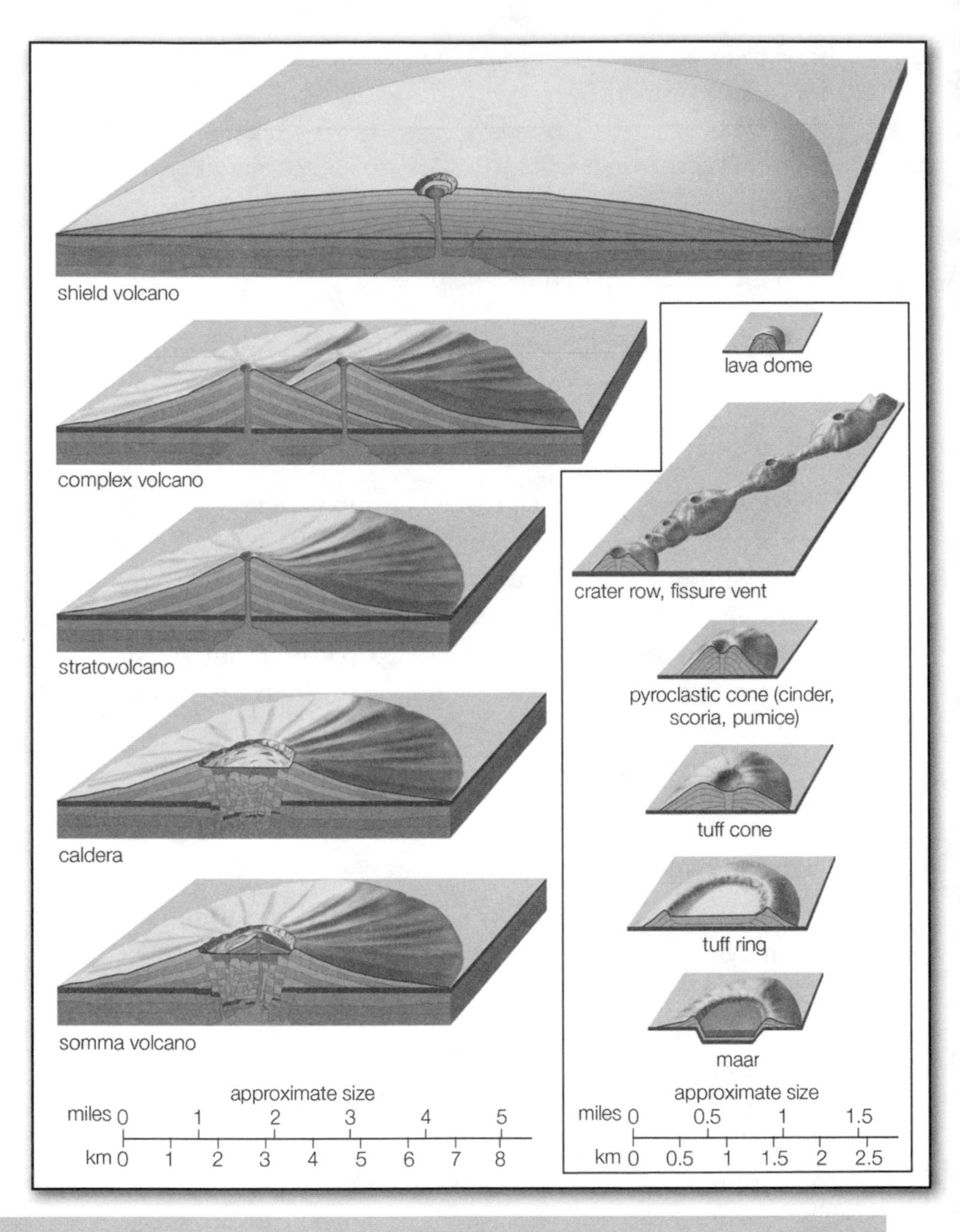

The landforms shown at left and right are vertically exaggerated, and those shown at right are out of scale to those shown at left. In reality a cinder cone would be approximately one-tenth the size of a stratovolcano. Encyclopædia Britannica, Inc.

flows. The alternating layers (strata) of ash and lava are not continuous, blanketlike deposits; rather, they are overlapping lobes or tongues of ash and lava. For this reason many geologists refer to stratovolcanoes as composite volcanoes.

Shield Volcanoes

Structures of this type are large, dome-shaped mountains built of lava flows. Their name derives from their similarity in shape to a warrior's shield lying face up. Shield volcanoes are usually composed of basalt. Small shield volcanoes may form rapidly from almost continuous eruptions, but the larger shields are formed over a span of about 1 million years by hundreds of thousands of effusive eruptions of fluid lavas from their summits and rift zones. The slopes of shield volcanoes are gentle, seldom exceeding 6°. The summits, which are nearly flat, are generally indented by cliff-walled craters or calderas. The Hawaiian volcano Mauna Loa is a typical shield volcano. Its elongate shape records a long history of fluid lava flows not only from its summit but from its two persistent rift zones.

Submarine Volcanoes

These structures occur in various forms, but many are cone-shaped seamounts. Some ancient island volcanoes were eroded flat or covered with a coral cap at sea level before they sank below the sea surface as they and the crust supporting them cooled and became denser. These flat-topped seamounts are called guyots. Most of the active submarine volcanoes that are known occur at shallow depths beneath the sea. They are recognized because their explosive eruptions can be detected and located by hydrophones. Active submarine volcanoes at depths of a few thousand metres are probably common, particularly along oceanic spreading centres, but the water pressure at these depths reduces explosive boiling, and so the eruptions are difficult to detect. One exception to this is the submarine volcano Loihi, a seamount whose summit

Momotombo Volcano (left) and Momotombito Island, viewed across Lake Managua, Nicaragua. Byron Augustin/D. Donne Bryant Stock

Ol Doinyo Lengai, volcano near Lake Natron, northern Tanzania. Robert Francis/Robert Harding Picture Library

caldera is 1 km (0.6 mile) below sea level and 30 km (19 miles) southeast of the island of Hawaii. Although eruptions of this youngest volcano of the Hawaiian chain have not been directly observed, seismographs detected swarms of earthquakes at shallow depths beneath the summit of Loihi in 1971–72, 1975, and 1996. Observers in a submersible research vessel from the University of Hawaii dove to Loihi as the 1996 earthquakes waned; they discovered a new collapse crater at the summit and fine white "dust" that greatly reduced visibility but saw no red lava or erupting vents. A submarine eruption has not yet been directly observed in progress.

Calderas

Most calderas—large circular or oval depressions more than 1 km (0.6 mile) in diameter—have been formed by inward collapse of landforms after large amounts of magma have been expelled from underground. Many are surrounded by steep cliffs, and some are filled with lakes. The terms *crater* and *caldera* are often used synonymously, but calderas are larger than craters. A crater can occur inside a caldera, as at Taal Lake in the Philippines, but not the reverse. Calderas are often associated with large eruptions (those producing volumes of 10 cubic km [2.4 cubic miles] or more) of dacitic or rhyolitic magma that form pyroclastic plateaus.

Calderas also occur on shield volcanoes. These calderas are thought to form when large rift eruptions or lateral intrusions remove tremendous quantities of magma from the shallow magma chambers beneath the summit, leaving the ground above the chambers with no support. The collapse and refilling of calderas on active Hawaiian volcanoes probably recur many times during a volcano's lifetime.

Whether a volcano is designated a caldera, shield volcano, or stratovolcano with a caldera depends on the principal landform feature. For example, Crater Lake in Oregon in the northwestern United States is designated a caldera, but Kilauea in Hawaii is designated a shield volcano even though it has a large summit caldera.

Complex Volcanoes

Such structures are mixed landforms. In most cases, they occur because of changes either in eruptive habit or in location of the principal vent area. A stratovolcano may form a large explosion crater that later becomes filled by a lava dome, or several new cones and craters may develop on a caldera's rim. One stratovolcano may have multiple summits when individual cones overlap one another. The Three Sisters volcanic complex in Oregon is an example of a complex volcano with three summits.

Pyroclastic Cones

Pyroclastic cones (also called cinder cones or scoria cones) such as Cerro Negro in Nicaragua are relatively small, steep (about 30°) volcanic landforms built of loose pyroclastic fragments, most of which are cinder-sized. The fragments cool sufficiently during their flight through the air so that they do not weld together when they strike one another. Generally, the crater from which the cinder fragments were ejected is located in the centre of the cone. In areas with strong prevailing winds, however, the crater may be upwind of the cone. The rock type involved in pyroclastic cones is generally basalt or basaltic andesite, and the eruption type is either the moderately explosive Vulcanian or the gentler Hawaiian, which produces high lava fountains.

Some cinder cones such as Parícutin in Mexico grow during a single eruption. Parícutin rises approximately

Eruption of Cerro Negro volcano, Nicaragua, November 1969. Cerro Negro is a cinder cone type of volcano that was born of a series of eruptions beginning in 1850. It still periodically blankets the surrounding countryside with ash. U.S. Department of the Interior, Geological Survey

410 metres (1,345 feet) from its base to its summit and is 1 km (0.6 mile) wide; it formed during nearly continuous eruptions from 1943 to 1952. Cinder cones also form at some vents on shield volcanoes, but these are not considered to be separate, individual volcanoes. Certain cinder cones have multiple eruptions, but, if activity continues for thousands to tens of thousands of years from the same vent, it is likely that they will develop into stratovolcanoes or complex volcanoes.

Pumice cones are structures similar to cinder cones, but they are made up of volcanic glass fragments so riddled with gas-bubble holes (vesicles) that they resemble a sponge and are very lightweight. Less common pyroclastic landforms include maars, low-relief craters often filled with water and surrounded by a rim of ejected material that was probably formed by explosive interaction of magma and groundwater; and tuff rings and tuff cones, which are landforms built of compacted pyroclastic deposits. Tuff rings and cones resemble maars, but they have higher rims and are not filled with water. Tuff rings are only about 5 metres (16 feet) high, with craters roughly at ground level. Tuff cones are higher and steeper, with craters above ground level. Punchbowl and Diamond Head on Oahu island, Hawaii, are famous examples of tuff cones.

Volcanic Fields

Such areas have many geologically young cinder cones or other features that have not been individually identified as separate volcanoes. If the conduits through which magma ascends to the surface are scattered over a broad area, many short-lived volcanoes are formed rather than a major volcano with repeated eruptions. The area in which Parícutin formed is a volcanic field with dozens of prehistoric—but geologically young—cinder cones and lava flows. The most likely place for the birth of a new volcano is in a known volcanic field.

Fissure Vents

These features constitute the surface trace of dikes (underground fractures filled with magma). Most dikes measure about 0.5 to 2 metres (1.5 to 6.5 feet) in width and several kilometres in length. The dikes that feed fissure vents reach the surface from depths of a few kilometres. Fissure vents are common in Iceland and along the radial rift zones of shield volcanoes.

In Iceland the volcanic vents often are long fissures parallel to the rift zone where lithospheric plates are diverging. Renewed eruptions generally occur from new parallel fractures offset by a few hundred to thousands of metres from the earlier fissures. This distribution of vents and voluminous eruptions of fluid basaltic lava usually build up a thick lava plateau rather than a single volcanic edifice. The largest effusive eruption of lava in recorded history occurred in 1783 in Iceland from the Laki fissure. This vent produced high lava fountains, a crater row 25 km (15.5 miles) long, and 565 square km (218 square miles) of basaltic lava flows with a volume of approximately 12 cubic km (2.9 cubic miles).

The radial fissure vents of Hawaiian volcanoes produce "curtains of fire" as lava fountains erupt along a portion of a fissure. These vents produce low ramparts of basaltic spatter on both sides of the fissure. More isolated lava fountains along the fissure produce crater rows of small spatter and cinder cones. The fragments that form a spatter cone are hot and plastic enough to weld together, while the fragments that form a cinder cone remain separate because of their lower temperature.

Lava Domes

Landforms of this sort consist of steep domal mounds of lava so viscous that the lava piles up over its vent without flowing away. The rock types that form lava domes are generally andesites, dacites, or rhyolites. Somehow these viscous lavas have lost much of their gas content in prior eruptions or during a slow rise to the surface. Even so, it is not unusual for an actively growing lava dome to have an explosive eruption that disrupts all or part of the dome. Many lava domes grow by internal intrusion of lava that causes swelling and oversteepening of the dome. Rockslides build up an apron of talus blocks around the lower sides of the dome. Lava domes can form mounds several hundred metres high with diameters ranging from several hundred to more than 1,000 metres (3,300 feet). Thick lava flows sometimes move short distances from

The lava dome of Mount St. Helens, May 16, 1984. Following the great eruption of May 18, 1980, a dome of lava grew intermittently in the crater of the volcano. By the time of this photograph, the dome measured 850 metres (2,800 feet) wide and 220 metres (725 feet) high. Courtesy of the U.S. Geological Survey; photograph, Lyn Topinka

the dome and distort its generally circular or oval shape. A good example of a lava dome is the one in the explosion crater at Mount St. Helens.

Other Volcanic Structures and Features

There are many types of volcanic forms and terms other than those described above. Some general terms that may be encountered include *volcanic cone* which is a descriptive term pertaining to shape with no implication of size, rock type, or genesis; and *explosion crater*, a large circular, elongate, or horseshoe-shaped excavation with ejected debris on its rim or flanks. A somma volcano, named for Mount Somma, a ridge on the slopes of Mount Vesuvius in Italy, is a caldera partially filled by a new central cone. In some areas, magma or still-hot igneous rocks at shallow depth leak gases through gas vents or interact with the groundwater system to create hot springs. These areas are known as hydrothermal regions, fumarole fields, or solfatara fields.

The Determinants of Size and Shape

The shape and size of a volcano are controlled by several factors. These include:

- The volume of volcanic products
- The interval length between eruptions
- The composition of volcanic products
- The variety of volcanic eruption types
- The geometry of the vent
- The environment into which the volcanic products are erupted

The volume of material released in any one eruption can vary enormously from a few cubic metres of magma to as much as 3,000 cubic km (720 cubic miles). A series of small eruptions usually builds up mounds close to the vent, whereas large-volume eruptions tend to disperse their products over a greater distance. Effusive eruptions form lava plateaus or gently sloping shield volcanoes; moderately explosive eruptions form stratovolcanoes; and giant explosive eruptions form plateaus of lava or ash flows and almost always form a caldera several kilometres in diameter over the eruption site. Naturally, since many other factors are involved in determining volcanic landforms, there are exceptions to these rules.

The chemical composition of magma affects its physical properties, which in turn have a major influence on the landform built by a volcanic eruption. Four common volcanic rock types are basalt, andesite, dacite, and rhyolite. As the silica content increases, these rock types generally become more viscous; as the magmatic gas content increases, they become more explosive. Other physical properties are, however, important in determining the character of lava flows. For example, hot basaltic lava produces flows with smooth to ropy surfaces. These flows, known as pahoehoe, tend to flow farther than the cooler aa flows of the same chemical composition that have rough, broken surfaces.

If a volcano has consistent eruption habits, its landform will reflect that character. The shape of the huge but gently sloping shield volcano Mauna Loa, for example, indicates a long record of eruption of fluid lava flows, while the beautiful, symmetrical shape of the stratovolcano Mount Fuji indicates a long record of moderately explosive eruptions from its summit that produce alternating layers of ash and lava. In contrast to simple shield and stratovolcanoes, many volcanoes change their eruptive habits—both in eruption type and in the location of their vents—over time. This results in a mixture of volcanic landforms called a complex volcano.

The geometry of the vent or vents also exerts profound control on volcanic landforms. Multiple point-source vents that erupt only once or at most a few times form a volcanic field of dozens of small cinder cones rather than a single large volcanic edifice. Volcanic vents in the form of long fissures usually build up a thick lava plateau (especially when erupting voluminous amounts of fluid lava) or a low volcanic mound. Hekla Volcano in Iceland is transitional between plateau-building fissure eruptions and eruptions from a single major vent that produce a symmetrical stratovolcano. Hekla erupts from a fissure that is parallel to the Mid-Atlantic Ridge and about 20 km (12 miles) in length. Viewed along the fissure, Hekla looks like a stratovolcano; perpendicular to the fissure, it appears as an elongate ridge.

Finally, but of great importance, is the environment where the volcanic products are erupted—into the atmosphere, under water, or under ice. Submarine volcanoes are surprisingly similar to their counterparts on land, but their slopes are generally steeper because water cools the lavas more rapidly. Deep submarine volcanism tends to be less explosive because the pressure of the water retards explosive boiling. Subglacial volcanism produces landforms that are dramatically different from those produced by subaerial volcanism. This is particularly apparent in Iceland, where glaciers covered the entire island 15,000 years ago, and large ice caps still cover extensive areas today. Fissure eruptions beneath the ice form steep ridges of broken lava fragments rather than lava-flow plateaus, while subglacial eruptions from point-source vents that erupt repeatedly form table mountains. Table mountain volcanoes have steep sides of pillow lavas—sacklike structures that form when flows of basaltic lava are extruded into the ocean, a deep lake, or a water-filled cavern within ice. These pillow structures are capped by several tens of metres of broken lava fragments from explosive shallow-water eruptions. The broken lava fragments in turn are overlain by shield-building lava flows erupted above the glacial surface.

HOT SPRINGS AND GEYSERS

Hot springs and geysers also are manifestations of volcanic activity. They result from the interaction of groundwater with magma or with solidified but still-hot igneous rocks at shallow depths.

Hot, or thermal, springs are features that contain water at temperatures substantially higher than the air temperature of the surrounding region. Most hot springs discharge groundwater that is heated by shallow intrusions of magma in volcanic areas. Some thermal springs, however, are not related to volcanic activity. In such cases, the water is heated by convective circulation: groundwater percolating downward reaches depths of a kilometre or more where the temperature of rocks is high because of the normal temperature gradient of Earth's crust—about 30 °C (54 °F) per kilometre in the first 10 km (6 miles).

Many of the colours in hot springs are caused by thermophilic (heat-loving) microorganisms. The cyanobacteria, one of the more common of these groups, grow in huge colonies called bacterial mats that form the colourful scums and slimes on the sides of hot springs. Various colours of cyanobacteria prefer specific conditions of water chemistry and temperature, thus providing a rough "thermometer" for hot springs: yellow, about 70 °C (160 °F); brown, about 60 °C (140 °F); and green, about 50 °C (120 °F) or lower.

A tremendous amount of heat is released by hot springs, and various applications of this geothermal energy have been developed. In certain areas, buildings and greenhouses are heated with water pumped from hot springs.

A type of hot spring known as a geyser spouts intermittent jets of water and steam. The term is derived from the Icelandic word *geysir*, meaning "to gush." This action is caused by the water in deep conduits beneath a geyser approaching or reaching the boiling point. At 300 metres (about 1,000 feet) below the surface, the boiling point of water increases to approximately 230 °C (450 °F) because of the increased pressure of the overlying water. As bubbles of steam or dissolved gas begin to form, rise, and expand, hot water spills from the geyser's vent, lowering the pressure on the water column below. Water at depth then momentarily exceeds its boiling point and flashes into steam, forcing additional water from the vent. This chain reaction continues until the geyser exhausts its supply of boiling water.

Yellowstone National Park in the United States is one of the most famous areas of hot springs and geysers in the world. The total heat flux from these thermal features is estimated to be 300 megawatts (300 million watts). The last great eruption at Yellowstone occurred about 630,000 years ago when some 1,000 cubic km (240 cubic miles) of rhyolitic pumice and ash were ejected in huge pyroclastic flows and resulted in the formation of a caldera—a large circular or oval depression caused by collapse of the surface following magma removal—approximately 45 by 75 km (28 by 47 miles) in size. Yellowstone Lake now occupies part of this giant caldera. Since that last great outburst, about 1,200 cubic km (288 cubic miles) of rhyolite lava flows and domes have erupted in numerous smaller events. The cooling roots of such past eruptions, or possibly the new intrusions of magma at shallow depth, are the heat sources for the Yellowstone hot springs and geysers.

Cross Section of a Geyser and Hot Spring

After a geyser stops spouting, the conduits at depth refill with groundwater, and reheating begins again. In geysers such as Yellowstone's Old Faithful, the spouting and recharge period is quite regular. This famous geyser has gushed to heights of 30 to 55 metres (100 to 180 feet) about every 90 minutes for more than 100 years. If Old Faithful's eruption lasts only a minute or two, the next interval will be shorter than average, while a four-minute eruption will be followed by a longer interval. Other geysers have much more erratic recharge times.

Old Faithful geyser, Upper Geyser Basin, Yellowstone National Park, Wyoming, U.S. George Marler/National Park Service

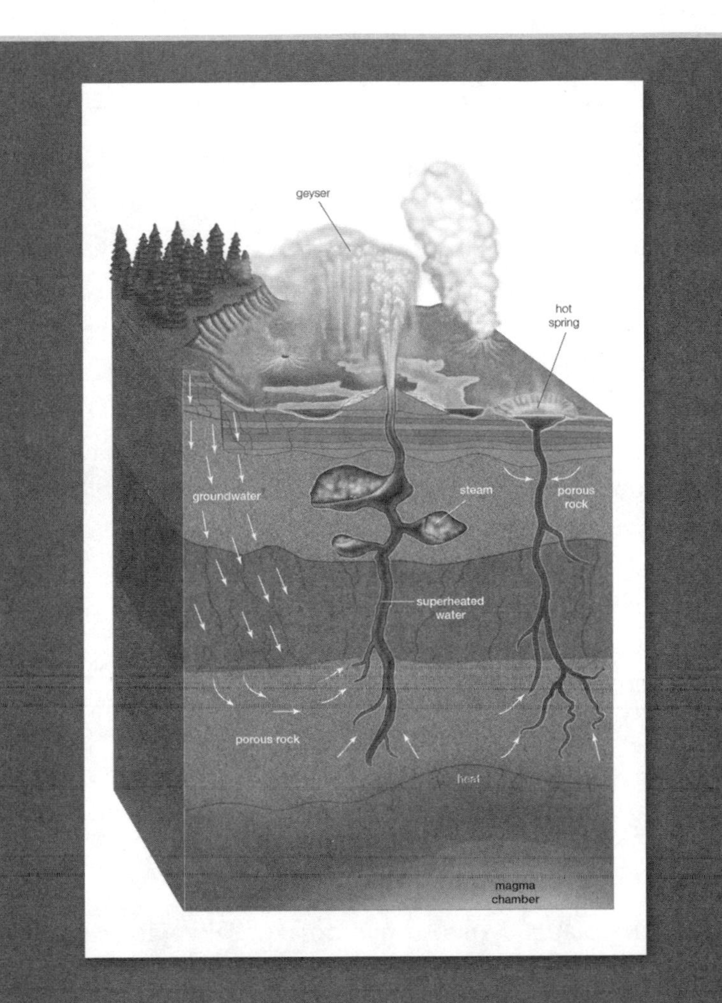

Groundwater percolates through porous rock into fractures deep underground, where heat from a nearby magma chamber superheats the pressurized water to a temperature above the boiling point of water at surface pressure. In hot springs the rising superheated water is cooled below the boiling point by groundwater before reaching the surface. In geysers the superheated water collects in underground pockets. There a small drop in pressure caused by the release of water at the surface flashes the superheated water into steam, which expands and ejects a column of steam and water into the air. When the supply of steam and hot water is exhausted, the spouting stops and the cycle begins again. Encyclopædia Britannica, Inc.

VOLCANISM AND TECTONIC ACTIVITY

Taking a more distant view of volcanic landforms from space, one can see that most volcanoes group together to form linear to arcuate belts across Earth's surface. It is now clear that these volcanic chains are closely related to global tectonic activity. Many active volcanoes are located in the so-called "Ring of Fire" made up of island arcs and mountain ranges bordering the Pacific Ocean. The concept of seafloor spreading and, more broadly, the theory of plate tectonics offer a logical explanation for the location of most volcanoes.

Volcanoes Related to Plate Boundaries

Topographic maps reveal the locations of large earthquakes and indicate the boundaries of the 12 major tectonic plates. For example, the Pacific Plate is bounded by the earthquake zones of New Zealand, New Guinea, the Mariana Islands, Japan, Kamchatka, the Aleutian Islands, western North America, the East Pacific Rise, and the Pacific-Antarctic Ridge.

Earth's plates, which move horizontally with respect to one another at a rate of a few centimetres per year, form three basic types of boundaries: convergent, divergent, and side-slipping. Japan and the Aleutian Islands are located on convergent boundaries where the Pacific Plate is moving beneath the adjacent continental plates—a process known as subduction. The San Andreas Fault system in California exemplifies a side-slipping boundary where the Pacific Plate is moving northwest relative to the North American Plate—a process called strike-slip, or transform, faulting. The East Pacific Rise is representative of a divergent boundary where the Pacific Plate and the Nazca Plate (west of South America) are moving apart—a process known as rifting.

Subduction Volcanoes

As an oceanic plate is subducted beneath a continental plate, seafloor sediments rich in water and carbon dioxide are carried beneath the overriding plate. These compounds may act as fluxes, reducing the melting temperature of magma. Although the process is not clearly understood, magma apparently forms and rises by buoyancy from a depth of 100 to 200 km (60 to 120 miles). Subduction-zone volcanoes occur on the overriding plate and are offset inland from the actual plate boundary along the ocean trench.

The rising subduction-zone magma is probably basaltic in composition and is formed by the partial melting of mantle rocks. As the rising magma moves slowly up through the continental crust of the overriding plate, however, two things may occur to increase significantly the silica content of the magma. Crystallization of olivine and pyroxene minerals from the basalt can leave the residual melt enriched in silica and depleted in magnesium, iron, and calcium. This process is called fractional crystallization. Also, basaltic magmas have enough excess heat to partially melt the continental host rocks through which they are ascending. Because continental rocks are generally higher in silica, potassium, and sodium than are oceanic rocks, this process of assimilation and mixing can also play an important role in producing the wide range of compositions that occur in rocks from subduction volcanoes.

The additional gas content of many magmas at subduction volcanoes (which, coupled with their often high-viscosity magma, makes them dangerously explosive) may be explained by more than one process. Additional water and carbon dioxide may come from both subducted seafloor sediments and assimilated crustal rocks. Furthermore, any fractional crystallization tends

Volcanic Activity and the Earth's Tectonic Plates

Volcanoes occur along both subduction and rift zones but are generally absent along strike-slip plate margins. Most subduction-related volcanoes are explosive and build stratovolcanoes, while rift volcanoes tend to be more effusive and build shield volcanoes, though there are exceptions to both these generalities. Subduction-related volcanoes erupt basalt, andesite, dacite, and rhyolite, andesite being the predominant rock type. Rift-related volcanoes, especially on the ocean floor, erupt mainly basalt.

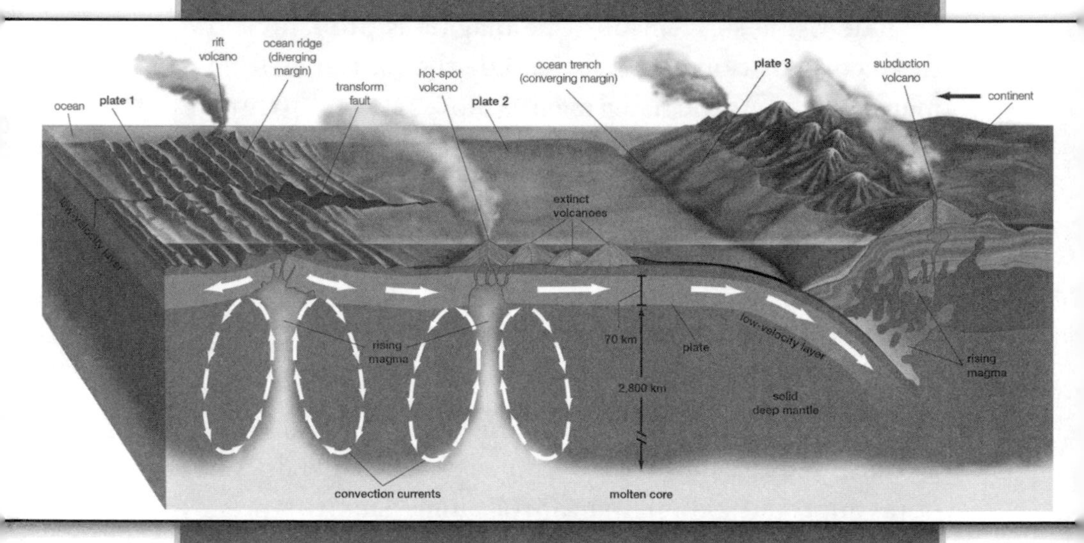

Stratovolcanoes tend to form at subduction zones, or convergent plate margins, where an oceanic plate slides beneath a continental plate and contributes to the rise of magma to the surface. At rift zones, or divergent margins, shield volcanoes tend to form as two oceanic plates pull slowly apart and magma effuses upward through the gap. Volcanoes are not generally found at strike-slip zones, where two plates slide laterally past each other. "Hot spot" volcanoes may form where plumes of lava rise from deep within the mantle to Earth's crust far from any plate margins. Encyclopædia Britannica, Inc.

The volcanoes on the western and northern margin of the Pacific Plate (New Zealand, New Guinea, Mariana Islands, Japan, Kamchatka, and the Aleutian Islands) are all subduction volcanoes. The rift volcanoes are largely hidden along the submarine crest of the East Pacific Rise and the Pacific-Antarctic Ridge at depths of 2 to 3 km (1.2 to 1.9 miles) below sea level. The Cascade volcanoes in the northwestern United States and the volcanoes in Mexico and Central America are related to the subduction under the North American Plate of the small Juan de Fuca and Cocos plates, which are on the east side of the Pacific Plate. Similarly, the volcanoes of the Andes are related to the subduction of the Nazca Plate beneath the South American Plate.

to concentrate volatile elements in the residual melt. If volcanic gases form separate fluid phases within batches of ascending magma (as carbon dioxide gas is most likely to do), these fluid phases may ascend more rapidly than the overall magma body and be concentrated in the upper portion. Sudden expansion of these hot volcanic gases at atmospheric pressure is the apparent reason for the highly explosive nature of many subduction volcanoes.

Rift Volcanoes

Rift volcanoes form when magma rises into the gap between diverging plates. They thus occur at or near actual plate boundaries. Measurements in Iceland suggest that the separation of plates is a continuous process but that the fracturing is intermittent, analogous to a rubber band that is slowly stretched until it snaps. Earthquake swarms and volcanic eruptions occur when the stretching exceeds the strength of the near-surface rocks, which then fracture along steeply dipping cracks parallel to the rift. Basaltic magma rising along these fractures causes Icelandic-type fissure eruptions.

Rift volcanoes in continental locations such as the East African Rift System are more complex. Assimilation of continental crust apparently gives them some of the characteristics more generally associated with subduction volcanoes, such as having a wider range of rock types and explosive habits.

Intraplate Volcanism

The 5 percent of known volcanoes in the world that are not closely related to plate margins are generally regarded as intraplate, or "hot-spot," volcanoes. A hot spot is believed to be related to the rising of a deep-mantle plume, which is caused by very slow convection of highly viscous material in Earth's mantle. As hot but solid mantle rock moves upward, partial melting may occur from the lowering of its pressure-dependent melting temperature. Where a lithospheric plate moves over a hot spot, a chain of volcanic islands may be created. As the plate moves, the older volcanoes are transported away from the magma source and become extinct. The younger, active volcanoes are clustered at the end of the chain over the hot spot. It is not known how a volcanic hot spot maintains its position for millions of years while a plate passes over it. Detailed seismic sounding of the mantle should increase the understanding of the mechanism controlling hot spots.

Hawaiian volcanoes are the best examples of hot-spot volcanoes. The five volcanoes that form the island of Hawaii at the southeast end of the Hawaiian chain are all less than one million years old. Two of these, Kilauea and Mauna Loa, are two of the most active volcanoes in the world. Northwestward along the Hawaiian chain each island is progressively older. The extinct volcano or volcanoes that formed the island of Kauai are about five million years old. Topographic maps show a major submarine continuation of the Hawaiian Ridge to the northwest of the Hawaiian Islands and then a dogleg bend into the Emperor Sea-mounts, which comprise an entirely submarine ridge continuing northward to the edge of the Pacific Plate.

Ages of rocks obtained by dredging and drilling the Emperor Seamounts indicate that they are a continuation of the Hawaiian chain and that the Hawaiian hot spot has been active for at least 80 million years. The Pacific Plate has moved over this centre of volcanism, first northward and later northwestward, at a rate of approximately 8 to 10 cm (3 to 4 inches) per year. The bend between the Emperor Seamounts and the Hawaiian Ridge occurred about 45 million years ago and indicates a significant shift in the direction of movement of the Pacific Plate.

Small, isolated intraplate volcanoes may not be produced by a hot spot but rather may be the result of deep fractures within the plates that allow pockets of magma to leak to the surface. These pockets originate in the low-velocity layer, so named because earthquake waves travel more slowly through the hot, plastically deforming rocks of this region than in the overlying rigid plates. The low-velocity layer begins about 50 to 150 km (30 to 90 miles) below the surface and extends to a depth of roughly 300 km (180 miles). A small amount (a few percent) of the low-velocity layer may be molten. Once a sufficient volume of magma forms in the subsurface, it tends to rise from its own buoyancy. Any fracture system at the plate margins or within the plates will facilitate this process.

VOLCANOES AND GEOTHERMAL ENERGY

Geothermal energy is plentiful, but geothermal power is not. Temperatures increase below Earth's surface at a rate of about 30 °C per km in the first 10 km (roughly 90 °F per mile in the first 6 miles) below the surface. This internal heat of Earth is an immense store of energy. In the upper 10 km of rock beneath the conterminous United States, it amounts to 3.3×10^{25} joules, or about 6,000 times the energy contained in the world's oil reserves. The problem in utilizing geothermal energy is extracting it.

The natural escape of Earth's heat through its surface averages only 0.06 watt per square metre (0.006 watt per square foot). To make geothermal power practical, some special situation must exist to concentrate Earth's heat energy in a small area. Underground reservoirs of steam or hot water that can be funneled into a drill hole provide this special situation. Some geothermal steam wells can produce 25 megawatts of thermal power, an amount equal to the normal heat flux of more than 400 square km (150 square miles) of land surface. The key to this concentration is the transfer of heat from deeper levels to the near surface by the ascending magma associated with volcanism. Magma at temperatures close to 1,200 °C (2,200 °F) moves upward to depths of only a few kilometres, where it transfers heat by conduction to groundwater. The groundwater then circulates by convection and forms large underground reservoirs of hot water and steam. Some of this thermal water may escape to the surface as hot springs or geysers.

Holes drilled into a subsurface geothermal system allow rapid transfer of hot water or steam to the surface. At the Geysers, a geothermal field north of San Francisco, superheated steam is directly tapped from porous underground reservoirs. In most other geothermal fields, the hot water is at or below its subsurface boiling temperature—about 300 °C (570 °F) at a depth of 1 km (0.6 mile). The hot water and steam produced from geothermal wells are used as the energy source to drive turbine generators in electric power plants. Hot water from lower-temperature geothermal reservoirs can be used for space heating and other applications. This form of geothermal power is utilized extensively in Iceland.

Some geothermal systems act as natural distilleries in the subsurface, dissolving trace amounts of gold, silver, and other rare elements from their host rocks. These elements may then be deposited at places where changes in temperature, pressure, or composition favour precipitation. Many hydrothermal ore deposits have been formed by once active—and in a few cases still active—geothermal systems. Gold is one more legacy of volcanism.

RELATED CONCEPTS

Several other phenomena characteristic of volcanic eruptions are presented below. Some phenomena, such as magma and pyroclastic flows, are common features of eruptions, whereas others, such as kimberlite eruptions and volcanic winters, are rare events. This section also includes a description of the scientific discipline of volcanology.

Bomb

A bomb is a mass of unconsolidated volcanic material that has a diameter greater than 64 mm (2.5 inches) and forms from clots of wholly or partly molten lava ejected during a volcanic eruption, partly solidifying during flight. The final shape is determined by the initial size, viscosity, and flight velocity of the lava bomb. Some, called spindle bombs, are shaped like a football or spindle of thread; others, called cow-dung or pancake bombs, are flattened on landing; and still others are ribbon-shaped. If bombs are still molten or plastic when they land (a characteristic of those formed during the relatively weak explosions of basaltic magma), they may partly fuse to form volcanic spatter. If their outer surfaces are solidified and the interior still plastic, gas expansion and impact may produce breadcrust bombs with a cracked skin.

Fumarole

A fumarole is a vent in Earth's surface from which steam and volcanic gases are emitted. The major source of the water vapour emitted by fumaroles is groundwater heated by bodies of magma lying relatively close to the surface. Carbon dioxide, sulfur dioxide, and hydrogen sulfide are usually emitted directly from the magma. Fumaroles are often present on active volcanoes during periods of relative quiet between eruptions.

Fumaroles are closely related to hot springs and geysers. In areas where the water table rises near the surface, fumaroles can become hot springs. A fumarole rich in sulfur gases is called a solfatara; a fumarole rich in carbon dioxide is called a mofette.

Kimberlite Eruption

Kimberlite eruptions are small but powerful volcanic events caused by the rapid ascent of kimberlites—a type of intrusive igneous rock originating in the asthenosphere—through the lithosphere and onto the surface of Earth. Kimberlites are thought to rise through a series of fissures in the rock. They form vertical pipelike structures that penetrate the surrounding rock. Unlike other kinds of eruptions, magma does not collect in a subsurface reservoir prior to the eruption. In addition, many surface depressions resulting from kimberlite eruptions contain deposits of diamonds.

As the kimberlite pipes approach the surface, decreasing pressure above allows some of the volatile materials in the magma (such as water and carbon dioxide) to become gaseous, and these gases expand rapidly. Should the pipes encounter rock layers containing groundwater, the water is vaporized and additional expansion occurs. Such expansion widens the pipes and produces an explosive event at the surface as upward-rushing gases dislodge rocks and create a craterlike depression.

The last kimberlite eruption is thought to have taken place more than 25 million years ago, and some scientists note that most occurred during the Cretaceous Period (145 million to about 65.5 million years ago). Since that time, depressions caused by kimberlite eruptions have undergone substantial erosion. During and after the eruption, the depression is often filled with breccia, a type of lithified sedimentary rock consisting of angular and subangular fragments rather than rounded clasts. Breccias that form during kimberlite eruptions are made up of rising kimberlite and the walls of the surrounding rock. When eroded, such a depression exposes a vertical funnel-shaped pipe that resembles a volcanic neck with the exception of the brecciated filling. If the eruption was explosive, these pipes, called diatremes, typically assume carrot-shaped profiles. In cases where the eruption is slower and corrodes the surrounding rock, diatremes may be bowl-shaped.

During their ascent, kimberlite pipes may pass through a region of the lower lithosphere called the diamond stability field, an area of high pressure where carbon can be transformed into diamonds. Diamonds that intersect the rising pipe may be pushed along by or carried within the magma to the surface. Although there is evidence that diamonds and other ejected materials can fall several kilometres away from the crater during an explosive event, most present-day discoveries of kimberlite diamonds occur within the remains of eroded craters.

Magma

Magma is defined as molten or partially molten underground rock from which igneous rocks form. It usually consists of silicate liquid, although carbonate and sulfide melts occur as well. Magma migrates either at depth or to Earth's surface and is ejected as lava. Suspended crystals and fragments of unmelted rock may be transported in the magma; dissolved volatiles may separate as bubbles and some liquid may crystallize during movement. Several interrelated physical properties determine the characteristics of magma, including chemical composition, viscosity, dissolved gases, and temperature.

As magma cools, crystals form in a systematic manner, which is most simply expressed in the form of Bowen's reaction series; early high-temperature crystals will tend to react with the liquid to form other minerals at lower temperatures. Two series are recognized: (1) a discontinuous reaction series, which from high to low temperatures is composed of olivine, orthopyroxene, clinopyroxene, amphibole, and biotite; and (2) a continuous reaction series, represented by high-temperature calcium-rich plagioclase to low-temperature sodium-rich plagioclase. Numerous variations can occur during crystallization to influence the resulting rock. Such variations include separation of early crystals from liquid, preventing a reaction; cooling of magma too rapidly for reactions to occur; and loss of volatiles, which may remove some components from the magma. Transport and emplacement of magma is strongly affected by its viscosity and by the fracture characteristics of rocks through which it moves. Viscosity is reduced by water and a lower silica content.

Mofette

A mofette (French: "noxious fume"; also spelled *moffette*) is a fumarole, or gaseous volcanic vent, that has a temperature well below the boiling point of water, though above the temperature of the surrounding air, and that is generally rich in carbon dioxide and perhaps methane and other hydrocarbons. When the winds are right, the issuing gases may drift and settle into nearby hollows or small valleys and cause the asphyxiation of animals and birds wandering in the areas. Such potentially deadly hollows have been noted in the Absaroka Range near Yellowstone National Park in Wyoming, U.S., and at the base of Iceland's Hekla volcano.

Volcanic Winter

This phenomenon occurs as cooling at Earth's surface resulting from the deposition of massive amounts of volcanic ash and sulfur aerosols in the stratosphere. Sulfur aerosols reflect incoming solar radiation and absorb terrestrial radiation. Together these processes cool the troposphere below. If sulfur aerosol loading is significant enough, it can result in climate changes at the global scale for years after the event, causing crop failures, cooler temperatures, and atypical weather conditions across the planet.

Explosive volcanic eruptions are capable of sending pulverized rock, sulfur dioxide (SO_2), and hydrogen sulfide (H_2S) into the stratosphere. Although volcanic ash can decrease regional visibility for a few months after the eruption, sulfur compounds injected into the stratosphere form sulfur aerosols that can reflect a portion of incoming sunlight for several years. As the concentration of sulfur aerosols increases in this region of the atmosphere, greater reflection occurs. Surface heating declines as a result, and thus cooler temperatures predominate at Earth's surface. Compared with the underlying troposphere, the stratosphere is relatively devoid of atmospheric turbulence, and thus these aerosols may remain in the stratosphere for several years before settling out.

There is evidence that volcanic winters have occurred several times throughout Earth's history, with varying degrees of severity. One of the more severe episodes of volcanic winter occurred sometime between 71,000 and 74,000 years ago when Mount Toba, a volcano on the island of Sumatra, expelled possibly as much as 2,800 cubic km (about 670 cubic miles) of ash into the stratosphere. Ice-core evidence suggests that average air temperatures worldwide plunged by 3–5 °C (5.4–9.0 °F) for years after the eruption. (Some model simulations estimate that this temperature decline may have been as much as 10 °C [18 °F] in the Northern Hemisphere in the first year after the eruption.) Some scientists maintain that this event sent the planet into a severe ice age that nearly caused the extinction of modern humans.

From June 1783 to February 1784 the Laki fissure in Iceland extruded about 12.5 cubic km (3 cubic miles) of lava that covered about 565 square km (220 square miles)—considered the greatest lava eruption on Earth in historical times. The enormous quantity of volcanic gas that was released caused a conspicuous haze over most of continental Europe. Some scientists link the presence of this haze over the region to the severity of the winter of 1783–84 in the Northern Hemisphere.

During the 19th century two volcanoes in the Indonesian archipelago were associated with volcanic winters. The first event was caused by the eruption of Mount Tambora, a volcano on the island of Sumbawa. It expelled about 100 cubic km (24 cubic miles) of ash into the atmosphere in 1815. This event had the effect of reducing the average global temperature by as much as 3 °C (5.4 °F) in 1816, causing the "year without a summer" in parts of North America and Europe.

The second event was caused by the eruption of Krakatoa in 1883. This eruption discharged nearly 21 cubic km (5 cubic miles) of rock fragments, destroying much of the island of Krakatoa, and the surrounding region was plunged into darkness for two and a half days because of ash in the air. The fine dust drifted several times around Earth, causing spectacular red and orange sunsets throughout the following year. Some scientists contend that this eruption upset weather patterns for years afterward. In 1928, after a period of renewed volcanic activity, a new island called Anak Krakatau ("Child of Krakatoa") emerged from the ocean in the spot where the original volcano once existed.

More recently, gases and ash from Mount Pinatubo, a volcano located on the island of Luzon in the Philippines, cooled the world's climate by about 0.5 °C (0.9 °F) for a few years after the volcano erupted in 1991.

Volcanism

Volcanism (also spelled *vulcanism*) includes any of the various processes and phenomena associated with the surficial discharge of molten rock, pyroclastic fragments, or hot water and steam, including volcanoes, geysers, and fumaroles. Although volcanism is best known on Earth, there is evidence that it has been important in the development of the other terrestrial planets—Mercury, Venus, and Mars—as well as some natural satellites such as Earth's Moon and Jupiter's moon Io.

On Earth, volcanism occurs in several distinct geologic settings. Most of these are associated with the boundaries of the enormous, rigid plates that make up the lithosphere—the crust and upper mantle. The majority of active terrestrial volcanoes (roughly 80 percent) and related phenomena occur where two lithospheric plates converge and one overrides the other, forcing it down into the mantle to be reabsorbed. Long curved chains of islands known as island arcs form at such subduction zones. Volcanoes of the explosive type make up many of the islands of a single arc or the inner row of islands of a double arc. All such islands that border the Pacific basin are built up from the seafloor, usually by the extrusion of basaltic and andesitic magmas.

A second major site of active volcanism is along the axis of the oceanic ridge system, where the plates move apart on both sides of the ridge and magma wells up from the mantle, creating new ocean floor along the trailing edges of both plates. Virtually all of this volcanic activity occurs underwater. In a few places the oceanic ridges are sufficiently elevated above the deep seafloor that they emerge from the ocean, and subaerial volcanism occurs. Iceland is the best-known example. The magmas that are erupted along the oceanic ridges are basaltic in composition.

A relatively small number of volcanoes occur within plates far from their margins. Some, as exemplified by the volcanic islands of Hawaii that lie in the interior of the Pacific Plate, are thought to occur because of plate movement over a "hot spot" from which magmas can penetrate to the surface. These magmas characteristically generate a chain of progressively older volcanoes that mark the direction of past motion of the plate over a particular hot spot. The active volcanoes of the East African Rift Valley also occur within a plate (the African Plate), but they appear to result from a different mechanism—possibly the beginning of a new region of plates moving apart.

VOLCANOLOGY

This discipline of the geologic sciences is concerned with all aspects of volcanic phenomena.

Volcanology (also spelled *vulcanology*) deals with the formation, distribution, and classification of volcanoes as well as with their structure and the kinds of materials ejected during an eruption (such as pyroclastic flows, lava, dust, ash, and volcanic gases). It also involves research on the relationships between volcanic eruptions and other large-scale geologic processes such as plate tectonics, mountain building, and earthquakes. One of the chief objectives of this research is determining the nature and causes of volcanic eruptions for the purpose of forecasting their occurrence. Another practical concern of volcanology is securing data that may aid in locating commercially valuable deposits of ores, particularly those of certain sulfide minerals.

Interest in volcanic phenomena extends back to ancient times. The eruption of Mount Vesuvius in 79 CE was recorded in considerable detail by Pliny the Younger. Studies of volcanoes, however, were not conducted systematically until the 19th century. Since that time volcanology has become an important branch of physical geology. Specialists in the field, using the principles and methods of geophysics and geochemistry and the tools of seismology and geodesy, have obtained much knowledge of processes that occur within Earth's interior

Chapter 3

Earthquakes

Earthquakes refer to any sudden shaking of the ground caused by the passage of seismic waves through Earth's rocks. Seismic waves are produced when some form of energy stored in the Earth's crust is suddenly released, usually when masses of rock straining against one another suddenly fracture and "slip." Earthquakes occur most often along geologic faults, narrow zones where rock masses move in relation to one another. The major fault lines of the world are located at the fringes of the huge tectonic plates that make up Earth's crust.

Little was understood about earthquakes until the emergence of seismology at the beginning of the 20th century. Seismology, which involves the scientific study of all aspects of earthquakes, has yielded answers to such long-standing questions as why and how earthquakes occur.

About 50,000 earthquakes large enough to be noticed without the aid of instruments occur annually over the

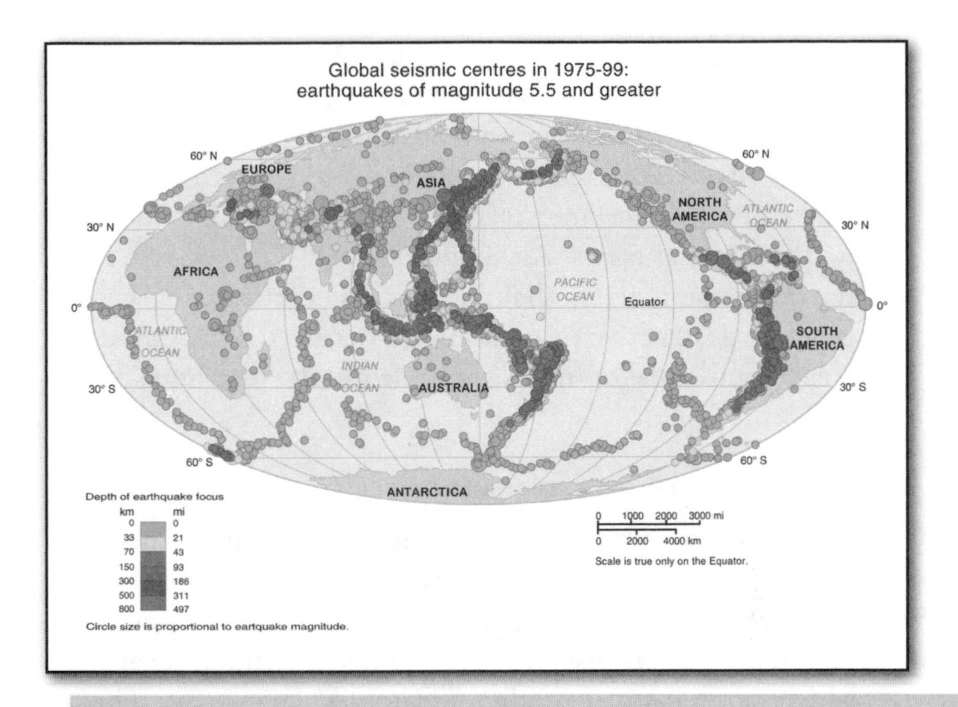

Distribution of seismic centres around the world where an earthquake with a magnitude of at least 5.5 occurred between 1975 and 1999. Encyclopædia Britannica, Inc.

entire Earth. Of these, approximately 100 are of sufficient size to produce substantial damage if their centres are near areas of habitation. Very great earthquakes occur on average about once per year. Over the centuries they have been responsible for millions of deaths and an incalculable amount of damage to property.

THE NATURE OF EARTHQUAKES

Since earthquakes have the potential to cause extensive damage and great loss of life, scientists have long attempted to understand how they occur, their immediate and secondary effects, and the forces that govern how intense they are. The most common forces that spawn earthquakes are associated with plate movement and volcanism; however, they can be generated artificially. The strength felt from a given earthquake event depends largely on one's distance away from the focus of the earthquake as well as the intensity of the seismic waves produced by the shifting rocks. Although damage often occurs in regions experiencing shaking ground, earthquakes can generate destructive tsunamis in the oceans that can affect areas thousands of miles away from the earthquake's source.

The Causes of Earthquakes

Earth's major earthquakes occur mainly in belts coinciding with the margins of tectonic plates. This has long been apparent from early catalogs of felt earthquakes and is even more readily discernible in modern seismicity maps, which show instrumentally determined epicentres. The most important earthquake belt is the Circum-Pacific Belt, which affects many populated coastal regions around the Pacific Ocean—for example, those of New Zealand, New Guinea, Japan, the Aleutian Islands, Alaska, and the western coasts of North and South America. It is estimated that 80 percent of the energy presently released in earthquakes comes from those whose epicentres are in this belt. The seismic activity is by no means uniform throughout the belt, and there are a number of branches at various points. Because at many places the Circum-Pacific Belt is associated with volcanic activity, it has been popularly dubbed the "Pacific Ring of Fire."

A second belt, known as the Alpide Belt, passes through the Mediterranean region eastward through Asia and joins the Circum-Pacific Belt in the East Indies. The energy released in earthquakes from this belt is about 15 percent of the world total. There also are striking connected belts of seismic activity, mainly along oceanic ridges—including those in the Arctic Ocean, the Atlantic Ocean, and the western Indian Ocean—and along the rift valleys of East Africa. This global seismicity distribution is best understood in terms of its plate tectonic setting.

Natural Forces

Earthquakes are caused by the sudden release of energy within some limited region of the rocks of Earth. The energy can be released by elastic strain, gravity, chemical reactions, or even the motion of massive bodies. Of all these the release of elastic strain is the most important cause, because this form of energy is the only kind that can be stored in sufficient quantity in Earth to produce major disturbances. Earthquakes associated with this type of energy release are called tectonic earthquakes.

Tectonics

Tectonic earthquakes are explained by the so-called elastic rebound theory, formulated by the American geologist Harry Fielding Reid after the San Andreas Fault ruptured in 1906, generating the great San Francisco earthquake. According to the theory, a tectonic earthquake occurs when strains in rock masses have accumulated to a point where the resulting stresses exceed the strength of the rocks, and sudden fracturing results. The fractures propagate rapidly through the rock, usually tending in the same direction and sometimes extending many kilometres along a local zone of weakness. In 1906, for instance, the San Andreas Fault slipped along a plane 430 km (270 miles) long. Along this line the ground was displaced horizontally as much as 6 metres (20 feet).

As a fault rupture progresses along or up the fault, rock masses are flung in opposite directions and thus spring back to a position where there is less strain. At any one point this movement may take place not at once but rather in irregular steps; these sudden slowings and restartings give rise to the vibrations that propagate as seismic waves. Such irregular properties of fault rupture are now included in the modeling of earthquake sources, both physically and mathematically. Roughnesses along the fault are referred to as asperities, and places where the rupture slows or stops are said to be fault barriers. Fault rupture starts at the earthquake focus, a spot that in many cases is close to 5–15 km under the surface. The rupture propagates in one or both directions over the fault plane until stopped or slowed at a barrier. Sometimes, instead of being stopped at the barrier, the fault rupture recommences on the far side; at other times the stresses in the rocks break the barrier, and the rupture continues.

Earthquakes have different properties depending on the type of fault slip that causes them. The usual fault model has a "strike" (that is, the direction from north taken by a horizontal line in the fault plane) and a "dip" (the angle from the horizontal shown by the steepest slope in the fault). The lower wall of an inclined fault is called the footwall. Lying over the footwall is the hanging wall. When rock masses slip past each other parallel to the strike, the movement is known as strike-slip faulting. Movement parallel to the dip is called dip-slip faulting. Strike-slip faults are right lateral or left lateral, depending on whether the block on the opposite side of the fault from an observer has moved to the right or left. In dip-slip faults, if the hanging-wall block moves downward relative to the footwall block, it is called "normal" faulting; the opposite motion, with the hanging wall moving upward relative to the footwall, produces reverse or thrust faulting.

All known faults are assumed to have been the seat of one or more earthquakes in the past, though tectonic movements along faults are often slow, and most geologically ancient faults are now aseismic (that is, they no longer cause earthquakes). The actual faulting associated with an earthquake may be complex, and it is often not clear whether in a particular earthquake the total energy issues from a single fault plane.

Observed geologic faults sometimes show relative displacements on the order of hundreds of kilometres over geologic time, whereas the sudden slip offsets that produce seismic waves may range from only several centimetres to tens of metres. In the 1976 Tangshan earthquake, for example, a surface strike-slip of about one metre was observed along the causative fault east of Beijing, and in the 1999 Taiwan earthquake the Chelung-pu fault slipped up to eight metres vertically.

Volcanism

A separate type of earthquake is associated with volcanic activity and is called a volcanic earthquake. Yet it is likely that even in such cases the disturbance is the result of a sudden slip of rock masses adjacent to the volcano and the consequent release of elastic strain energy. The stored energy, however, may in part be of hydrodynamic origin due to heat provided by magma moving in reservoirs beneath the volcano or to the release of gas under pressure.

There is a clear correspondence between the geographic distribution of volcanoes and major earthquakes, particularly in the Circum-Pacific Belt and along oceanic ridges. Volcanic vents, however, are generally several hundred kilometres from the epicentres of most major shallow earthquakes, and many earthquake sources occur nowhere near active volcanoes. Even in cases where an earthquake's focus occurs directly below structures marked by volcanic vents, there is probably no immediate causal connection between the two activities; most likely both are the result of the same tectonic processes.

Artificial Induction

Earthquakes are sometimes caused by human activities, including the injection of fluids into deep wells, the detonation of large underground nuclear explosions, the excavation of mines, and the filling of large reservoirs. In the case of deep mining, the removal of rock produces changes in the strain around the tunnels. Slip on adjacent, preexisting faults or outward shattering of rock into the new cavities may occur. In fluid injection, the slip is thought to be induced by premature release of elastic strain, as in the case of tectonic earthquakes, after fault surfaces are lubricated by the liquid. Large underground nuclear explosions have been known to produce slip on already strained faults in the vicinity of the test devices.

Reservoir Induction

Of the various earthquake-causing activities cited above, the filling of large reservoirs is among the most important. More than 20 significant cases have been documented in which local seismicity has increased following the impounding of water behind high dams. Often, causality cannot be substantiated, because no data exists to allow comparison of earthquake occurrence before and after the reservoir was filled. Reservoir-induction effects are most marked for reservoirs exceeding 100 metres (330 feet) in depth and 1 cubic km (0.24 cubic mile) in volume. Three sites where such connections have very probably occurred are the Hoover Dam in the United States, the Aswan High Dam in Egypt, and the Kariba Dam on the border between Zimbabwe and Zambia. The most generally accepted explanation for earthquake occurrence in such cases assumes that rocks near the reservoir are already strained from regional tectonic forces to a point where nearby faults are almost ready to slip. Water in the reservoir adds a pressure perturbation that triggers the fault rupture. The pressure effect is perhaps enhanced by the fact that the rocks along the fault have lower strength because of increased water-pore pressure. These factors notwithstanding, the filling of most large reservoirs has not produced earthquakes large enough to be a hazard.

The specific seismic source mechanisms associated with reservoir induction have been established in a few cases. For the main shock at the Koyna Dam and Reservoir in India (1967), the evidence favours strike-slip faulting motion. At both the Kremasta Dam in Greece (1965) and the Kariba Dam in Zimbabwe-Zambia (1961), the generating mechanism was dip-slip on normal faults. By contrast, thrust mechanisms have been determined for sources of earthquakes at the lake behind Nurek Dam in Tajikistan. More than 1,800 earthquakes occurred during the first nine years after water was impounded in this 317-metre-deep reservoir in 1972, a rate amounting to four times the average number of shocks in the region prior to filling.

Seismology and Nuclear Explosions

In 1958 representatives from several countries, including the United States and the Soviet Union, met to discuss the technical basis for a nuclear test-ban treaty. Among the matters considered was the feasibility of developing effective means with which to detect underground nuclear explosions and to distinguish them seismically from earthquakes. After that conference, much special research was directed to seismology, leading to major advances in seismic signal detection and analysis.

Recent seismological work on treaty verification has involved using high-resolution seismographs in a worldwide network, estimating the yield of explosions, studying wave attenuation in Earth, determining wave amplitude and frequency spectra discriminants, and applying seismic arrays. The findings of such research have shown that underground nuclear explosions, compared with natural earthquakes, usually generate seismic waves through the body of Earth that are of much larger amplitude than the surface waves. This telltale difference along with other types of seismic evidence suggest that an international monitoring network of 270 seismographic stations could detect and locate all seismic events over the globe of magnitude 4 and above (corresponding to an explosive yield of about 100 tons of TNT).

The Effects of Earthquakes

Earthquakes have varied effects, including changes in geologic features, damage to man-made structures, and impact on human and animal life. Most of these effects occur on solid ground, but, since most earthquake foci are actually located under the ocean bottom, severe effects are often observed along the margins of oceans.

Surface Phenomena

Earthquakes often cause dramatic geomorphological changes, including ground movements—either vertical or horizontal—along geologic fault traces; rising, dropping, and tilting of the ground surface; changes in the flow of groundwater; liquefaction of sandy ground; landslides; and mudflows. The investigation of topographic changes is aided by geodetic measurements, which are made systematically in a number of countries seriously affected by earthquakes.

Earthquakes can do significant damage to buildings, bridges, pipelines, railways, embankments, and other structures. The type and extent of damage inflicted are related to the strength of the ground motions and to the behaviour of the foundation soils. In the most intensely damaged region, called the meizoseismal area, the effects of a severe earthquake are usually complicated and depend on the topography and the nature of the surface materials. They are often more severe on soft alluvium and unconsolidated sediments than on hard rock. At distances of more than 100 km (60 miles) from the source, the main damage is caused by seismic waves traveling along the surface. In mines there is frequently little damage below depths of a few hundred metres even though the ground surface immediately above is considerably affected.

Earthquakes are frequently associated with reports of distinctive sounds and lights. The sounds are generally low-pitched and have been likened to the noise of an underground train passing through a station. The occurrence of such sounds is consistent with the passage of high-frequency seismic waves through the ground. Occasionally, luminous flashes, streamers, and bright balls have been reported in the night sky during earthquakes. These lights have been attributed to electric induction in the air along the earthquake source.

Tsunamis

Following certain earthquakes, very long-wavelength water waves in oceans or seas sweep inshore. More properly called seismic sea waves or tsunamis (*tsunami* is a Japanese word for "harbour wave"), they are commonly referred to as tidal waves, although the attractions of the Moon and Sun play no role in their formation. They sometimes come ashore to great heights—tens of metres above mean tide level—and may be extremely destructive.

The usual immediate cause of a tsunami is sudden displacement in a seabed sufficient to cause the sudden raising or lowering of a large body of water. This deformation may be the fault source of an earthquake, or it may be a submarine landslide arising from an earthquake. Large volcanic eruptions along shorelines, such as those of

Thera (*c.* 1580 BCE) and Krakatoa (1883 CE), have also produced notable tsunamis. The most destructive tsunami ever recorded occurred on Dec. 26, 2004, after an earthquake displaced the seabed off the coast of Sumatra, Indonesia. More than 200,000 people were killed by a series of waves that flooded coasts from Indonesia to Sri Lanka and even washed ashore on the Horn of Africa.

Following the initial disturbance to the sea surface, water waves spread in all directions. Their speed of travel in deep water is given by the formula (*gh*), where *h* is the sea depth and *g* is the acceleration of gravity. This speed may be considerable—100 metres per second (225 miles per hour) when *h* is 1,000 metres (3,300 feet). However, the amplitude (that is, the height of disturbance) at the

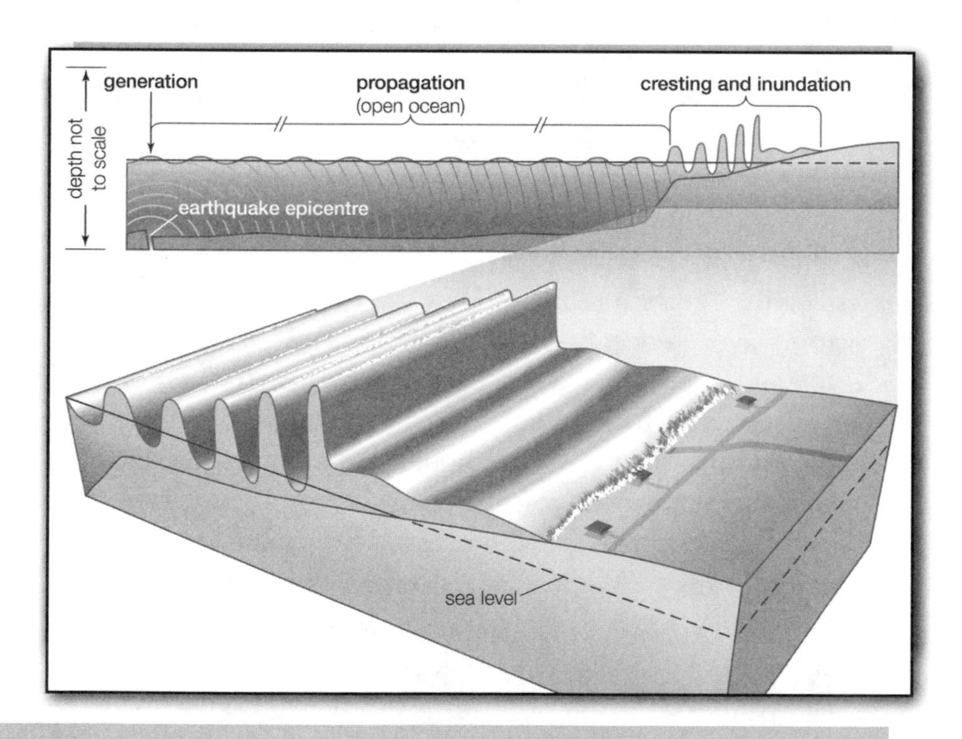

After being generated by an undersea earthquake or landslide, a tsunami may propagate unnoticed over vast reaches of open ocean before cresting in shallow water and inundating a coastline. Encyclopædia Britannica, Inc.

water surface does not exceed a few metres in deep water, and the principal wavelength may be on the order of hundreds of kilometres; correspondingly, the principal wave period—that is, the time interval between arrival of successive crests—may be on the order of tens of minutes. Because of these features, tsunami waves are not noticed by ships far out at sea.

When tsunamis approach shallow water, however, the wave amplitude increases. The waves may occasionally reach a height of 20 to 30 metres above mean sea level in U- and V-shaped harbours and inlets. They characteristically do a great deal of damage in low-lying ground around such inlets. Frequently, the wave front in the inlet is nearly vertical, as in a tidal bore, and the speed of onrush may be on the order of 10 metres per second. In some cases there are several great waves separated by intervals of several minutes or more. The first of these waves is often preceded by an extraordinary recession of water from the shore, which may commence several minutes or even half an hour beforehand.

Organizations, notably in Japan, Siberia, Alaska, and Hawaii, have been set up to provide tsunami warnings. A key development is the Seismic Sea Wave Warning System, an internationally supported system designed to reduce loss of life in the Pacific Ocean. Centred in Honolulu, it issues alerts based on reports of earthquakes from circum-Pacific seismographic stations.

Seiches

Seiches are rhythmic motions of water in nearly landlocked bays or lakes that are sometimes induced by earthquakes and tsunamis. Oscillations of this sort may last for hours or even for a day or two.

The great Lisbon earthquake of 1755 caused the waters of canals and lakes in regions as far away as Scotland and

Sweden to go into observable oscillations. Seiche surges in lakes in Texas, in the southwestern United States, commenced between 30 and 40 minutes after the 1964 Alaska earthquake, produced by seismic surface waves passing through the area.

A related effect is the result of seismic waves from an earthquake passing through the seawater following their refraction through the seafloor. The speed of these waves is about 1.5 km (0.9 mile) per second, the speed of sound in water. If such waves meet a ship with sufficient intensity, they give the impression that the ship has struck a submerged object. This phenomenon is called a seaquake.

The Intensity and Magnitude of Earthquakes

Earthquake intensity, or "strength," and earthquake magnitude, or the "size" of the seismic waves, are distinct features of earthquakes that relate to the amount of energy released by the shifting rocks.

Intensity Scales

The violence of seismic shaking varies considerably over a single affected area. Because the entire range of observed effects is not capable of simple quantitative definition, the strength of the shaking is commonly estimated by reference to intensity scales that describe the effects in qualitative terms. Intensity scales date from the late 19th and early 20th centuries, before seismographs capable of accurate measurement of ground motion were developed. Since that time, the divisions in these scales have been associated with measurable accelerations of the local ground shaking. Intensity depends, however, in a complicated way not only on ground accelerations but also on the periods and other features of seismic waves, the distance of the measuring point from the source, and the local geologic structure. Furthermore, earthquake intensity, or

Modified Mercalli Scale of Earthquake Intensity

• I. Not felt. Marginal and long-period effects of large earthquakes.
• II. Felt by persons at rest, on upper floors, or otherwise favourably placed to sense tremors.
• III. Felt indoors. Hanging objects swing. Vibrations are similar to those caused by the passing of light trucks. Duration can be estimated.
• IV. Vibrations are similar to those caused by the passing of heavy trucks (or a jolt similar to that caused by a heavy ball striking the walls). Standing automobiles rock. Windows, dishes, doors rattle. Glasses clink, crockery clashes. In the upper range of grade IV, wooden walls and frames creak.
• V. Felt outdoors; direction may be estimated. Sleepers awaken. Liquids are disturbed, some spilled. Small objects are displaced or upset. Doors swing, open, close. Pendulum clocks stop, start, change rate.
• VI. Felt by all; many are frightened and run outdoors. Persons walk unsteadily. Pictures fall off walls. Furniture moves or overturns. Weak plaster and masonry cracks. Small bells ring (church, school). Trees, bushes shake.
• VII. Difficult to stand. Noticed by drivers of automobiles. Hanging objects quivering. Furniture broken. Damage to weak masonry. Weak chimneys broken at roof line. Fall of plaster, loose bricks, stones, tiles, cornices. Waves on ponds; water turbid with mud. Small slides and caving along sand or gravel banks. Large bells ringing. Concrete irrigation ditches damaged.
• VIII. Steering of automobiles affected. Damage to masonry; partial collapse. Some damage to reinforced masonry; none to reinforced masonry designed to resist lateral forces. Fall of stucco and some masonry walls. Twisting, fall of chimneys, factory stacks, monuments, towers, elevated tanks. Frame houses moved on foundations if not bolted down; loose panel walls thrown out. Decayed pilings broken off. Branches broken from trees. Changes in flow or temperature of springs and wells. Cracks in wet ground and on steep slopes.

• IX. General panic. Weak masonry destroyed; ordinary masonry heavily damaged, sometimes with complete collapse; reinforced masonry seriously damaged. Serious damage to reservoirs. Underground pipes broken. Conspicuous cracks in ground. In alluvial areas, sand and mud ejected; earthquake fountains, sand craters.
• X. Most masonry and frame structures destroyed with their foundations. Some well-built wooden structures and bridges destroyed. Serious damage to dams, dikes, embankments. Large landslides. Water thrown on banks of canals, rivers, lakes, and so on. Sand and mud shifted horizontally on beaches and flat land. Railway rails bent slightly.
• XI. Rails bent greatly. Underground pipelines completely out of service.
• XII. Damage nearly total. Large rock masses displaced. Lines of sight and level distorted. Objects thrown into air.

With the use of an intensity scale, it is possible to summarize such data for an earthquake by constructing isoseismal curves, which are lines that connect points of equal intensity. If there were complete symmetry about the vertical through the earthquake's focus, isoseismals would be circles with the epicentre (the point at the surface of Earth immediately above where the earthquake originated) as the centre. However, because of the many unsymmetrical geologic factors influencing intensity, the curves are often far from circular. The most probable position of the epicentre is often assumed to be at a point inside the area of highest intensity. In some cases, instrumental data verify this calculation, but not infrequently the true epicentre lies outside the area of greatest intensity.

strength, is distinct from earthquake magnitude, which is a measure of the amplitude, or size, of seismic waves as specified by a seismograph reading.

A number of different intensity scales have been set up during the past century and applied to both current and ancient destructive earthquakes. For many years the most widely used was a 10-point scale devised in 1878 by Michele Stefano de Rossi and François-Alphonse Forel. The scale now generally employed in North America is the Mercalli scale, as modified by Harry O. Wood and Frank Neumann in 1931, in which intensity is considered to be more suitably graded. A 12-point abridged form of the modified Mercalli scale is provided below. Modified Mercalli intensity VIII is roughly correlated with peak accelerations of about one-quarter that of gravity (g = 9.8 metres, or 32.2 feet, per second squared) and ground velocities of 20 cm (8 inches) per second. Alternative scales have been developed in both Japan and Europe for local conditions. The European (MSK) scale of 12 grades is similar to the abridged version of the Mercalli.

Earthquake Magnitude

Earthquake magnitude is a measure of the "size," or amplitude, of the seismic waves generated by an earthquake source and recorded by seismographs. (The types and nature of these waves are described in the section "Seismic Waves," p. 247.) Because the size of earthquakes varies enormously, it is necessary for purposes of comparison to compress the range of wave amplitudes measured on seismograms by means of a mathematical device. In 1935 the American seismologist Charles F. Richter set up a magnitude scale of earthquakes as the logarithm to base 10 of the maximum seismic wave amplitude (in thousandths of a millimetre) recorded on a standard seismograph (the Wood-Anderson torsion pendulum seismograph) at a distance of 100 km (60 miles) from the earthquake epicentre. Reduction of amplitudes observed at various distances to the amplitudes expected at the standard distance of 100 km is made on the basis of empirical tables. Richter magnitudes M_L are computed on the assumption that the ratio of the maximum wave amplitudes at two given distances is the same for all earthquakes and is independent of azimuth.

Richter first applied his magnitude scale to shallow-focus earthquakes recorded within 600 km of the epicentre in the southern California region. Later, additional empirical tables were set up, whereby observations made at distant stations and on seismographs other than the standard type could be used. Empirical tables were extended to cover earthquakes of all significant focal depths and to enable independent magnitude estimates to be made from body- and surface-wave observations.

At the present time a number of different magnitude scales are used by scientists and engineers as a measure of the relative size of an earthquake. The *P*-wave magnitude (M_b), for one, is defined in terms of the amplitude of the *P* wave recorded on a standard seismograph. Similarly, the surface-wave magnitude (M_s) is defined in terms of the logarithm of the maximum amplitude of ground motion for surface waves with a wave period of 20 seconds.

As defined, an earthquake magnitude scale has no lower or upper limit. Sensitive seismographs can record earthquakes with magnitudes of negative value and have recorded magnitudes up to about 9.0. (The 1906 San Francisco earthquake, for example, had a Richter magnitude of 8.25.)

A scientific weakness is that there is no direct mechanical basis for magnitude as defined above. Rather, it is an empirical parameter analogous to stellar magnitude assessed by astronomers. In modern practice a more soundly based mechanical measure of earthquake size is used—namely, the seismic moment (M_o). Such a parameter is related to the angular leverage of the forces that produce the slip on the causative fault. It can be calculated both from recorded seismic waves and from field measurements of the size of the fault rupture. Consequently, seismic moment provides a more uniform scale of earthquake size based on classical mechanics. This measure allows a more scientific magnitude to be used called moment magnitude (M_w). It is proportional to the logarithm of the seismic moment; values do not differ greatly from M_s values for moderate earthquakes. Given the above definitions, the great Alaska earthquake of 1964, with a Richter magnitude (M_L) of 8.3, also had the values $M_s = 8.4$, $M_o = 820 \times 10^{27}$ dyne centimetres, and $M_w = 9.2$.

Earthquake Energy

Energy in an earthquake passing a particular surface site can be calculated directly from the recordings of seismic ground motion, given, for example, as ground velocity. Such recordings indicate an energy rate of 10^5 watts per square metre (9,300 watts per square foot) near a moderate-size earthquake source. The total power output of a rupturing fault in a shallow earthquake is on the order of 10^{14} watts, compared with the 10^5 watts generated in rocket motors.

The surface-wave magnitude M_s has also been connected with the surface energy E_s of an earthquake by empirical formulas. These give $E_s = 6.3 \times 10^{11}$ and 1.4×10^{25} ergs for earthquakes of $M_s = 0$ and 8.9, respectively. A unit increase in M_s corresponds to approximately a 32-fold increase in energy. Negative magnitudes M_s correspond to the smallest instrumentally recorded earthquakes, a magnitude of 1.5 to the smallest felt earthquakes, and one of 3.0 to any shock felt at a distance of up to 20 km (12 miles). Earthquakes of magnitude 5.0 cause light damage near the epicentre; those of 6.0 are destructive over a restricted area; and those of 7.5 are at the lower limit of major earthquakes.

The total annual energy released in all earthquakes is about 10^{25} ergs, corresponding to a rate of work between 10 million and 100 million kilowatts. This is approximately one one-thousandth the annual amount of heat escaping from Earth's interior. Ninety percent of the total seismic energy comes from earthquakes of magnitude 7.0 and higher—that is, those whose energy is on the order of 10^{23} ergs or more.

Frequency

There also are empirical relations for the frequencies of earthquakes of various magnitudes. Suppose N to be the average number of shocks per year for which the magnitude lies in a range about M_s. Then $\log_{10} N = a - bM_s$ fits the data well both globally and for particular regions; for example, for shallow earthquakes worldwide, $a = 6.7$ and $b = 0.9$ when $M_s > 6.0$. The frequency for larger earthquakes therefore increases by a factor of about 10 when the magnitude is diminished by one unit. The increase in frequency with reduction in M_s falls short, however, of matching the decrease in the energy E. Thus, larger earthquakes are overwhelmingly responsible for most of the total seismic energy release. The number of earthquakes per year with $M_b > 4.0$ reaches 50,000.

THE OCCURRENCE OF EARTHQUAKES

Earthquakes are the result of one plate, or portion of a plate, sliding against another. They may be preceded or followed by small shocks. Although the depth at which earthquake foci occurs can vary, most are considered shallow.

Tectonic Associations

Global seismicity patterns had no strong theoretical explanation until the dynamic model called plate tectonics was developed during the late 1960s. This theory holds that Earth's upper shell, or lithosphere, consists of nearly a dozen large, quasi-stable slabs called plates. The thickness of each of these plates is roughly 80 km (50 miles). The plates move horizontally relative to neighbouring plates at a rate of 1 to 10 cm (0.4 to 4 inches) per year over a shell of lesser strength called the asthenosphere. At the plate edges where there is contact between adjoining plates, boundary tectonic forces operate on the rocks, causing physical and chemical changes in them. New lithosphere is created at oceanic ridges by the upwelling and cooling of magma from Earth's mantle. The horizontally moving plates are believed to be absorbed at the ocean trenches, where a subduction process carries the lithosphere downward into Earth's interior. The total amount of lithospheric material destroyed at these subduction zones equals that generated at the ridges.

Seismological evidence (such as the location of major earthquake belts) is everywhere in agreement with this tectonic model. Earthquake sources are concentrated along the oceanic ridges, which correspond to divergent plate boundaries. At the subduction zones, which are associated with convergent plate boundaries, intermediate- and deep-focus earthquakes mark the location of the upper part of a dipping lithosphere slab. The focal mechanisms indicate that the stresses are aligned with the dip of the lithosphere underneath the adjacent continent or island arc.

Some earthquakes associated with oceanic ridges are confined to strike-slip faults, called transform faults, that offset the ridge crests. The majority of the earthquakes occurring along such horizontal shear faults are characterized by slip motions. Also in agreement with the plate tectonics theory is the high seismicity encountered along the edges of plates where they slide past each other. Plate boundaries of this kind, sometimes called fracture zones, include the San Andreas Fault in California and the North

Anatolian fault system in Turkey. Such plate boundaries are the site of interplate earthquakes of shallow focus.

The low seismicity within plates is consistent with the plate tectonic description. Small to large earthquakes do occur in limited regions well within the boundaries of plates; however, such intraplate seismic events can be explained by tectonic mechanisms other than plate boundary motions and their associated phenomena.

Shallow, Intermediate, and Deep Foci

Most parts of the world experience at least occasional shallow earthquakes—those that originate within 60 km (40 miles) of Earth's outer surface. In fact, the great majority of earthquake foci are shallow. It should be noted, however, that the geographic distribution of smaller earthquakes is less completely determined than more severe quakes, partly because the availability of relevant data is dependent on the distribution of observatories.

Of the total energy released in earthquakes, 12 percent comes from intermediate earthquakes—that is, quakes with a focal depth ranging from about 60 to 300 km. About 3 percent of total energy comes from deeper earthquakes. The frequency of occurrence falls off rapidly with increasing focal depth in the intermediate range. Below intermediate depth the distribution is fairly uniform until the greatest focal depths, of about 700 km (430 miles), are approached.

The deeper-focus earthquakes commonly occur in patterns called Benioff zones that dip into Earth, indicating the presence of a subducting slab. Dip angles of these slabs average about 45°, with some shallower and others nearly vertical. Benioff zones coincide with tectonically active island arcs such as Japan, Vanuatu, Tonga, and the

Aleutians, and they are normally but not always associated with deep ocean trenches such as those along the South American Andes. Exceptions to this rule include Romania and the Hindu Kush mountain system. In most Benioff zones, intermediate- and deep-earthquake foci lie in a narrow layer, although recent precise hypocentral locations in Japan and elsewhere show two distinct parallel bands of foci 20 km apart.

Aftershocks, Foreshocks, and Swarms

Usually, a major or even moderate earthquake of shallow focus is followed by many lesser-size earthquakes close to the original source region. This is to be expected if the fault rupture producing a major earthquake does not relieve all the accumulated strain energy at once. In fact, this dislocation is liable to cause an increase in the stress and strain at a number of places in the vicinity of the focal region, bringing crustal rocks at certain points close to the stress at which fracture occurs. In some cases an earthquake may be followed by 1,000 or more aftershocks a day.

Sometimes a large earthquake is followed by a similar one along the same fault source within an hour or perhaps a day. An extreme case of this is multiple earthquakes. In most instances, however, the first principal earthquake of a series is much more severe than the aftershocks. In general, the number of aftershocks per day decreases with time. The aftershock frequency is roughly inversely proportional to the time since the occurrence of the largest earthquake of the series.

Most major earthquakes occur without detectable warning, but some principal earthquakes are preceded by foreshocks. In another common pattern, large numbers of small earthquakes may occur in a region for months without a major earthquake. In the Matsushiro region of Japan, for instance, there occurred between August 1965 and August 1967 a series of hundreds of thousands of earthquakes, some sufficiently strong (up to Richter magnitude 5) to cause property damage but no casualties. The maximum frequency was 6,780 small earthquakes on April 17, 1966. Such series of earthquakes are called earthquake swarms. Earthquakes associated with volcanic activity often occur in swarms, though swarms also have been observed in many nonvolcanic regions.

Notable Earthquakes in History					
Year	Affected Area	Magnitude	Intensity	Approximate Number of Deaths	Comments
c. 1500 BCE	Knossos, Crete (Greece)	...	X	...	One of several events that leveled the capital of Minoan civilization, this quake accompanied the explosion of the nearby volcanic island of Thera.
27 BCE	Thebes (Egypt)	...	...	...	This quake cracked one of the statues known as the Colossi of Memnon, and for almost two centuries the "singing Memnon" emitted musical tones on certain mornings as it was warmed by the Sun's rays.

Notable Earthquakes in History					
Year	Affected Area	Magnitude	Intensity	Approximate Number of Deaths	Comments
CE 62	Pompeii and Herculaneum (Italy)	...	X	...	These two prosperous Roman cities had not yet recovered from the quake of 62 when they were buried by the eruption of Mount Vesuvius in 79.
115	Antioch (Antakya, Turkey)	...	XI	...	A centre of Hellenistic and early Chritian culture, Antioch suffered many devastating quakes; this one almost killed the visiting Roman emperor Trajan.
1556	Shaanxi province (China)	...	IX	830,000	This may have been the deadliest earthquake ever recorded.
1650	Cuzco (Peru)	8.1	VIII	...	Many of Cuzco's Baroque monuments date to the rebuillding of the city after this quake.
1692	Port Royal (Jamaica)	...	...	2,000	Much of this British West Indies port, a notorious haven for buccaneers and slave traders, sank beneath the sea following the quake.
1693	southeastern Sicily (Italy)	...	XI	93,000	Syracuse, Catania, and Ragusa were almost completely destroyed but were rebuilt with a Baroque splendour that still attracts tourists.

Notable Earthquakes in History					
Year	Affected Area	Magnitude	Intensity	Approximate Number of Deaths	Comments
1755	Lisbon, Portugal	...	XI	62,000	The Lisbon earthquake of 1755 was felt as far away as Algiers and caused a tsunami that reached the Caribbean.
1780	Tabriz (Iran)	7.7	...	200,000	This ancient highland city was destroyed and rebuilt, as it had been in 791, 858, 1041, and 1721, and would be again in 1927.
1811–12	New Madrid, Mo. (U.S.)	8.0 to 8.8	XII	...	A series of quakes at the New Madrid Fault caused few deaths, but the New Madrid earthquake of 1811–12 rerouted portions of the Mississippi River and was felt from Canada to the Gulf of Mexico.
1812	Caracas (Venezuela)	9.6	X	26,000	A provincial town in 1812, Caracas recovered and eventually became Venezuela's capital.
1835	Concepción, Chile	8.5	...	35	British naturalist Charles Darwin, witnessing this quake, marveled at the power of Earth to destroy cities and alter landscapes.
1886	Charleston, S.C., U.S.	...	IX	60	This was one of the largest quakes ever to hit the eastern United States.

Notable Earthquakes in History					
Year	Affected Area	Magnitude	Approximate Number of Deaths	Intensity	Comments
1895	Ljubljana (Slovenia)	6.1	VIII	...	Modern Ljubljana is said to have been born in the rebuilding after this quake.
1906	San Francisco, Calif., U.S.	7.9	XI	700	San Francisco still dates its modern develoment from the San Francisco earthquake of 1906 and the resulting fires.
1908	Messina and Reggio di Calabria, Italy	7.5	XII	110,000	These two cities on the Strait of Messina were almost completely destroyed in what is said to be Europe's worst earthquake ever.
1920	Gansu province, China	8.5	...	200,000	Many of the deaths in this quake-prone province were caused by huge landslides.
1923	Tokyo-Yokohama, Japan	7.9	...	142,800	Japan's capital and its principal port, located on soft alluvial ground, suffered severely from the Tokyo-Yokohama earthquake of 1923.
1931	Hawke Bay, New Zealand	7.9	...	256	The bayside towns of Napier and Hastings were rebuilt in an Art Deco style that is now a great tourist attraction.
1935	Quetta (Pakistan)	7.5	X	20,000	The capital of Balochistan province was severely damaged in the most destructive quake to hit South Asia in the 20th century.

Notable Earthquakes in History					
Year	Affected Area	Magnitude	Intensity	Approximate Number of Deaths	Comments
1948	Ashgabat (Turkmenistan)	7.3	X	176,000	Every year, Turkmenistan commemorates the utter destruction of its capital in this quake.
1950	Assam, India	8.7	X	574	The largest quake ever recorded in South Asia killed relatively few people in a lightly populated region along the indo-Chinese border.
1960	Valdivia and Puerto Montt, Chile	9.5	X	I 5,700	The Chile earthquake of 1960, the largest quake ever recorded in the world, produced a tsunami that crossed the Pacific Ocean to Japan, where it killed more than 100 people.
1963	Skopje, Macedonia	6.9	X	1,070	The capital of Macedonia had to be rebuilt almost completely following this quake.
1964	Prince William Sound, Alaska, U.S.	9.2	...	131	Anchorage, Seward, and Valdez were damaged, but most deaths in the Alaska earthquake of 1964 were caused by tsunamis in Alaska and as far away as California.
1972	Managua, Nicaragua	6.2	...	10,000	The centre of the capital of Nicaragua was almost completely destroyed and has never been rebuilt.

Notable Earthquakes in History					
Year	Affected Area	Magnitude	Intensity	Approximate Number of Deaths	Comments
1976	Guatemala City, Guatemala	7.5	IX	23,000	Rebuilt following a series of devastating quakes in 1917-18, the capital of Guatemala again suffered great destruction.
1976	Tangshan, China	8.0	X	242,000	In the Tangshan earthquake of 1976, this industrial city was almost completely destroyed in the worst earthquake disaster in modern history.
1985	Michoacán state and Mexico City, Mexico	8.1	IX	10,000	The centre of Mexico City, built largely on the soft subsoil of an ancient lake, suffered great damage in the Mexico City earthquake of 1985.
1988	Spitak and Gyumri, Armenia	6.8	X	25,000	This quake destroyed nearly one-third of Armenia's industrial capacity.
1989	Loma Prieta, Calif., U.S.	7.1	IX	62	This first sizable movement of the San Andreas Fault since 1906 collapsed a section of the San Francisco-Oakland Bay Bridge.
1994	Northridge, Calif., U.S.	6.8	IX	60	Centred in the urbanized San Fernando Valley, this quake collapsed freeways and some buildings, but damage was limited by earthquake-resistant construction.

Notable Earthquakes in History					
Year	Affected Area	Magnitude	Intensity	Approximate Number of Deaths	Comments
1995	Kobe, Japan	6.9	XI	5,502	The Great Hanshin Earthquake destroyed or damaged 200,000 buildings and left 300,000 people homeless.
1999	Izmit, Turkey	7.4	X	17,000	The industrial city of Izmit and the naval base at Gölcük were heavily damaged.
1999	Nan-t'ou county, Taiwan	7.7	X	2,400	The Taiwan earthquake of 1999, the worst to hit Taiwan since 1935, provided a wealth of digitized data for seismic and engineering studies.
2001	Bhuj, Gujarat state, India	8.0	X	20,000	This quake, possibly the deadliest ever to hit India, was felt across India and Pakistan.
2003	Bam, Iran	6.6	IX	26,000	This ancient Silk Road fortress city, built mostly of mud brick, was almost completely destroyed.
2004	Aceh province, Sumatra, Indonesia	9.	...	200,000	The deaths resulting from this offshore quake actually were caused by a tsunami that, in addition to killing more than 150,000 in Indonesia, killed people as far away as Sri Lanka and Somalia.

Notable Earthquakes in History					
Year	Affected Area	Magnitude	Intensity	Approximate Number of Deaths	Comments
2005	Azad Kashmir (Pakistani administered Kashmir)	7.6	VIII	80,000	This shock (perhaps the deadliest ever to strike South Asia) left hundreds of thousands of people exposed to the coming winter weather.
2008	Sichuan province, China	7.9	...	69,000	This quake left over 5 million people homeless across the region, and over half of Beichuan City was destroyed by the initial seismic event and the release of water from a lake.
2010	Port-au-Prince, Haiti	7.0	...	200,000 (at time of printing)	The combination of a high population density in Haiti's capital and a lack of building codes rendered up to one million people—one tenth of the population—homeless.

Data source: National Oceanic and Atmospheric Administration, National Geophysical Data Center, Significant Earthquake Database, a searchable online database using the *Catalog of Significant Earthquakes 2150 B.C.-1991 A.D.*, with addenda.

SIGNIFICANT EARTHQUAKES

Earthquakes are among the most destructive natural events. On land, the upheaval caused by these phenomenon can cause landslides and collapse buildings, leading to tremendous numbers of human fatalities. In the oceans, the sudden movement of the seafloor rarely produces loss of life and property damage directly; however, tsunamis generated by such movement can promulgate across entire oceans to harm populations thousands of miles away. The following section details a number of earthquake events notable for the tolls they took on human lives.

The Aleppo Earthquake of 1138

This earthquake, among the deadliest ever recorded, struck the Syrian city of Aleppo (Ḥalab) on Oct. 11, 1138. The city suffered extensive damage, and it is estimated that 230,000 people were killed.

Aleppo is located in northern Syria. The region, which sits on the boundary between the Arabian geologic plate and the African plate, is part of the Dead Sea Fault system. In the early 12th century this ancient Muslim city was home to tens of thousands of residents. On Oct. 10, 1138, a small shock shook the region, and some residents fled to surrounding towns. The main quake occurred the following day. As the city walls crumbled, rocks cascaded into the streets. Aleppo's citadel collapsed, killing hundreds of residents.

Although Aleppo was the largest community affected by the earthquake, it likely did not suffer the worst of the damage. European Crusaders had constructed a citadel at nearby Ḥorim, which was leveled by the quake. A Muslim fort at Al-Atārib was destroyed as well, and several smaller towns and manned forts were reduced to rubble. The quake was allegedly felt as far away as Damascus, about 220 miles (350 km) to the south. The Aleppo earthquake was the first of several occurring between 1138 and 1139 that devastated areas in northern Syria and western Turkey.

The Shaanxi Province Earthquake of 1556

On Jan. 23, 1556, a massive earthquake, believed to be the deadliest one ever recorded, occurred in Shaanxi province in northern China.

The earthquake (estimated at magnitude 8) struck Shaanxi and neighbouring Shanxi province to the east early on Jan. 23, 1556, killing or injuring an estimated 830,000 people. This massive death toll is thought to have reduced the population of the two provinces by about 60 percent. Local annals (which date to 1177 BCE) place the epicentre of the earthquake around Huaxian in Shaanxi. These annals, which record 26 other destructive earthquakes in the province, describe the destruction caused by the 1556 earthquake in a level of vivid detail that is unique among these records. Though the quake lasted only seconds, it leveled mountains, altered the path of rivers, caused massive flooding, and ignited fires that burned for days.

The local records indicate that, in addition to inspiring searches for the causes of earthquakes, this particular quake led the people in the region affected to search for ways to minimize the damage caused by such disasters. Many of the casualties in the quake were people who had been crushed by falling buildings. Thus, in the aftermath of the 1556 quake, many of the stone buildings that had been leveled were replaced with buildings made of softer, more earthquake-resistant materials, such as bamboo and wood.

The 1556 Shaanxi earthquake is associated with three major faults, which form the boundaries of the Wei River basin. All 26 of the earthquakes recorded in the annals had epicentres in this basin.

The Lisbon Earthquake of 1755

A series of earthquakes shook the port city of Lisbon, Port., on the morning of Nov. 1, 1755, causing serious damage and killing an estimated 60,000 people in Lisbon alone. Violent shaking demolished large public buildings and about 12,000 dwellings. Because November 1 is All Saints' Day, a large part of the population was attending mass at the moment the earthquake struck; the churches, unable to withstand the seismic shock, collapsed, killing or injuring thousands of worshippers.

Modern research indicates that the main seismic source was faulting of the seafloor along the tectonic plate boundaries of the mid-Atlantic. The earthquake generated a tsunami that produced waves about 20 feet (6 metres) high at Lisbon and 65 feet (20 metres) high at Cádiz, Spain. The waves traveled westward to Martinique in the Caribbean Sea, a distance of 3,790 miles (6,100 km), in 10 hours and there reached a height of 13 feet (4 metres) above mean sea level. Damage was even reported in Algiers, 685 miles (1,100 km) to the east. The total number of persons killed included those who perished by drowning and in fires that burned throughout Lisbon for about six days following the shock. Depictions of the earthquakes in art and literature continued for centuries, making the "Great Lisbon Earthquake," as it came to be known, a seminal event in European history.

The New Madrid Earthquakes of 1811–12

A series of three large earthquakes occurred near New Madrid in southern Missouri on Dec. 16, 1811 (magnitude from 8.0 to 8.5), and on Jan. 23 (magnitude 8.4) and Feb. 7, 1812 (magnitude 8.8). There were numerous aftershocks, of which 1,874 were large enough to be felt in Louisville, Ky., about 180 miles (300 km) away. The principal shock produced seismic waves of sufficient amplitude to shake down chimneys in Cincinnati, Ohio, about 360 miles (600 km) away. The waves were felt as far away as Canada in the north and the Gulf Coast in the south. The area of significant shaking was about 38,600 square miles (100,000 square km), considerably greater than the area involved in the San Francisco earthquake of 1906. Subsequently it was discovered that North American continental earthquakes, such as the Missouri shocks, produce greater shaking than

TOP: *Tree with a double set of roots, formed in the aftermath of the New Madrid earthquakes (1811–12). The ground sank by several feet, creating low areas that were flooded by the Mississippi River.* U.S. Geological Survey

BOTTOM: *Landslide trench and ridge in the Chickasaw Bluffs east of Reelfoot Lake, Tenn., resulting from the New Madrid earthquakes (1811–12).* U.S. Geological Survey

do comparable shocks along the Pacific coast. In one region roughly 150 miles long by 37 miles wide (240 km by 60 km), the ground sank 3 to 9 feet (1 to 3 metres) and was covered by inflowing river water. In certain locations, forests were overthrown or ruined by the loss of soil shaken from the roots of the trees.

The Messina Earthquake and Tsunami

An earthquake and subsequent tsunami devastated southern Italy on Dec. 28, 1908. The double catastrophe almost completely destroyed Messina, Reggio di Calabria, and dozens of nearby coastal towns.

What was likely the most powerful recorded earthquake to hit Europe began at about 5:20 AM local time. Its epicentre was under the Strait of Messina, which separates the island of Sicily from the province of Calabria, the "toe" of Italy's geographical "boot." The main shock lasted for more than 20 seconds, and its magnitude reached 7.5 on the Richter scale. The tsunami that followed brought waves estimated to be 40 feet (13 metres) high crashing down on the coasts of northern Sicily and southern Calabria. More than 80,000 people were killed in the disaster. Many of the survivors were relocated to other Italian cities; others emigrated to the United States.

Experts long surmised that the tsunami resulted from seafloor displacement caused by the earthquake. However, research completed in the early 21st century suggested that an underwater landslide, unrelated to the earthquake, triggered the ensuing tsunami.

The Tokyo-Yokohama Earthquake of 1923

This earthquake, also called the Great Kanto earthquake, with a magnitude of 7.9 devastated the Tokyo-Yokohama metropolitan area near noon on Sept. 1, 1923. The death toll from this shock was estimated at more than 140,000.

The San Francisco Earthquake of 1906

A major earthquake with a magnitude of 7.9 occurred on April 18, 1906, at 5:12 AM off the northern California coast. The San Andreas Fault slipped along a segment about 270 miles (430 km) long, extending from San Juan Bautista in San Benito county to Humboldt county, and from there perhaps out under the sea to an unknown distance. The shaking was felt from Los Angeles in the south to Coos Bay, Oregon, in the north. Damage was severe in San Francisco and in other towns situated near the fault, including San Jose, Salinas, and Santa Rosa. At least 700 people were killed. In San Francisco the earthquake started a fire that destroyed the central business district. Geologic field studies of this earthquake led to the detailed formation of the theory that elastic rebound of strained faults causes the shaking associated with earthquakes.

Crowds watching the fires set off by the earthquake in San Francisco in 1906. Photo by Arnold Genthe. Library of Congress, Washington, D.C.

More than half of the brick buildings and one-tenth of the reinforced concrete structures collapsed. Many hundreds of thousands of houses were either shaken down or burned. The shock started a tsunami that reached a height of 39.5 feet (12 metres) at Atami on Sagami Gulf, where it destroyed 155 houses and killed 60 persons. The only comparable Japanese earthquake in the 20th century was at Kōbe on Jan. 16, 1995; about 5,500 people died amid considerable damage, which included widespread fires in the city and a landslide in nearby Nishinomiya.

The Chile Earthquake of 1960

This earthquake originated off the coast of Chile on May 22, 1960, with a moment magnitude of 9.5. The fault-displacement source of this earthquake, the largest in the world in the 20th century, extended over a distance of about 680 miles (1,100 km) along the southern Chilean coast. The cause was major underthrusting of the Pacific Plate under South America. Casualties included about 5,700 killed and 3,000 injured, and property damage in southern Chile amounted to roughly $550 million. Tsunamis triggered by the faulting caused human fatalities and property destruction in Hawaii, Japan, and the West Coast of the United States.

The Alaska Earthquake of 1964

An earthquake that occurred in south-central Alaska on March 27, 1964, with a Richter scale magnitude of 9.2, this event released at least twice as much energy as the San Francisco earthquake of 1906 and was felt on land over an area of almost 502,000 square miles (1,300,000 square km). The death toll was only 131 because of the low density of the state's population, but property damage was high. The earthquake tilted an area of at least 46,442 square miles (120,000 square km). Landmasses were thrust up locally as high as 82 feet (25 metres) to the east of a line extending northeastward from Kodiak Island through the western part of Prince William Sound. To the west, land sank as much as 8 feet (2.5 metres). Extensive damage in coastal areas resulted from submarine landslides and tsunamis. Tsunami damage occurred as far away as Crescent City, Calif. The occurrence of tens of thousands of aftershocks indicates that the region of faulting extended about 620 miles (1,000 km) along the North Pacific Plate subduction zone.

The Ancash Earthquake of 1970

This earthquake, also called the Great Peruvian earthquake, originated off the coast of Peru on May 31, 1970, and caused massive landslides. More than 65,000 people died.

The epicentre of the earthquake was under the Pacific Ocean, about 15 miles (25 km) west of the Peruvian fishing port of Chimbote, in the Ancash department of north-central Peru. It occurred at about 3:20 PM local time and had a moment magnitude of 7.9. The effects of the quake could be felt from the northern city of Chiclayo south to the capital city of Lima, a distance of more than 400 miles (650 km). The most damage occurred in the coastal towns near the epicentre and in the Santa River valley. The destruction was exacerbated by the construction techniques used in the area; many homes and buildings were constructed using adobe, with many built on unstable soil.

Tens of thousands of people were killed or injured when their homes or businesses collapsed, and a significant number of victims died as the result of landslides triggered by the quake. The most destructive landslide fell from Peru's highest mountain, Mount Huascarán, located in the west-central Andes. Fast-moving snow and earth swallowed the village of Yungay, buried much of Ranrahirca, and devastated other villages in the area.

The Tangshan Earthquake of 1976

Striking on July 28, 1976, with a magnitude of 8.0, this earthquake nearly razed the Chinese coal-mining and industrial city of Tangshan, located about 68 miles (110 km) east of Beijing. The death toll, thought to be one of the largest in recorded history, was officially reported as 242,000 persons, but it may have been as high as 655,000. At least 700,000 more people were injured, and property damage was extensive, reaching even to Beijing. Most of the fatalities resulted from the collapse of unreinforced masonry homes where people were sleeping.

The Mexico City Earthquake of 1985

The Mexico City earthquake possessed a moment magnitude of 8.0 whose main shock occurred at 7:18 AM on Sept. 19, 1985. The cause was a fault slip along the subduction slab under the Pacific coast of Mexico. Although 250 miles (400 km) from the epicentre, Mexico City suffered major building damage, and more than 10,000 of its inhabitants were reported killed. The highest intensity was in the central city, which is constructed on a former lake bed. The ground motion there measured five times that in the outlying districts, which have different soil foundations.

The San Francisco–Oakland Earthquake of 1989

This major earthquake, also called the Loma Prieta earthquake, shook the San Francisco Bay Area, California, U.S., on Oct. 17, 1989. The strongest earthquake to hit the area since the San Francisco earthquake of 1906, it caused more than 60 deaths, thousands of injuries, and widespread property damage.

The earthquake was triggered by a slip along the San Andreas Fault. Its epicentre was in the Forest of Nisene Marks State Park, near Loma Prieta peak in the Santa

Cruz mountains, northeast of Santa Cruz and approximately 60 miles (100 km) south of San Francisco. It began just after 5:00 PM local time and lasted approximately 15 seconds, with a magnitude of 7.1. The most severe damage was suffered by San Francisco and Oakland, but communities throughout the region, including Alameda, Santa Clara, Santa Cruz, and Monterey, also were affected. San Francisco's Marina district was particularly hard hit because it had been built on filled land (comprising loose, sandy soil), and the unreinforced masonry buildings in Santa Cruz (many of which were 50 to 100 years old) failed spectacularly.

The earthquake significantly damaged the transportation system of the Bay Area. The collapse of the Cypress Street Viaduct (Nimitz Freeway) caused most of the earthquake-related deaths. The San Francisco–Oakland Bay Bridge was also damaged when a span of the top deck collapsed. In the aftermath, all bridges in the area underwent seismic retrofitting to make them more resistant to earthquakes.

Remarkably, the earthquake struck just before the start of the third game of the 1989 World Series, which was being played in San Francisco's Candlestick Park between two Bay Area baseball teams, the San Francisco Giants and the Oakland Athletics. The disaster's occurrence during a major live television broadcast meant that news of the earthquake, as well as aerial views provided by the Goodyear blimp, reached a large audience. The baseball championship, which was suspended for 10 days, would come to be known as the "Earthquake Series."

The Northridge Earthquake of 1994

The Northridge earthquake occurred in the densely populated San Fernando Valley in southern California, U.S., on Jan. 17, 1994. The third major earthquake to occur in the state in 23 years (after the 1971 San Fernando Valley and 1989 San Francisco–Oakland earthquakes), the Northridge earthquake was the state's most destructive one since the San Francisco earthquake of 1906 and the costliest one in U.S. history.

The earthquake occurred just after 4:30 AM local time along a previously undiscovered blind thrust fault in the San Fernando Valley. Its epicentre was in Northridge, a suburb located about 20 miles (32 km) west-northwest of downtown Los Angeles. The major shock lasted 10–20 seconds and registered a magnitude of 6.7.

Fatality estimates range from just under 60 to more than 70 people killed, with most studies placing the number at around 60. The timing of the earthquake (early morning during a federal holiday) is thought to have prevented a higher death toll, as most residents were in their beds, rather than on failed freeways or in other collapsed structures (such as office buildings or parking lots). Most of the casualties occurred in wood-frame apartment buildings, popular in the San Fernando Valley, and particularly in those with weak first floors or lower-level parking garages.

Property damage was severe and widespread; although the worst damage was sustained by communities in the western and northern San Fernando Valley, other areas of Los Angeles county were affected, as were parts of Ventura, Orange, and San Bernardino counties. The percentage of buildings completely destroyed was relatively low in light of the strength of the ground motions. Nevertheless, tens of thousands of buildings were damaged, with many "red-tagged" as unsafe to enter and many more restricted to limited entry ("yellow-tagged"). A significant portion of the transportation system around Los Angeles was shut down, as sections of major freeways (including the Santa

Monica Freeway and the Golden State Freeway) collapsed and numerous bridges sustained heavy damage. Fires that broke out in the San Fernando Valley and in Venice and Malibu caused additional harm.

The extent of the property damage in an area so well-prepared for earthquakes was staggering. Accordingly, a number of legislative changes were made in the aftermath of the Northridge earthquake. Most significantly, the state created the California Earthquake Authority, a publicly managed but privately funded organization offering basic residential earthquake insurance.

The Kōbe Earthquake of 1995

The large-scale Kōbe earthquake (Japanese: Hanshin-Awaji Daishinsai; "Great Hanshin-Awaji Earthquake Disaster") shook the Ōsaka-Kōbe (Hanshin) metropolitan area of western Japan; it was among the strongest, deadliest, and costliest to ever strike that country.

The earthquake, also called the Great Hanshin earthquake, hit at 5:46 AM on Tuesday, Jan. 17, 1995, in the southern part of Hyogo prefecture, west-central Honshu. It lasted about 20 seconds and registered as a magnitude 6.9 (7.3 on the Richter scale). Its epicentre was the northern part of Awaji Island in the Inland Sea, 12.5 miles (20 km) off the coast of the port city of Kōbe; the quake's focus was about 10 miles (16 km) below the earth's surface. The Hanshin region (the name is derived from the characters used to write Ōsaka and Kōbe) is Japan's second largest urban area, with more than 11 million inhabitants; with the earthquake's epicentre located as close as it was to such a densely populated area, the effects were overwhelming. Its estimated death toll of 6,400 made it the worst earthquake to hit Japan since the Tokyo-Yokohama (Great Kantō) earthquake of 1923, which had killed more

Building knocked off its foundation by the January 1995 earthquake in Kōbe, Japan. Dr. Roger Hutchison/NGDC

than 140,000. The Kōbe quake's devastation included 40,000 injured, more than 300,000 homeless residents, and in excess of 240,000 damaged homes, with millions of homes in the region losing electric or water service. Kōbe was the hardest hit city with 4,571 fatalities, more than 14,000 injured, and more than 120,000 damaged structures, more than half of which were fully collapsed. Portions of the Hanshin Expressway linking Kōbe and Ōsaka also collapsed or were heavily damaged during the earthquake.

The earthquake was notable for exposing the vulnerability of the infrastructure. Authorities who had proclaimed the superior earthquake-resistance capabilities of Japanese construction were quickly proved wrong by the collapse of numerous supposedly earth-quake-

Burning and collapsed buildings in Kōbe, Japan, after the January 1995 earthquake. Dr. Roger Hutchison/NGDC

resistant buildings, rail lines, elevated highways, and port facilities in the Kōbe area. Although most of the buildings that had been constructed according to new building codes withstood the earthquake, many others, particularly older wood-frame houses, did not. The transportation network was completely paralyzed, and the inadequacy of national disaster preparedness was also exposed. The government was heavily criticized for its slow and ineffectual response, as well as its initial refusal to accept help from foreign countries.

In the aftermath of the Kōbe disaster, roads, bridges, and buildings were reinforced against another earthquake, and the national government revised its disaster response policies (its response to the 2004 quake in Niigata prefecture was much faster and more effective). An emergency transportation network was also devised, and evacuation centres and shelters were set up in Kōbe by the Hyogo prefectural government.

The İzmit Earthquake of 1999

Also referred to as the Kocaeli or the Gölcük earthquake, this devastating event, centred near the city of İzmit in northwestern Turkey, occurred on Aug. 17, 1999. Thousands of people were killed, and large parts of a number of mid-sized towns and cities were destroyed.

The earthquake, which occurred on the northernmost strand of the North Anatolian fault system, struck just after 3:00 AM local time. Its epicentre was about 7 miles (11 km) southeast of İzmit. The initial shock lasted less than a minute and registered a magnitude of 7.6. It was followed by two moderate aftershocks on August 19, about 50 miles (80 km) west of the original epicentre. More than 17,000 people were killed and an estimated 500,000 left homeless as thousands of buildings—chief among them the Turkish navy headquarters in Gölcük and the Tüpraş oil refinery in İzmit—collapsed or were heavily damaged. High casualty figures were reported in the towns of Gölcük, Derince, Darıca, and Sakarya (Adapazarı). Farther west, in Istanbul, the earthquake caused hundreds of fatalities and widespread destruction.

The rescue and relief effort was spearheaded by the Turkish Red Crescent and the Turkish army, with many international aid agencies joining in. The immediate support offered by Greece led to a thaw in the often-contentious relationship between the two neighbouring countries. Because most of the casualties resulted from the collapse of residential buildings, there was a strong public outcry against private contractors, who were accused of poor workmanship and of using cheap, inadequate materials. Some contractors were criminally prosecuted, but very few were found guilty. Public opinion also condemned officials who had failed to enforce building codes regarding earthquake-resistant designs.

The Taiwan Earthquake of 1999

This earthquake began at 1:47 AM local time on Sept. 21, 1999, below an epicentre 93 miles (150 km) south of Taipei, Taiwan. The death toll was 2,400 and some 10,000 people were injured. Thousands of houses collapsed, making more than 100,000 people homeless. The magnitude of the main shock was 7.7, resulting in about 10,000 buildings irreparably damaged and 7,500 partially damaged.

The earthquake, also called the 1999 Chi Chi earthquake, was produced by thrust faulting along the Chelung-pu fault in central Taiwan. The hanging wall thrust westward and upward along a line almost 60 miles (100 km) long, with uplift ranging from more than 3 feet (1 metre) in the south to 26 feet (8 metres) in the north. Many roads and bridges were damaged at their intersections with the fault displacement. The earthquake provided a wealth of observations for seismological research and engineering design; it is considered preeminent in the recording of strong ground shaking and crustal movement in the era of modern digital seismographs.

The Bhuj Earthquake of 2001

The Bhuj earthquake was a massive event that occurred on Jan. 26, 2001, in the Indian state of Gujarat, on the Pakistani border.

The earthquake struck near the town of Bhuj on the morning of India's annual Republic Day (celebrating the creation of the Republic of India in 1950), and it was felt throughout much of northwestern India and parts of Pakistan. The moment magnitude of the quake was 7.7 (6.9 on the Richter scale). In addition to killing more than

20,000 people and injuring more than 150,000 others, the quake left hundreds of thousands homeless and destroyed or damaged more than a million buildings. A large majority of the local crops were ruined as well. Many people were still living in makeshift shelters a year later.

The Kashmir Earthquake

A disastrous earthquake centred in the Pakistan-administered portion of the Kashmir region and the North-West Frontier Province (NWFP) of Pakistan, the Kashmir earthquake also affected adjacent parts of India and Afghanistan. At least 79,000 people were killed and more than 32,000 buildings collapsed in Kashmir, with additional fatalities and destruction reported in India and Afghanistan.

The devastating earthquake struck on Saturday, Oct. 8, 2005, at 8:50 AM local time (03:50 UTC), with its epicentre approximately 65 miles (105 km) north-northeast of Islamabad, the capital of Pakistan. Measured at a magnitude of 7.6 (slightly less than that of the 1906 San Francisco quake), the earthquake caused major destruction in northern Pakistan, northern India, and Afghanistan, an area that lies on an active fault caused by the northward tectonic drift of the Indian subcontinent. The tremors were felt at a distance of up to 620 miles (1,000 km), as far away as Delhi and Punjab in northern India. The property loss caused by the quake left an estimated four million area residents homeless. The severity of the damage and the high number of fatalities were exacerbated by poor construction in the affected areas.

The Sichuan Earthquake of 2008

On May 12, 2008, a magnitude-7.9 earthquake brought enormous devastation to the mountainous central region of Sichuan province in southwestern China. The epicentre was in the city of Wenchuan, and some 80 percent of the structures in the area were flattened. Whole villages and towns in the mountains were destroyed, and many schools collapsed. China's government quickly deployed 130,000 soldiers and other relief workers to the stricken area, but the damage from the earthquake made many remote villages difficult to reach, and the lack of modern rescue equipment caused delays that might have contributed to the number of deaths. In the aftermath, millions of people were left homeless, and some 90,000 were counted as dead or missing in the final assessment. Hundreds of dams, including two major ones, were found to have sustained damage. Some 200 relief workers were reported to have died in mud slides in the affected area, where damming of rivers and lakes by rocks, mud, and earthquake debris made flooding a major threat.

The Haiti Earthquake of 2010

This large-scale earthquake occurred Jan. 12, 2010, at 4:53 PM, some 15 miles (24 km) southwest of the Haitian capital of Port-au-Prince. The initial shock registered a magnitude of 7.0 and was soon followed by two aftershocks of magnitudes 5.9 and 5.5. More aftershocks occurred in the following days, including another one of magnitude 5.9 that struck on January 20. Seismologists asserted that minor tremors would likely persist for months or even years. Haiti had not been hit by an earthquake of such enormity since the 18th century.

The earthquake was generated by the movement of the Caribbean tectonic plate eastward along the Enriquillo–Plantain Garden strike-slip fault system, a transform boundary that separates the Gonâve microplate—the fragment of the North American Plate upon which Haiti is situated—from the Caribbean Plate. Occurring at a depth of 8.1 miles (13 km), the temblor was fairly shallow, which increased the degree of shaking at the Earth's surface. The collapsed buildings defining the landscape of the disaster area came as a consequence of Haiti's lack of building codes. Without adequate reinforcement, the buildings disintegrated under the force of the quake. It was estimated that some three million people were affected by the quake—nearly one-third of the country's total population. Of these, up to one million were left homeless.

THE STUDY OF EARTHQUAKES

The scientific discipline that is concerned with the study of earthquakes and of the propagation of seismic waves within Earth is called seismology. A branch of geophysics, it has provided much information about the composition and state of the planet's interior.

The goals of seismological investigations may be local or regional, as in the attempt to determine subsurface faults and other structures in petroleum or mineral exploration, or they may be of global significance, as in attempts to determine structural discontinuities in Earth's interior, the geophysical characteristics of island arcs, oceanic trenches, or mid-oceanic ridges, or the elastic properties of Earth materials generally.

In recent years, attention has been devoted to earthquake prediction and, more successfully, to assessing seismic hazards at different geographic sites in an effort to reduce the risks of earthquakes. The physics of seismic fault sources have been better determined and modeled for computer analysis. Moreover, seismologists have studied quakes induced by human activities, such as impounding water behind high dams and detonating underground nuclear explosions. The objective of the latter research is to find ways of discriminating between explosions and natural earthquakes. In order to predict where and when earthquakes will occur, scientists must first develop an understanding of the seismic waves that move through Earth and traverse along its surface. The measurement of these phenomena by seismometers, seismographs, and other instruments near fault lines (both on land and at the bottom of the ocean) allows scientists to detect earthquake patterns and construct models of earthquake behaviour. Such models can help structural engineers design buildings better able to withstand the forces generated by earthquakes. These tools also allow scientists to predict more accurately the time, location, and strength of impending earthquakes to warn people in affected areas.

SEISMIC WAVES

The vibration generated by an earthquake, explosion, or similar energetic source and propogated within Earth or along its surface is called a seismic wave. Earthquakes produce different types of seismic waves. Each type is classified according to the depth and medium in which it propagates.

The Principal Types of Seismic Waves

Seismic waves generated by an earthquake source are commonly classified into four main types. The first two, the *P* (or primary) and *S* (or secondary) waves, propagate within the body of Earth, while the third and fourth, consisting of Love and Rayleigh waves, propagates along its surface. The existence of these types of seismic waves was mathematically predicted during the 19th century, and modern comparisons show that there is a close correspondence between such theoretical calculations and actual measurements of the seismic waves.

The *P* seismic waves travel as elastic motions at the highest speeds. They are longitudinal waves that can be

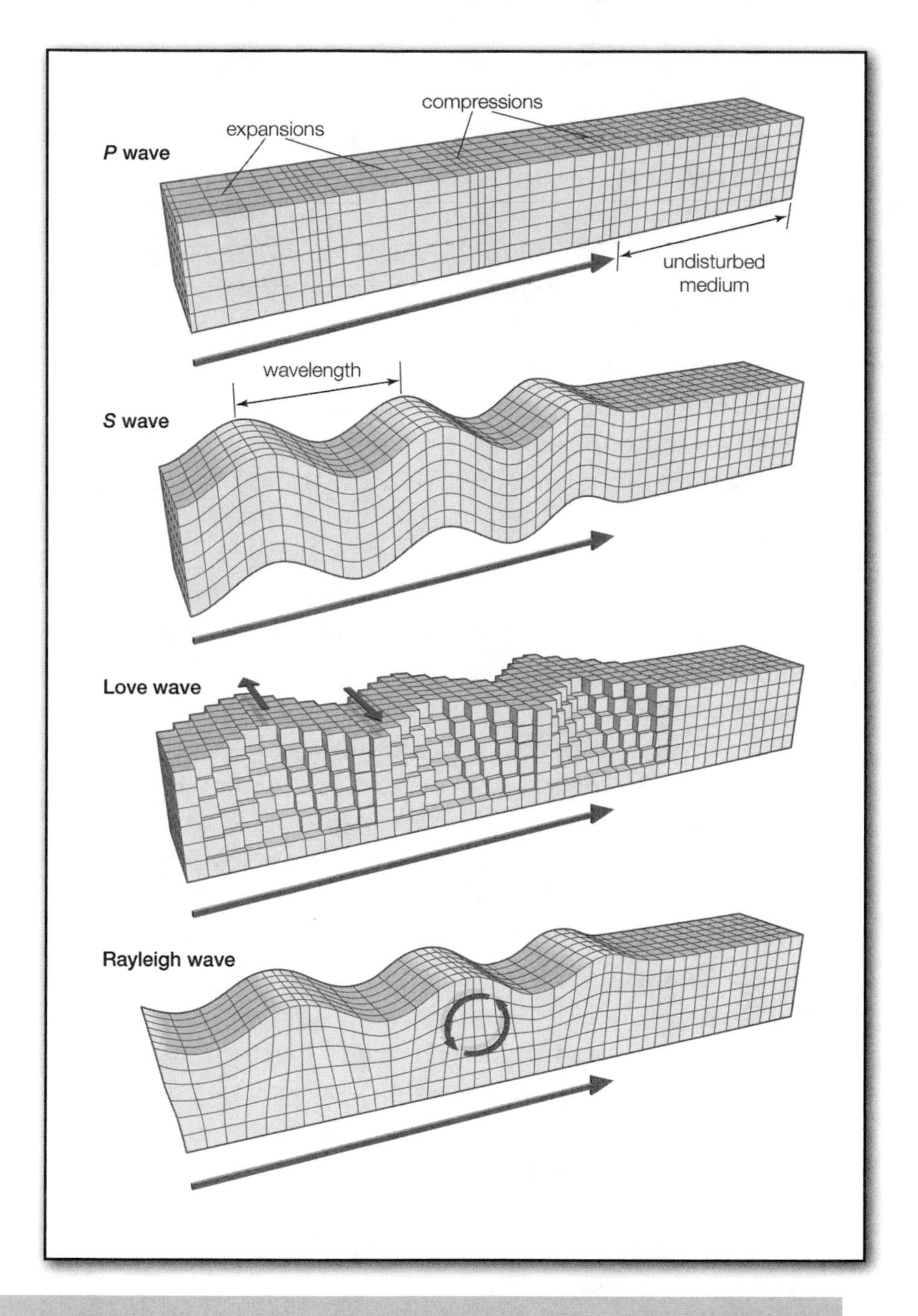

The main types of seismic waves: P, S, Love, and Rayleigh. Encyclopædia Britannica, Inc.

transmitted by both solid and liquid materials in Earth's interior. With *P* waves, the particles of the medium vibrate in a manner similar to sound waves—the transmitting media is alternately compressed and expanded. The slower type of body wave, the *S* wave, travels only through solid material. With *S* waves, the particle motion is transverse to the direction of travel and involves a shearing of the transmitting rock.

Because of their greater speed, *P* waves are the first to reach any point on Earth's surface. The first *P*-wave onset starts from the spot where an earthquake originates. This point, usually at some depth within Earth, is called the focus, or hypocentre. The point at the surface immediately above the focus is known as the epicentre.

Of the two surface seismic waves, Love waves--named after the British seismologist A. E. H. Love, who first predicted their existence—travel faster. They follow along after the *P* and *S* waves have passed through the body of the planet. They are propagated when the solid medium near the surface has varying vertical elastic properties. Displacement of the medium by the wave is entirely perpendicular to the direction of propagation and has no vertical or longitudinal components. The energy of Love waves, like that of other surface waves, spreads from the source in two directions rather than in three, and so these waves produce a strong record at seismic stations even when originating from distant earthquakes.

The other principal surface waves are called Rayleigh waves after the British physicist Lord Rayleigh, who first mathematically demonstrated their existence. Both love and Rayleigh waves involve horizontal particle motion bu only the latter type has vertical ground displacements. Rayeigh waves travel along the free surface of an elastic solid such as Earth. Their motion is a combination of longitudinal compression and dilation that results in an elliptical motion of points on the surface. Of all seismic waves, Rayleigh waves spread out most in time, producing a long wave duration on seismographs. Even at substantial distances from the source inalluvial basins, Love and Rayleigh waves they cause much of the shaking felt during earthquakes.

The Properties of Seismic Waves

At all distances from the focus, mechanical properties of the rocks, such as incompressibility, rigidity, and density, play a role in the speed with which the waves travel and the shape and duration of the wave trains. The layering of the rocks and the physical properties of surface soil also affect wave characteristics. In most cases, elastic behaviour occurs in earthquakes, but strong shaking of surface soils from the incident seismic waves sometimes results in nonelastic behaviour, including slumping (that is, the downward and outward movement of unconsolidated material) and the liquefaction of sandy soil.

When a seismic wave encounters a boundary that separates rocks of different elastic properties, it undergoes reflection and refraction. There is a special complication because conversion between the wave types usually also occurs at such a boundary: an incident *P* or *S* wave can yield reflected *P* and *S* waves and refracted *P* and *S* waves. Boundaries between structural layers also give rise to diffracted and scattered waves. These additional waves are in part responsible for the complications observed in ground motion during earthquakes. Modern research is concerned with computing synthetic records of ground motion that are realistic in comparison with observed ground shaking, using the theory of waves in complex structures.

The frequency range of seismic waves is large, from as high as the audible range (greater than 20 hertz) to as low as the frequencies of the free oscillations of the whole Earth, with the gravest period being 54 minutes. Attenuation of the waves in rock imposes high-frequency limits, and in small to moderate earthquakes the dominant frequencies extend in surface waves from about 1 to 0.1 hertz.

The amplitude range of seismic waves is also great in most earthquakes. Displacement of the ground ranges from 10^{-10} to 10^{-1} metre (4^{-12} to 4 inches). In the greatest earthquakes the ground amplitude of the predominant *P* waves may be several centimetres at periods of two to five seconds. Very close to the seismic sources of great earthquakes, investigators have measured large wave amplitudes with accelerations of the ground exceeding that of gravity (9.8 metres, or 32.2 feet, per second squared) at high frequencies and ground displacements of 1 metre at low frequencies.

The Measurement of Seismic Waves

The amplitude and frequency of seismic waves can be measured by a variety of instruments.

Seismographs and Accelerometers

Seismographs are used to measure ground motion in both earthquakes and microseisms (small oscillations described below). Most of these instruments are of the pendulum type. Early mechanical seismographs had a pendulum of large mass (up to several tons) and produced seismograms by scratching a line on smoked paper on a rotating drum. In later instruments, seismograms were recorded by means of a ray of light from the mirror of a galvanometer through which passed an electric current generated by electromagnetic induction when the pendulum of the seismograph moved. Technological developments in electronics have given rise to higher-precision pendulum seismometers and sensors of ground motion. In these instruments the electric voltages produced by motions of the pendulum or the equivalent are passed through electronic circuitry to amplify and digitize the ground motion for more exact readings.

Generally speaking, seismographs are divided into three types: short-period, long- (or intermediate-) period, and ultralong-period, or broadband, instruments. Short-period instruments are used to record *P* and *S* body waves with high magnification of the ground motion. For this purpose, the seismograph response is shaped to peak at a period of about one second or less. The intermediate-period instruments of the type used by the World-Wide Standardized Seismographic Network (described in the section "Earthquake Observatories") had a response maximum at about 20 seconds. Recently, in order to provide as much flexibility as possible for research work, the trend has been toward the operation of very broadband seismographs with digital representation of the signals. This is usually accomplished with very long-period pendulums and electronic amplifiers that pass signals in the band between 0.005 and 50 hertz.

When seismic waves close to their source are to be recorded, special design criteria are needed. Instrument sensitivity must ensure that the largest ground movements can be recorded without exceeding the upper scale limit of the device. For most seismological and engineering purposes the wave frequencies that must be recorded are higher than 1 hertz, and so the pendulum or its equivalent can be small. For this reason accelerometers that measure the rate at which the ground velocity is changing have an advantage for strong-motion recording. Integration is then performed to estimate ground velocity and displacement. The ground accelerations to be registered range up to two times that of gravity. Recording such accelerations can be accomplished mechanically with short torsion suspensions or force-balance mass-spring systems.

Because many strong-motion instruments need to be placed at unattended sites in ordinary buildings for periods of months or years before a strong earthquake occurs, they usually record only when a trigger mechanism is actuated with the onset of ground motion. Solid-state memories are now used, particularly with digital recording instruments, making it possible to preserve the first few seconds before the trigger starts the permanent recording and to store digitized signals on magnetic cassette tape or on a memory chip. In past design absolute timing was not provided on strong-motion records but only accurate relative time marks; the present trend, however, is to provide Universal Time (the local mean time of the prime meridian) by means of special radio receivers, small crystal clocks, or GPS (global positioning system) receivers from satellite clocks.

The prediction of strong ground motion and response of engineered structures in earthquakes depends critically on measurements of the spatial variability of earthquake intensities near the seismic wave source. In an effort to secure such measurements, special arrays of strong-motion seismographs have been installed in areas of high seismicity around the world. Large-aperture seismic arrays (linear dimensions on the order of 1 to 10 km, or 0.6 to 6 miles) of strong-motion accelerometers can now be used to improve estimations of speed, direction of propagation, and types of seismic wave components. Particularly important for full understanding of seismic wave patterns at the ground surface is measurement of the variation of wave motion with depth. To aid in this effort, special digitally recording seismometers have been installed in deep boreholes.

Ocean-Bottom Measurements

Because 70 percent of Earth's surface is covered by water, there is a need for ocean-bottom seismometers to augment the global land-based system of recording stations. Field tests have established the feasibility of extensive long-term recording by instruments on the seafloor. Japan already has a semipermanent seismograph system of this type that was placed on the seafloor off the Pacific coast of central Honshu in 1978 by means of a cable.

Because of the mechanical difficulties of maintaining permanent ocean-bottom instrumentation, different systems have been considered. They all involve placement of instruments on the bottom of the ocean, though they employ various mechanisms for data transmission. Signals may be transmitted to the ocean surface for retransmission by auxiliary apparatus or transmitted via cable to a shore-based station. Another system is designed to release its recording device automatically, allowing it to float to the surface for later recovery.

The use of ocean-bottom seismographs should yield much-improved global coverage of seismic waves and provide new information on the seismicity of oceanic regions. Ocean-bottom seismographs will enable investigators to determine the details of the crustal structure of the seafloor and, because of the relative thinness of the oceanic crust, should make it possible to collect clear seismic information about the upper mantle. Such systems are also expected to provide new data on plate boundaries, on the origin and propagation of microseisms, and on the nature of ocean-continent margins.

Measuring Microseisms

Small ground motions known as microseisms are commonly recorded by seismographs. These weak wave motions are not generated by earthquakes, and they complicate accurate recording of the latter. However, they are of scientific interest because their form is related to the Earth's surface structure.

Some microseisms have local causes—for example, those due to traffic or machinery or due to local wind effects, storms, and the action of rough surf against an extended steep coast. Another class of microseisms exhibits features that are very similar on records traced at earthquake observatories that are widely separated, including approximately simultaneous occurrence of maximum amplitudes and similar wave frequencies. These microseisms may persist for many hours and have more or less regular periods of about five to eight seconds. The largest amplitudes of such microseisms are on the order of 10^{-3} cm (0.0004 inch) and occur in coastal regions. The amplitudes also depend to some extent on local geologic structure. Some microseisms are produced when large standing water waves are formed far out at sea. The period of this type of microseism is half that of the standing wave.

The Observation of Earthquakes

Earthquake Observatories

Worldwide during the late 1950s, there were only about 700 seismographic stations, which were equipped with seismographs of various types and frequency responses. Few instruments were calibrated; actual ground motions could not be measured, and timing errors of several seconds were common. The World-Wide Standardized Seismographic Network (WWSSN), the first modern worldwide standardized system, was established to help remedy this situation. Each station of the WWSSN had six seismographs—three short-period and three long-period seismographs. Timing and accuracy were maintained by crystal clocks, and a calibration pulse was placed daily on each record. By 1967 the WWSSN consisted of about 120 stations distributed over 60 countries. The resulting data provided the basis for significant advances in research on earthquake mechanisms, global tectonics, and the structure of Earth's interior.

By the 1980s a further upgrading of permanent seismographic stations began with the installation of digital equipment by a number of organizations. Among the global networks of digital seismographic stations now in operation are the Seismic Research Observatories in boreholes 100 metres (330 feet) deep and modified high-gain, long-period surface observatories. The Global Digital Seismographic Network in particular has remarkable capability, recording all motions from Earth tides to microscopic ground motions at the level of local ground noise. At present there are about 128 sites. With this system the long-term seismological goal will have been accomplished to equip global observatories with seismographs that can record every small earthquake anywhere over a broad band of frequencies.

Locating Earthquake Epicentres

Many observatories make provisional estimates of the epicentres of important earthquakes. These estimates provide preliminary information locally about particular earthquakes and serve as first approximations for the calculations subsequently made by large coordinating centres.

If an earthquake's epicentre is less than 105° away from an observatory, the epicentre's position can often be estimated from the readings of three seismograms recording perpendicular components of the ground motion. For a shallow earthquake the epicentral distance is indicated by the interval between the arrival times of *P* and *S* waves; the azimuth and angle of wave emergence at the surface are indicated by a comparison of the sizes and directions of the first movements shown in the seismograms and by the relative sizes of later waves, particularly surface waves. It should be noted, however, that in certain regions the first wave movement at a station arrives from a direction differing from the azimuth toward the epicentre. This anomaly is usually explained by strong variations in geologic structures.

When data from more than one observatory are available, an earthquake's epicentre may be estimated from the times of travel of the *P* and *S* waves from source to recorder. In many seismically active regions, networks of seismographs with telemetry transmission and centralized timing and recording are common. Whether analog or digital recording is used, such integrated systems greatly simplify observatory work: multichannel signal displays make identification and timing of phase onsets easier and more reliable. Moreover, online microprocessors can be programmed to pick automatically, with some degree of confidence, the onset of a significant common phase, such as *P*, by correlation of waveforms from parallel network channels. With the aid of specially designed computer programs, seismologists can then locate distant earthquakes to within about 10 km (6 miles) and the epicentre of a local earthquake to within a few kilometres.

Catalogs of earthquakes felt by humans and of earthquake observations have appeared intermittently for many centuries. The earliest known list of instrumentally recorded earthquakes with computed times of origin and epicentres is for the period 1899–1903. In subsequent years, cataloging of earthquakes has become more uniform and complete. Especially valuable is the service provided by the International Seismological Centre (ISC) at Newbury, Eng. Each month it receives more than 1,000,000 readings from more than 2,000 stations worldwide and preliminary estimates of the locations of approximately 1,600 earthquakes from national and regional agencies and observatories. The ISC publishes a monthly bulletin—with about a two-year delay—that provides all available information on each of more than 5,000 earthquakes.

Various national and regional centres control networks of stations and act as intermediaries between individual stations and the international organizations. Examples of long-standing national centres include the Japan Meteorological Agency and United States National Earthquake Information Center in Colorado (a subdivision of the United States Geological Survey). These centres normally make estimates of the magnitudes, epicentres, origin times, and focal depths of local earthquakes. On the Internet, data on global seismicity is continually accessible through the Web site of the Incorporated Research Institutions for Seismology (IRIS).

An important research technique is to infer the character of faulting in an earthquake from the recorded seismograms. For example, observed distributions of the directions of the first onsets in waves arriving at the Earth's surface have been effectively used. Onsets are called "compressional" or "dilatational" according to whether the direction is away from or toward the focus, respectively. A polarity pattern becomes recognizable when the directions of the *P*-wave onsets are plotted on a map—there are broad areas in which the first onsets are predominantly compressions, separated from predominantly dilatational areas by nodal curves near which the *P*-wave amplitudes are abnormally small.

In 1926 the American geophysicist Perry E. Byerly used patterns of *P* onsets over the entire globe to infer the orientation of the fault plane in a large earthquake. The polarity method yields two *P*-nodal curves at Earth's surface; one curve is in the plane containing the assumed fault, and the other is in the plane (called the auxiliary plane) that passes through the focus and is perpendicular to the forces of the plane. The recent availability of worldwide broad-based digital recording has enabled computer programs to be written that estimate the fault mechanism and seismic moment from the complete pattern of seismic wave arrivals. Given a well-determined pattern at a number of earthquake observatories, it is possible to locate two planes, one of which is the plane containing the fault.

Earthquake Prediction

The Observation and Interpretation of Precursory Phenomena

The search for periodic cycles in earthquake occurrence is an old one. Generally, periodicities in time and space for major earthquakes have not been widely detected or accepted. One problem is that long-term earthquake catalogs are not homogeneous in their selection and reporting. The most extensive catalog of this kind comes from China and begins about 700 BCE. The catalog contains some information on about 1,000 destructive earthquakes. The sizes of these earthquakes have been assessed from the reports of damage, intensity, and shaking.

Another approach to the statistical occurrence of earthquakes involves the postulation of trigger forces that initiate the rupture. Such forces have been attributed to severe weather conditions, volcanic activity, and tidal forces, for example. Usually correlations are made between the physical phenomena assumed to provide the trigger and the repetition of earthquakes. Inquiry must always be made to discover whether a causative link is actually present, but in no cases to the present has a trigger mechanism, at least for moderate to large earthquakes, been unequivocally found that satisfies the various necessary criteria.

Statistical methods also have been tried with populations of regional earthquakes. It has been suggested, but never established generally, that the slope b of the regression line between the logarithm of the number of earthquakes and the magnitude for a region may change characteristically with time. Specifically, the claim is that the b value for the population of foreshocks of a major earthquake may be significantly smaller than the mean b value for the region averaged over a long interval of time.

The elastic rebound theory of earthquake sources allows rough prediction of the occurrence of large shallow earthquakes. Harry F. Reid gave, for example, a crude forecast of the next great earthquake near San Francisco. (The theory also predicted, of course, that the place would be along the San Andreas or an associated fault.) The geodetic data indicated that during an interval of 50 years relative displacements of 3.2 metres (10.5 feet) had occurred at distant points across the fault. The maximum elastic-rebound offset along the fault in the 1906 earthquake was 6.5 metres. Therefore, $(6.5 \div 3.2) \times 50$, or about 100, years would again elapse before sufficient strain accumulated for the occurrence of an earthquake comparable to that of 1906. The premises are that the regional strain will grow uniformly and that various constraints have not been altered by the great 1906 rupture itself (such as by the onset of slow fault slip). Such strain rates are now being more adequately measured along a number of active faults such as the San Andreas, using networks of GPS sensors.

For many years prediction research has been influenced by the basic argument that strain accumulates in the rock masses in the vicinity of a fault and results in crustal deformation. Deformations have been measured in the horizontal direction along active faults (by trilateration and triangulation) and in the vertical direction by precise leveling and tiltmeters. Some investigators believe that changes in groundwater level occur prior to earthquakes; variations of this sort have been reported mainly from China. Because water levels in wells respond to a complex array of factors such as rainfall, such factors will have to be removed if changes in water level are to be studied in relation to earthquakes.

The theory of dilatancy (that is, an increase in volume) of rock prior to rupture once occupied a central position in discussions of premonitory phenomena of earthquakes, but it now receives less support. It is based on the observation that many solids exhibit dilatancy during deformation. For earthquake prediction the significance of dilatancy, if real, is in its effects on various measurable quantities of Earth's crust, such as seismic velocities, electric resistivity, and ground and water levels. The best-studied consequence is the effect on seismic velocities. The influence of internal cracks and pores on the elastic properties of rocks can be clearly demonstrated in laboratory measurements of those properties as a function of hydrostatic pressure. In the case of saturated rocks, experiments predict—for shallow earthquakes—that dilatancy occurs as a portion of the crust is stressed to failure, causing a decrease in the velocities of seismic waves. Recovery of velocity is brought about by subsequent rise of the pore pressure of water, which also has the effect of weakening the rock and enhancing fault slip.

Strain buildup in the focal region may have measurable effects on other observable properties, including electrical conductivity and gas concentration. Because the electrical conductivity of rocks depends largely on interconnected water channels within the rocks, resistivity may increase before the cracks become saturated. As pore fluid is expelled from the closing cracks, the local water table would rise and concentrations of gases such as radioactive radon would increase. No unequivocal confirming measurements have yet been published.

Geologic methods of extending the seismicity record back from the present also are being explored. Field studies indicate that the sequence of surface ruptures along major active faults associated with large earthquakes can sometimes be constructed. An example is the series of large earthquakes in Turkey in the 20th century, which were caused mainly by successive westward ruptures of the North Anatolian Fault. Liquefaction effects preserved in beds of sand and peat have provided evidence—when radiometric dating methods are used—for large paleoearthquakes extending back for more than 1,000 years in many seismically active zones, including the Pacific Northwest coast of the United States.

Less well-grounded precursory phenomena, particularly earthquake lights and animal behaviour, sometimes draw more public attention than the precursors discussed above. Many reports of unusual lights in the sky and abnormal animal behaviour preceding earthquakes are known to seismologists, mostly in anecdotal form. Both these phenomena are usually explained in terms of a release of gases prior to earthquakes and electric and acoustic stimuli of various types. At present there is no definitive experimental evidence to support claims that animals sometimes sense the coming of an earthquake.

Methods of Reducing Earthquake Hazards

Considerable work has been done in seismology to explain the characteristics of the recorded ground motions in earthquakes. Such knowledge is needed to predict ground motions in future earthquakes so that earthquake-resistant structures can be designed. Although earthquakes cause death and destruction through such secondary effects as landslides, tsunamis, fires, and fault rupture, the greatest losses—both of lives and of property—result from the collapse of man-made structures during the violent shaking of the ground. Accordingly, the most effective way to mitigate the damage of earthquakes from an engineering standpoint is to design and construct structures capable of withstanding strong ground motions.

Interpreting Recorded Ground Motions

Most elastic waves recorded close to an extended fault source are complicated and difficult to interpret uniquely. Understanding such near-source motion can be viewed as a three-part problem. The first part stems from the generation of elastic waves by the slipping fault as the moving rupture sweeps out an area of slip along the fault plane within a given time. The pattern of waves produced is dependent on several parameters, such as fault dimension and rupture velocity. Elastic waves of various types radiate from the vicinity of the moving rupture in all directions. The geometry and frictional properties of the fault critically affect the pattern of radiation from it.

The second part of the problem concerns the passage of the waves through the intervening rocks to the site and the effect of geologic conditions. The third part involves the conditions at the recording site itself, such as topography and highly attenuating soils. All these questions must be considered when estimating likely earthquake effects at a site of any proposed structure.

Experience has shown that the ground strong-motion recordings have a variable pattern in detail but predictable regular shapes in general (except in the case of strong multiple earthquakes). In a strong horizontal shaking of the ground near the fault source, there is an initial segment of

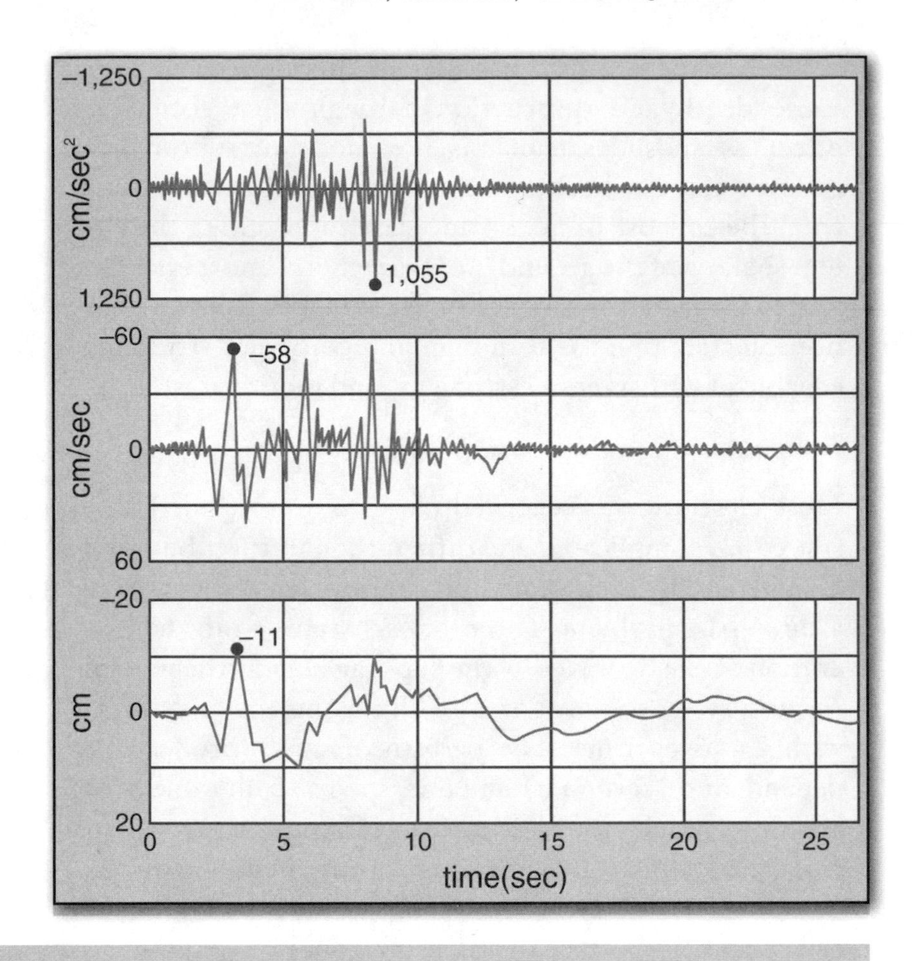

Recording of the San Fernando earthquake, near Pacoima Dam, California, 1971, showing (top) ground acceleration, (centre) velocity, and (bottom) displacement. Encyclopædia Britannica, Inc.

motion made up mainly of *P* waves, which frequently manifest themselves strongly in the vertical motion. This is followed by the onset of *S* waves, often associated with a longer-period pulse of ground velocity and displacement related to the near-site fault slip or fling. This pulse is often enhanced in the direction of the fault rupture and normal to it. After the *S* onset there is shaking that consists of a mixture of *S* and *P* waves, but the *S* motions become dominant as the duration increases. Later, in the horizontal component, surface waves dominate, mixed with some *S* body waves. Depending on the distance of the site from the fault and the structure of the intervening rocks and soils, surface waves are spread out into long trains.

Constructing Seismic Hazard Maps

In many regions, seismic expectancy maps or hazard maps are now available for planning purposes. The anticipated intensity of ground shaking is represented by a number called the peak acceleration or the peak velocity.

To avoid weaknesses found in earlier earthquake hazard maps, the following general principles are usually adopted today:

1. The map should take into account not only the size but also the frequency of earthquakes.
2. The broad regionalization pattern should use historical seismicity as a database, including the following factors: major tectonic trends, acceleration attenuation curves, and intensity reports.
3. Regionalization should be defined by means of contour lines with design parameters referred to ordered numbers on neighbouring contour lines (this procedure minimizes sensitivity concerning the exact location of boundary lines between separate zones).
4. The map should be simple and not attempt to microzone the region.
5. The mapped contoured surface should not contain discontinuities, so that the level of hazard progresses gradually and in order across any profile drawn on the map.

Developing Resistant Structures

Developing engineered structural designs that are able to resist the forces generated by seismic waves can be achieved either by following building codes based on hazard maps or by appropriate methods of analysis. Many countries reserve theoretical structural analyses for the larger, more costly, or critical buildings to be constructed in the most seismically active regions, while simply requiring that ordinary structures conform to local building codes. Economic realities usually determine the goal, not of preventing all damage in all earthquakes but of minimizing damage in moderate, more common earthquakes and ensuring no major collapse at the strongest intensities. An essential part of what goes into engineering decisions on design and into the development and revision of earthquake-resistant design codes is therefore seismological, involving measurement of strong seismic waves, field studies of intensity and damage, and the probability of earthquake occurrence.

Earthquake risk can also be reduced by rapid post-earthquake response. Strong-motion accelerographs have been connected in some urban areas, such as Los Angeles, Tokyo, and Mexico City, to interactive computers. The recorded waves are correlated with seismic intensity scales and rapidly displayed graphically on regional maps via the World Wide Web.

The Exploration of Earth's Interior with Seismic Waves

Seismological data on Earth's deep structure come from several sources. These include *P* and *S* waves in earthquakes and nuclear explosions, the dispersion of surface waves from distant earthquakes, and vibrations of the whole Earth from large earthquakes.

One of the major aims of seismology is to infer the minimum set of properties of Earth's interior that will explain recorded seismic wave trains in detail. Notwithstanding the tremendous progress made in the exploration of Earth's deep structure during the first half of the 20th century, realization of this goal was severely limited until the 1960s because of the laborious effort required to evaluate theoretical models and to process the large amounts of earthquake data recorded. The application of high-speed computers with their enormous storage and rapid retrieval capabilities opened the way for major advances in both theoretical work and data handling.

Since the mid-1970s, researchers have studied realistic models of Earth's structure that include continental and oceanic boundaries, mountains, and river valleys rather than simple structures such as those involving variation only with depth. In addition, various technical developments have benefited observational seismology. For example, the implications of seismic exploratory techniques developed by the petroleum industry (such as seismic reflection) have been recognized and the procedures adopted. Equally significant has been the application of three-dimensional imaging methods to the exploration of Earth's deep structure. This has been made possible by the development of very fast microprocessors and computers with peripheral display equipment.

Seismological Tomography

The major method for determining the structure of Earth's deep interior is the detailed analysis of seismograms of seismic waves. (Such earthquake readings also provide estimates of wave velocities, density, and elastic and inelastic parameters in Earth.) The primary procedure is to measure the travel times of various wave types, such as *P* and *S*, from their source to the recording seismograph.

First, however, identification of each wave type with its ray path through Earth must be made.

Rays corresponding to waves that have been reflected at Earth's outer surface (or possibly at one of the interior discontinuity surfaces) are denoted as *P P*, *P S*, *S P*, *P S S*, and so on. For example, *P S* corresponds to a wave that is of *P* type before surface reflection and of *S* type afterward. In addition, there are rays such as *p P P*, *s P P*, and *s P S*, the symbols *p* and *s* corresponding to an initial ascent to the outer surface as *P* or *S* waves, respectively, from a deep focus.

An especially important class of rays is associated with a discontinuity surface separating the central core of Earth from the mantle at a depth of about 2,900 km (1,800 miles) below the outer surface. The symbol *c* is used to indicate an upward reflection at this discontinuity. Thus, if a *P* wave travels down from a focus to the discontinuity surface in question, the upward reflection into an *S* wave is recorded at an observing station as the ray *P c S* and similarly with *P c P*, *S c S*, and *S c P*. The symbol *K* is used to denote the part (of *P* type) of the path of a wave that passes through the liquid central core. Thus, the ray *S K S* corresponds to a wave that starts as an *S* wave, is refracted into the central core as a *P* wave, and is refracted back into the mantle, wherein it finally emerges as an *S* wave. Such rays as *S K K S* correspond to waves that have suffered an internal reflection at the boundary of the central core.

The discovery of the existence of an inner core in 1936 by the Danish seismologist Inge Lehmann made it necessary to introduce additional basic symbols. For paths of waves inside the central core, the symbols *i* and *I* are used analogously to *c* and *K* for the whole Earth; therefore, *i* indicates reflection upward at the boundary between the outer and inner portions of the central core, and *I*

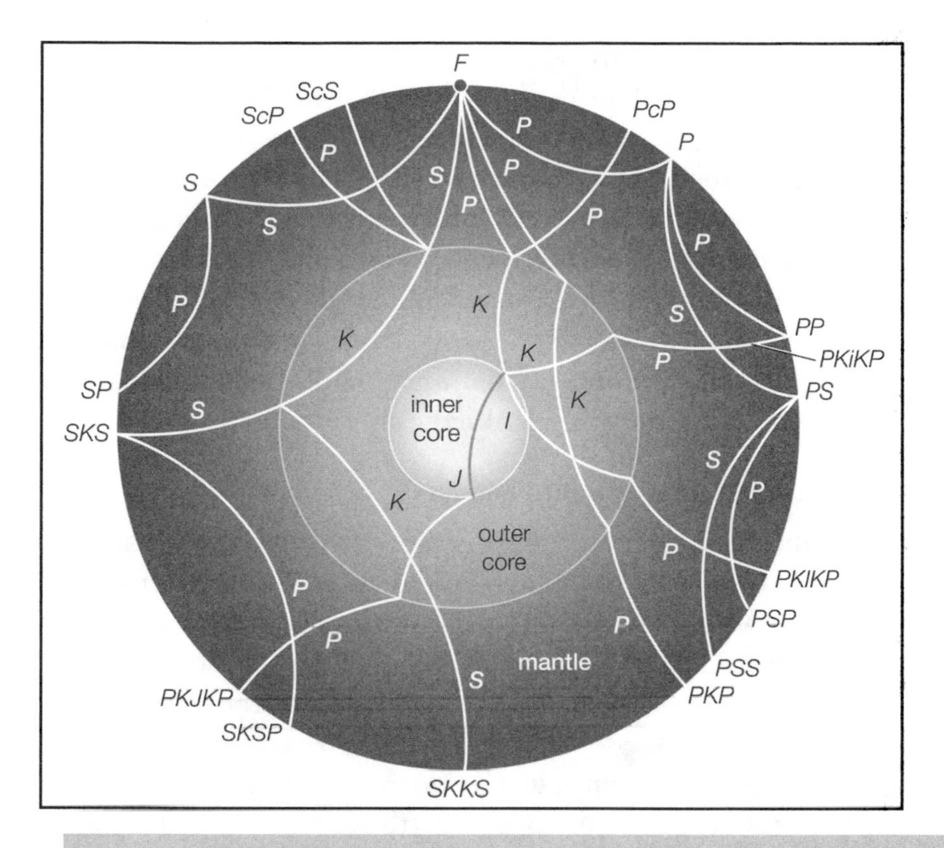

Seismic ray types in Earth's interior from an earthquake at F. Encyclopædia Britannica, Inc.

corresponds to the part (of *P* type) of the path of a wave that lies inside the inner portion. Thus, for instance, discrimination needs to be made between the rays *P K P*, *P K i K P*, and *P K I KP*. The first of these corresponds to a wave that has entered the outer part of the central core but has not reached the inner core, the second to one that has been reflected upward at the inner core boundary, and the third to one that has penetrated into the inner portion.

By combining the symbols *p*, *s*, *P*, *S*, *c*, *K*, *i*, and *I* in various ways, notation is developed for all the main rays associated with body earthquake waves. The symbol *J* has been introduced to correspond to *S* waves in the inner core, should evidence ever be found for such waves.

Finally, the use of times of travel along rays to infer hidden structure is analogous to the use of X-rays in medical tomography. The method involves reconstructing an image of internal anomalies from measurements made at the outer surface. Nowadays, hundreds of thousands of travel times of *P* and *S* waves are available in earthquake catalogs for the tomographic imaging of Earth's interior and the mapping of internal structure.

The Structure of Earth's Interior

Studies with earthquake recordings have given a picture inside the Earth of a solid but layered and flow-patterned mantle about 2,900 km (1,800 miles) thick, which in places lies within 10 km (6 miles) of the surface under the oceans.

The thin surface rock layer surrounding the mantle is the crust, whose lower boundary is called the Mohorovičić discontinuity. In normal continental regions the crust is about 30 to 40 km thick; there is usually a superficial low-velocity sedimentary layer underlain by a zone in which seismic velocity increases with depth. Beneath this zone there is a layer in which *P*-wave velocities in some places fall from 6 to 5.6 km per second. The middle part of the crust is characterized by a heterogeneous zone with *P* velocities of nearly 6 to 6.3 km per second. The lowest layer of the crust (about 10 km thick) has significantly higher *P* velocities, ranging up to nearly 7 km per second.

In the deep ocean there is a sedimentary layer that is about 1 km thick. Underneath is the lower layer of the oceanic crust, which is about 4 km thick. This layer is inferred to consist of basalt that formed where extrusions of basaltic magma at oceanic ridges have been added to the upper part of lithospheric plates as they spread away from the ridge crests. This crustal layer cools as it moves away from the ridge crest, and its seismic velocities increase correspondingly.

Below the mantle lies a shell that is 2,255 km thick, which seismic waves show to have the properties of a liquid. At the very centre of the planet is a separate solid core with a radius of 1,216 km. Recent work with observed

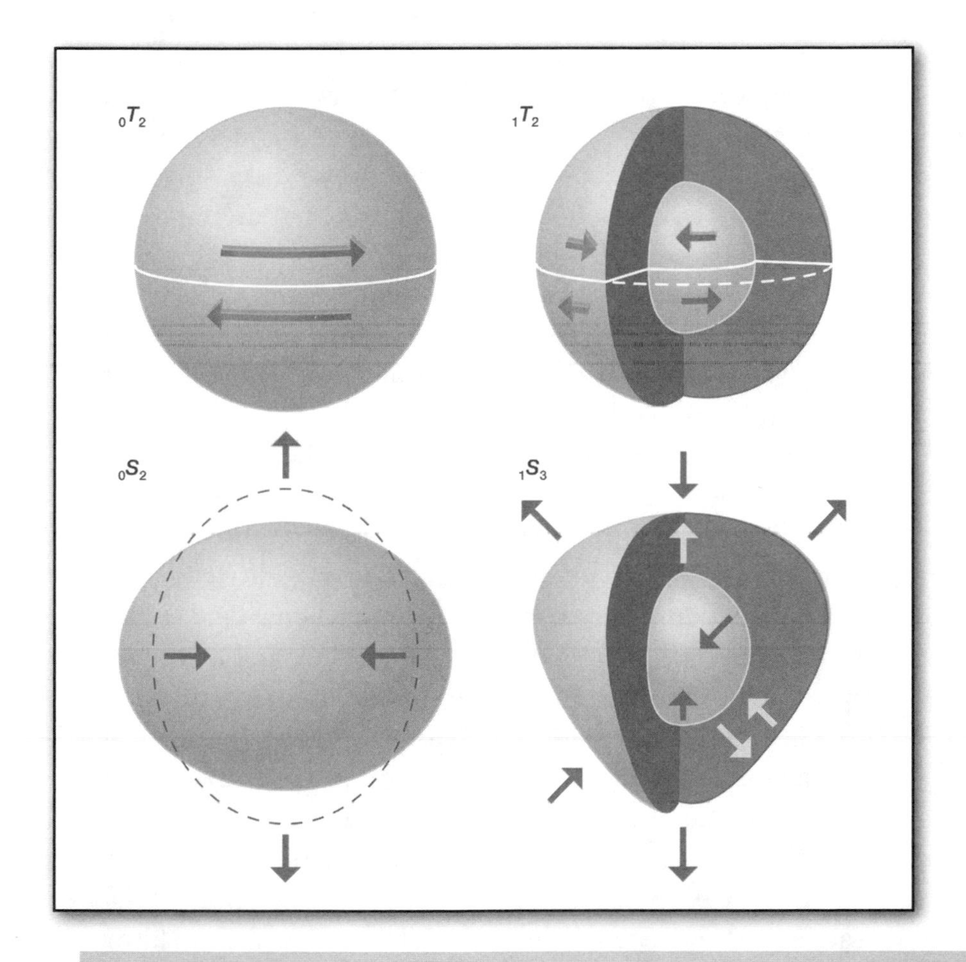

Displacements of Earth in four types of free vibrations. Encyclopædia Britannica, Inc.

seismic waves has revealed three-dimensional structural details inside Earth, especially in the crust and lithosphere, under the subduction zones, at the base of the mantle, and in the inner core. These regional variations are important in explaining the dynamic history of the planet.

Long-Period Oscillations of the Globe

Sometimes earthquakes are large enough to cause the whole Earth to ring like a bell. The deepest tone of vibration of the planet is one with a period (the length of time between the arrival of successive crests in a wave train) of 54 minutes. Knowledge of these vibrations has come from a remarkable extension in the range of periods of ground movements that can be recorded by modern digital long-period seismographs that span the entire allowable spectrum of earthquake wave periods: from ordinary *P* waves with periods of tenths of seconds to vibrations with periods on the order of 12 and 24 hours such as those that occur in Earth tidal movements.

The measurements of vibrations of the whole Earth provide important information on the properties of the interior of the planet. It should be emphasized that these free vibrations are set up by the energy release of the earthquake source but continue for many hours and sometimes even days. For an elastic sphere such as Earth, two types of vibrations are known to be possible. In one type, called *S* modes, or spheroidal vibrations, the motions of the elements of the sphere have components along the radius as well as along the tangent. In the second type, which are designated as *T* modes, or torsional vibrations, there is shear but no radial displacements. The nomenclature is *n S l* and *n T l*, where the letters *n* and *l* are related to the surfaces in the vibration at which there is zero motion. The subscript *n* gives a count of the number of

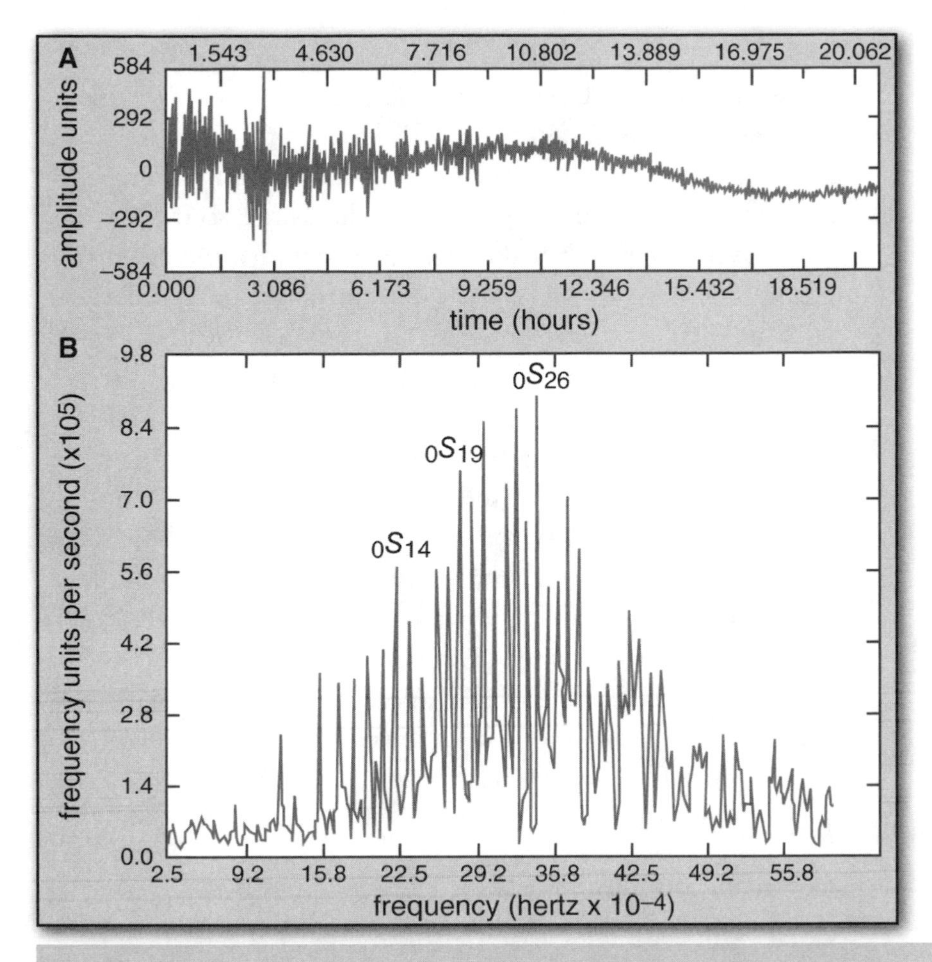

(A) Recorded ground motion for 20 hours at Whiskeytown, California, in the large Indonesian earthquake, 1977. (B) Frequency spectrum of Earth's oscillations from that record. Encyclopædia Britannica, Inc.

internal zero-motion (nodal) surfaces, and *l* indicates the number of surface nodal lines.

Several hundred types of *S* and *T* vibrations have been identified and the associated periods measured. The amplitudes of the ground motion in the vibrations have been determined for particular earthquakes, and, more important, the attenuation of each component vibration has been measured. The dimensionless measure of this decay constant is called the quality factor *Q*. The greater the value of *Q*, the less the wave or vibration damping. Typically, for ${}_{0}S_{10}$ and ${}_{0}T_{10}$, the *Q* values are about 250.

Recent research has shown that observations of long-period oscillations of Earth discriminate fairly finely between different Earth models. In applying the observations to improve the resolution and precision of such representations of the planet's internal structure, a considerable number of Earth models are set up, and all the periods of their free oscillations are computed and checked against the observations. Models can then be successively eliminated until only a small range remains. In practice, the work starts with existing models; efforts are made to amend them by sequential steps until full compatibility with the observations is achieved, within the uncertainties of the observations. Even so, the resulting computed Earth structure is not a unique solution to the problem.

Extraterrestrial Seismic Phenomena

Space vehicles have carried equipment to the surface of the Moon and Mars with which to record seismic waves, and seismologists on Earth have received telemetered signals from seismic events in both cases.

By 1969, seismographs had been placed at six sites on the Moon during the U.S. Apollo missions. Recording of seismic data ceased in September 1977. The instruments detected between 600 and 3,000 moonquakes during each year of their operation, though most of these seismic events were very small. The ground noise on the lunar surface is low compared with that of Earth, so that the seismographs could be operated at very high magnifications. Because there was more than one station on the Moon, it was possible to use the arrival times of *P* and *S* waves at the lunar stations from the moonquakes to determine foci in the same way as is done on Earth.

Moonquakes are of three types. First, there are the events caused by the impact of lunar modules, booster rockets, and meteorites. The lunar seismograph stations were able to detect meteorites hitting the Moon's surface more than 1,000 km (600 miles) away. The two other types of moonquakes had natural sources in the Moon's interior: they presumably resulted from rock fracturing, as on Earth. The most common type of natural moonquake had deep foci, at depths of 600 to 1,000 km; the less common variety had shallow focal depths.

Seismological research on Mars has been less successful. Only one of the seismometers carried to the Martian surface by the U.S. Viking landers during the mid-1970s remained operational, and only one potential marsquake was detected in 546 Martian days.

RELATED CONCEPTS

A number of other important concepts related to the study of earthquakes are presented below. The majority of these terms describe the kinds of locations in which earthquakes are likely to occur or the instrumentation used to measure these phenomena.

Circum-Pacific Belt

This zone of earthquake epicentres (points on the surface directly above the foci, or origination points, of earthquakes) surrounds the Pacific Ocean and coincides with tectonic plate boundaries. For much of its length the belt follows chains of island arcs such as Tonga and New

Hebrides, the Philippines, Japan, the Kuril Islands, and the Aleutians, or arc-shaped features, such as the Andes. Volcanoes are associated with the Circum-Pacific Belt throughout its length; for this reason this encircling Pacific Ocean belt is often called the Ring of Fire. Deep ocean troughs bound the belt on the oceanic side; continental land masses lie behind. The Circum-Pacific Belt is the source of approximately 80 percent of the world's shallow-focus earthquakes and virtually all deep-focus earthquakes.

Fault

In geology, a fault is a planar or gently curved fracture in the rocks of Earth's crust, where compressional or tensional forces cause relative displacement of the rocks on the opposite sides of the fracture. Faults range in length from a few centimetres to many hundreds of kilometres, and displacement likewise may range from less than a centimetre to several hundred kilometres along the fracture surface (the fault plane). In some instances, the movement is distributed over a fault zone composed of many individual faults that occupy a belt hundreds of metres wide. The geographic distribution of faults varies; some large areas have almost none, others are cut by innumerable faults.

Faults may be vertical, horizontal, or inclined at any angle. Although the angle of inclination of a specific fault plane tends to be relatively uniform, it may differ considerably along its length from place to place. When rocks slip past each other in faulting, the upper or overlying block along the fault plane is called the hanging wall, or headwall; the block below is called the footwall. The fault strike is the direction of the line of intersection between the fault plane and the surface of Earth. The dip of a fault plane is its angle of inclination measured from the horizontal.

Types of Faulting in Tectonic Earthquakes

Faults are classified according to their angle of dip and their relative displacement. Normal dip-slip faults are produced by vertical compression as Earth's crust lengthens. The hanging wall slides down relative to the footwall. Normal faults are common; they bound many of the mountain ranges of the world and many of the rift valleys found along spreading margins of tectonic plates. Rift valleys are formed by the sliding of the hanging walls downward many thousands of metres, where they then become the valley floors.

A block that has dropped relatively downward between two normal faults dipping toward each other is called a graben. A block that has been relatively uplifted between two normal faults that dip away from each other is called a horst. A tilted block that lies between two normal faults dipping in the same direction is a tilted fault block.

Reverse dip-slip faults result from horizontal compressional forces caused by a shortening, or contraction, of the Earth's crust. The hanging wall moves up and over the footwall. Thrust

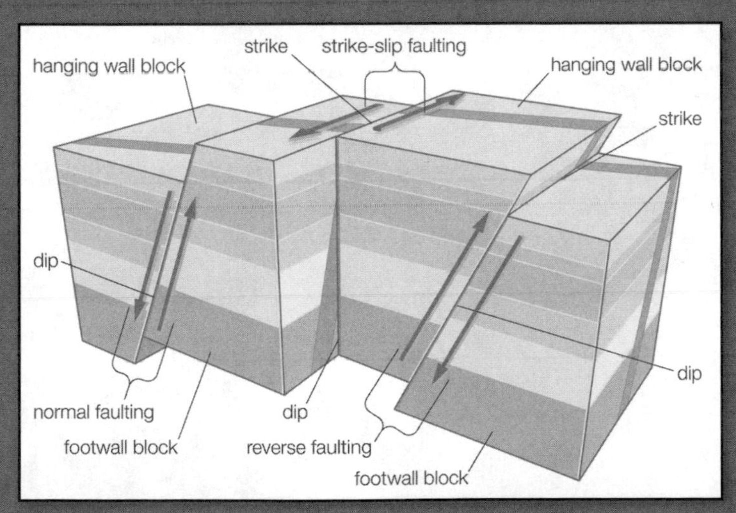

In normal and reverse faulting, rock masses slip vertically past each other. In strike-slip faulting, the rocks slip past each other horizontally. Encyclopædia Britannica, Inc.

faults are reverse faults that dip less than 45°. Thrust faults with a very low angle of dip and a very large total displacement are called overthrusts or detachments; these are often found in intensely deformed mountain belts. Large thrust faults are characteristic of compressive tectonic plate boundaries, such as those that have created the Himalayas and the subduction zones along the west coast of South America.

Strike-slip (also called transcurrent, wrench, or lateral) faults are similarly caused by horizontal compression, but they release their energy by rock displacement in a horizontal direction almost parallel to the compressional force. The fault plane is essentially vertical, and the relative slip is lateral along the plane. These faults are widespread. Many are found at the boundary between obliquely converging oceanic and continental tectonic plates. A well-known terrestrial example is the San Andreas Fault, which, during the San Francisco earthquake of 1906, had a maximum movement of 6 metres (20 feet).

Oblique-slip faults have simultaneous displacement up or down the dip and along the strike. The displacement of the blocks on the opposite sides of the fault plane usually is measured in relation to sedimentary strata or other stratigraphic markers, such as veins and dikes. The movement along a fault may be rotational, with the offset blocks rotating relative to one another.

Fault slip may polish smooth the walls of the fault plane, marking them with striations called slickensides, or it may crush them to a fine-grained, claylike substance known as fault gouge; when the crushed rock is relatively coarse-grained, it is referred to as fault breccia. Occasionally, the beds adjacent to the fault plane fold or bend as they resist slippage because of friction. Areas of deep sedimentary rock cover often show no surface indications of the faulting below.

Movement of rock along a fault may occur as a continuous creep or as a series of spasmodic jumps of a few metres during a few seconds. Such jumps are separated by intervals during which stress builds up until it overcomes the frictional forces along the fault plane and causes another slip. Most, if not all, earthquakes are caused by rapid slip along faults.

Richter Scale

The Richter scale is a widely used quantitative measure of the magnitude of an earthquake, devised in 1935 by American seismologist Charles F. Richter.

The Richter scale was originally devised to measure the magnitude of local earthquakes in southern California as recorded by a specific kind of seismograph. Current scientific practice has replaced the original Richter scale with other scales, including the body-wave magnitude scale and the moment magnitude scale, which have no restrictions regarding distance and type of seismograph used. Nevertheless, the Richter scale is still commonly cited in news reports of earthquake severity.

On the original Richter scale the smallest earthquakes measurable at that time were assigned values close to zero.

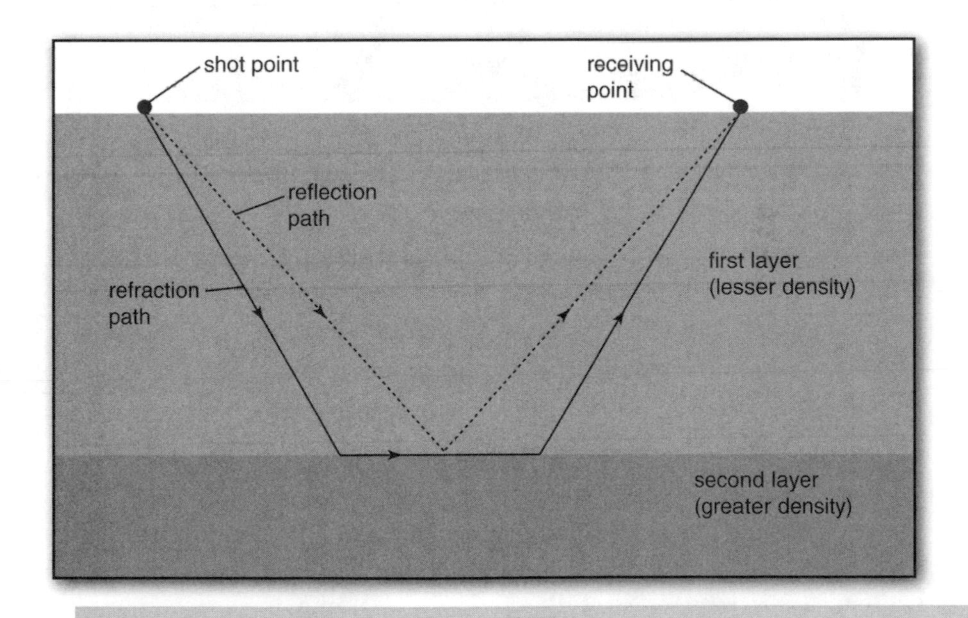

Simplified view of seismic survey methods. Encyclopædia Britannica, Inc.

Since modern seismographs can detect seismic waves even smaller than those originally chosen for zero magnitude, the Richter scale now measures earthquakes having negative magnitudes. Each increase of one unit on the scale represents a 10-fold increase in the magnitude of an earthquake—in other words, numbers on the Richter scale are proportional to the common (base 10) logarithms of maximum wave amplitudes. In theory the scale has no upper limit, but in practice no earthquake has ever been registered above magnitude 9.

RICHTER SCALE OF EARTHQUAKE MAGNITUDE

Magnitude Level	Catagory*	Effects	Earthquakes Per Year
less than 1.0 to 2.9	Micro	generally not felt by people, though recorded on local instruments	more than 100,000
3.0-3.9	Minor	felt by many people; no damage	12,000-100,000
4.0-4.9	Light	felt by all; minor breakage of objects	2,000-12,000
6.0-6.9	Strong	moderate damage in populated areas	20-200
7.0-7.9	Major	serious damage over large areas; loss of life	3-20
8.0 and higher	Great	severe destruction and loss of life over large areas	fewer than 3

SEISMIC BELT

A seismic belt is a narrow geographic zone on Earth's surface along which most earthquake activity occurs. The outermost layer of Earth (lithosphere) is made up of several large tectonic plates. The edges where these plates move against one another are the location of interplate earthquakes that produce the seismic belts. Island arcs, mountain chains, volcanism, deep ocean troughs, and oceanic ridges are often features of seismic belts. The two major seismic belts are the Circum-Pacific Belt, which surrounds the Pacific Ocean, and the Alpide Belt, which stretches from the Azores through the Mediterranean and Middle East to the Himalayas and Indonesia, where it joins the Circum-Pacific Belt. A purely oceanic seismic belt lies along the mid-Atlantic ridge.

SEISMIC SURVEY

A seismic survey is a method of investigating subterranean structure, particularly as related to exploration for petroleum, natural gas, and mineral deposits. The technique is based on determinations of the time interval that elapses between the initiation of a seismic wave at a selected shop point and the arrival of reflected or refracted impulses at one or more seismic detectors. Seismic air guns are commonly used to initiate the seismic waves. This technique has largely replaced the practice of exploding dynamite underground. Electric vibrators or falling weights (thumpers) may also be employed at sites where an underground explosion might cause damage—e.g., where caverns are present. Upon arrival at the detectors, the amplitude and timing of waves are recorded to give a seismogram (record of ground vibrations).

Generally, the density of rocks near the surface of Earth increases with depth. Seismic waves initiated at the shot point may reach the receiving point by reflection, refraction, or both. When the shot point is close to the receiving point, reflected waves usually reach the receiving point first. At greater distances, however, the seismic pulse travels faster by the refraction path because its velocity is greater along the top of the lower, denser layer than it is through the upper layer; in this case, the refracted wave arrives first.

Interpretation of the depths and media reached by seismic waves thus depends on the distance between shot points and receiving points and the densities of the strata. The results of a seismic survey may be presented in the form of a cross-sectional drawing of the subsurface structures as if cut by a plane through the shot point, the detector, and the centre of Earth. Such drawings are called seismic profiles.

Seismograph

A seismograph is an instrument that makes a record of seismic waves caused by an earthquake, explosion, or other Earth-shaking phenomenon. Seismographs are equipped with electromagnetic sensors that translate ground motions into electrical changes, which are processed and recorded by the instruments' analog or digital circuits. A record produced by a seismograph on a display screen or paper printout is called a seismogram. Although originally designed to locate natural earthquakes, seismographs have many other uses, such as petroleum exploration, investigation of Earth's crust and lower layers, and monitoring of volcanic activity.

Development of the First Seismographs

An early seismic instrument called the seismoscope made no time record of ground oscillations but simply indicated that shaking had occurred. A Chinese scholar, Chang Heng, invented such an instrument as early as 132 CE. It was cylindrical in shape with eight dragon heads arranged around its upper circumference, each with a ball in its mouth. Around the lower circumference were eight frogs, each directly under a dragon head. When an earthquake occurred, one of the balls was released from a dragon's mouth, probably by an internal pendulum, and was caught by a frog's mouth.

A device involving water spillage was developed in 17th-century Italy. Later a water-filled bowl and still later a cup filled with mercury were used for detecting earthquakes and tremors. In 1855 Luigi Palmieri of Italy designed a seismometer, an instrument that senses the amount of ground motion. Palmieri's seismometer consisted of several U-shaped tubes filled with mercury and oriented toward the different points of the compass. When the ground shook, the motion of the mercury made an electrical contact that stopped a clock and simultaneously started a recording drum on which the motion of a float on the surface of

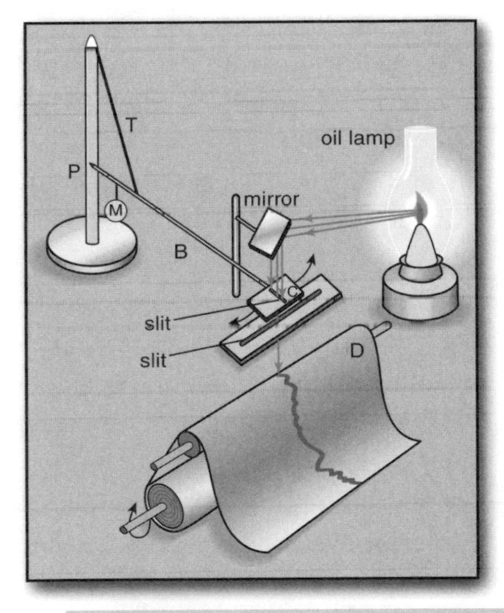

Horizontal pendulum seismograph, as invented by English seismologist John Milne in 1880. From *Bulletin of the Seismological Society of America* (1969), vol. 59, no. 1, p. 212

mercury was registered. This device thus indicated time of occurrence and the relative intensity and duration of the ground motion.

The basic problem in measuring ground motions is to attain a steady point that remains fixed when the ground moves. Various types of pendulums have been used for this purpose. The simplest type is a common pendulum in which a heavy mass is suspended by a wire or rod from a fixed point (as in a clock). Other forms are the inverted pendulum, in which a heavy mass is fixed to the upper end of a vertical rod pointed at its lower end, and the horizontal pendulum, in which a rod with a mass on its end is suspended at two points so as to swing in a nearly horizontal plane instead of a vertical plane. In 1840 a seismometer based on the common pendulum was installed near Comrie in Perthshire, Scotland.

Seismograph developments occurred rapidly in 1880 when Sir James Alfred Ewing, Thomas Gray, and John Milne, British scientists working in Japan, began to study earthquakes. Following a severe earthquake that occurred at Yokohama near Tokyo in that year, they organized the Seismological Society of Japan. Under its auspices various devices, forerunners of today's seismograph, were invented. Among the instruments constructed in this period was Milne's famous horizontal pendulum seismograph. In his design, a boom, to which the mass was attached, was suspended horizontally by a pivot and a silk thread fixed to a point above the pivot. A thin plate, in which a narrow slit was cut parallel to the boom, was attached to the end of the boom. A similar plate with a slit at right angles to the upper plate was fixed on the top of a box containing a recording drum. A ray of light from an oil lamp passed through both slits and formed a small spot of light on a sheet of light-sensitive graph paper (bromide paper) wrapped on the recording drum. Milne successfully used this seismograph to record several earthquakes in Japan; then, after returning to England, he established a small worldwide seismographic network using such instruments.

The horizontal pendulum seismograph was improved greatly after World War II. The Press-Ewing seismograph, developed in the United States for recording long-period waves, was widely used throughout the world. This device employed a Milne-type pendulum, but the pivot supporting the pendulum was replaced by an elastic wire to avoid friction.

Basic Principles of the Modern Seismograph

If a common pendulum is free to swing in one direction and if the ground moves rapidly in the direction of freedom of the pendulum while the pendulum is motionless, the pendulum will tend to remain in place through inertia. If the ground moves back and forth (oscillates) and if the period of ground motion (the time necessary for one complete oscillation) is sufficiently shorter than the period of free oscillation of the pendulum, the pendulum will again lag, and the movement of the ground relative to the pendulum can be recorded. The magnitude of this movement is commonly amplified electrically. When the period of the pendulum is comparable to that of the ground motion, the seismograph will not exactly record Earth's movement. The correction, however, can readily be computed mathematically.

In general, then, the seismograph is an instrument in which the relative motion of pendulum and ground is recorded. It is equally possible to take the ratio between the deflection of the pendulum and the velocity (or acceleration) of the ground. This ratio is called the velocity (or acceleration) sensitivity of the seismograph.

If free oscillation of the pendulum is not minimized, it will mask the proper recording of seismic waves. The simplest way to reduce (damp out) the free oscillation of a pendulum is to suspend it in a viscous (thick) liquid of which the resisting force is proportional to the velocity of the pendulum. In practice, the required resisting force is exerted by a special device called a damper. In an electromagnetic damper, the resisting force is created by electrical currents induced in a copper plate moving in a strong magnetic field.

The ground can move in any of three directions, two horizontal and one vertical. Because each kind of movement must be separately recorded, three pendulums, one for each direction, are needed for a complete seismograph.

Various methods of recording pendulum motion have been developed. In the mechanical method (now of historical interest only), a sheet of smoked paper was wrapped around a rotating drum, so mounted as to move with Earth. A moving pen connected to the pendulum pressed lightly on the paper. The rotating drum shifted slightly with each revolution so that recorded lines were not superimposed on each other. The drum rotated without interruption; one sheet of paper usually lasted 24 hours. Though this method was simple and economical, the seismograph had to have a heavy mass to overcome the friction between pen and paper. In consequence, some mechanical seismographs weighed one ton or more. In the more modern optical method, pendulum motion causes a mirror to move; light is reflected by this mirror onto photosensitive paper wrapped on a drum. Thus, there is no friction to affect the pendulum.

In the electromagnetic method, widely used today, a coil fixed to the mass of the pendulum moves in a magnetic field and creates an electric current. When the current is amplified electronically, high magnification is obtainable. Certain short-period seismographs of this type used for the observation of microearthquakes attain a magnification as high as 1,000,000 or more. In ordinary seismographic observation, the time of initiation of ground oscillations is recorded. Marks are placed on the seismogram once a minute; an extra one identifies the hour.

All the seismographs described so far measure oscillatory motions of the ground at a given point. The strain seismograph, in contrast, employs no pendulum, and its operation depends on changes in the distance between two points on the ground. This type of seismograph was devised in 1935.

Strong-motion seismographs, called accelerographs, are designed particularly to register intense movements of the ground, mainly for engineering purposes—i.e., anti-seismic construction in earthquake-prone areas such as Japan. Strong-motion seismographs employ accelerometers as sensors, record digitally directly on magnetic tape or memory chips, and can measure ground acceleration up to twice gravity. Networks of accelerographs are now operative in several earthquake regions (e.g., California, Japan, Taiwan, Mexico), offering continuous direct recording linked to computers and the World Wide Web. Data on ground shaking are thus available within minutes of a local damaging earthquake.

Applications of the Seismograph

A seismograph records oscillation of the ground caused by seismic waves that travel from their point of origin through Earth or along its surface. The seismogram of a nearby small earthquake is of simple pattern, showing the arrival of *P* waves (waves that vibrate in the direction of propagation), *S* waves (waves that vibrate at right angles to the direction of propagation), and surface waves. In the case of distant earthquakes or of nearby very large earthquakes, the seismogram pattern is more complicated because it shows various sorts of seismic waves that originate from one or many points but then may be reflected or refracted within Earth's crust before reaching the seismograph. The relation between the arrival time of the *P* and *S* waves and the epicentral distance—i.e., the distance from the point of origin—is expressed by a time-distance curve, in which the arrival time is read on the vertical axis and the epicentral distance on the horizontal axis. If the arrival times of various seismic waves are read on the seismogram at a station and compared with the standard time-distance curves, the epicentral distance from that station (the distance of the centre of the earthquake from the recording station) can be determined. If the epicentral distance from at least three stations is known, the origin of the earthquake can be calculated by simple trigonometric methods.

The eruption of a volcano is commonly accompanied by many small earthquakes, especially when a volcano resumes activity after a long dormant period. Observation with sensitive seismographs therefore plays an important role in the prediction of volcanic activity. Often a strong earthquake is preceded by small earthquakes. Observation of very small tremors with sensitive seismographs is helpful in predicting disastrous earthquakes.

Seismographs sometimes detect small and long-continuing oscillations of the ground, called microseisms, that do not originate as earthquakes. The occurrence of some microseisms is related to storms at sea.

Seismographs are used for detecting remote nuclear underground tests. In this activity, the relatively faint seismic waves generated by an underground explosion must be distinguished from natural tremors. If the seismic waves generated by an explosive charge are recorded by sensitive seismographs installed at various points in the neighbourhood of the explosion, the underground structure of the site can be determined by analyzing the time-distance curves of *P* waves, both direct waves and those reflected or refracted at the boundaries of underground layers. Depths of underground layers, their angle of inclination, and the speed of seismic waves in each layer can be determined. Since the discovery of a large oil field in the United States by this method in 1923, seismic surveying has made rapid progress and is now used for oil and gas exploration. The improvement in the instruments and techniques achieved after World War II made it possible to determine the structure of Earth's crust to a depth of 40 to 50 km (about 25 to 30 miles) by detonation of a small amount of explosive.

Ground motions caused by dynamite blasts in mines, quarries, and public works also can be measured by the seismograph. Preliminary examinations based on seismographic measurements make it possible to estimate the intensity of shocks and, thus, evaluate the possibilities of damage caused by a given amount of dynamite. Rock bursts, in which rocks are ejected suddenly in deep pits or tunnels, are caused by increase of stress in the surrounding rocks. Experience in mines shows that an increase of small shocks detectable by highly sensitive geophones—portable seismometers for field use—generally indicates a rock burst hazard.

Detection of vibrations on the lunar surface by seismographs is of fundamental importance in determining the internal structure, physical state, and tectonic (crustal) activity of the Moon. Moon seismographs were installed during the Apollo program starting in 1969. They contained three long-period seismometers and a single-component, short-period, vertical seismometer. Many moonquakes were recorded by these instruments. Similar instruments were placed on Mars by the Viking 1 and 2 landers in 1976 to determine the extent of seismic activity on that planet.

NOTED THINKERS

The modern scientific understanding of earthquakes owes much to the work of seismologists and geologists. Some of the more influential personages, such as August Edward Hough Love, who described surface waves, John Milne, who created the modern seismograph, and Charles Richter, who developed a widely used scale for assessing earthquake magnitude, are presented below.

Beno Gutenberg

(b. June 4, 1889, Darmstadt, Ger.—d. Jan. 25, 1960, Los Angeles, Calif., U.S.)

Beno Gutenberg was an American seismologist noted for his analyses of earthquake waves and the information they furnish about the physical properties of Earth's interior.

Gutenberg served as a professor of geophysics and director of the seismological laboratory at the California Institute of Technology, Pasadena, from 1930 to 1957, when he retired. He worked with Charles Richter to develop a method of determining the intensity of earthquakes. Calculating the energy released by present-day shallow earthquakes, they showed that three-quarters of that energy occurs in the Circum-Pacific belt. Gutenberg wrote several books, including *Earthquakes in North America* (1950); he edited *Internal Constitution of the Earth* (1939) and, with Richter, wrote *The Seismicity of the Earth* (1941).

Sir Harold Jeffreys

(b. April 22, 1891, Fatfield, Durham, Eng.—d. March 18, 1989, Cambridge),

Sir Harold Jeffreys was a British astronomer and geophysicist noted for his wide variety of scientific contributions.

Jeffreys was educated at Armstrong College, Newcastle-upon-Tyne (D.Sc., 1917), and St. John's College, University of Cambridge (M.A., 1917), and was a fellow at St. John's from 1914. He served in the Meteorological Office (1917–22), lectured in mathematics at Cambridge (1923–32), was reader in geophysics at Cambridge (1932–46), and was the university's Plumian professor of astronomy (1945–58). He was knighted in 1953.

In his work in astronomy, Jeffreys established that the four large outer planets (Jupiter, Saturn, Uranus, and Neptune) are very cold and devised early models of their planetary structure. His other astronomical work includes research into the origin of the solar system and the theory of the variation of latitude.

Sir Harold Jeffreys. Camera Press

In geophysics, he investigated the thermal history of Earth, was coauthor (1940) of the standard tables of travel times for earthquake waves, and was the first to demonstrate that the Earth's core is liquid. He explained the origin of monsoons and sea breezes and showed how cyclones are vital to the general circulation of the atmosphere. Jeffreys also published seminal works on probability theory and on methods of general mathematical physics.

Jeffreys was an effective critic of the mechanical feasibility of the theory of continental drift, a forerunner of modern plate tectonics. His skepticism of the possibility of convection in the Earth's mantle carried over to strong objections to plate tectonics as well—an opposition he maintained all his life in spite of mounting geophysical evidence that the theory was correct.

Jeffreys's honours included the Gold Medal of the Royal Astronomical Society (1937) and the Royal Medal of the Royal Society of London (1948). Among his principal works, many of which went through multiple editions in his lifetime, are *The Earth: Its Origin, History and Physical Constitution* (1924), *Theory of Probability* (1939), *Earthquakes and Mountains* (1935), and *Methods of Mathematical Physics* (1946), written with his wife, Lady Bertha Swirles Jeffreys. *The Collected Papers of Sir Harold Jeffreys* was published in six volumes from 1971 to 1977.

Augustus Edward Hough Love

(b. April 17, 1863, Weston-super-Mare, Somerset, Eng.—d. June 5, 1940, Oxford)

Augustus Edward Hough Love, a British geophysicist and mathematician, discovered a major type of seismic wave that was subsequently named for him.

Love held the Sedleian professorship of natural philosophy at the University of Oxford from 1899 to 1940. In his analysis of earthquake waves, Love made the assumption that Earth consists of concentric layers that differ in density and postulated the occurrence of a seismic wave confined to the surface layer, or crust, of Earth. This wave would be propagated as a result of the difference in density between the crust and underlying mantle. His prediction was confirmed by recordings of the behaviour of waves in the surface layer of Earth. He proposed a method—based on measurements of Love waves—to measure the thickness of Earth's crust. In addition to his work on geophysical theory, Love studied elasticity and wrote *A Treatise on the Mathematical Theory of Elasticity*, 2 vol. (1892–93).

John Michell

(b. 1724, Nottinghamshire, Eng.—d. April 21, 1793, Thornhill, Yorkshire)

A British geologist and astronomer, John Michell is considered one of the fathers of seismology, the science of earthquakes.

In 1760, the year in which he was elected a fellow of the Royal Society of London, Michell finished writing *Conjectures Concerning the Cause, and Observations upon the Phænomena of Earthquakes*, in which he presented the conclusions from his study of the disastrous Lisbon earthquake of 1755. He showed that the focus of that earthquake was underneath the Atlantic Ocean, and he proposed erroneously that the cause of earthquakes was high-pressure steam, created when water comes into contact with subterranean fires. His contributions to astronomy included the first realistic estimate of the distance between Earth and a star and the suggestion, later verified by the English astronomer John Herschel, that binary stars are physically close to and in orbit around each other.

Michell became Woodwardian Professor of Geology at the University of Cambridge in 1762 and rector of Thornhill in 1767. In 1750 he had published a major work on artificial magnets. He may have conceived the principle of the torsion balance independently of the French physicist Charles-Augustin de Coulomb. He hoped to use this instrument to determine the mean density of Earth. Although he died before finishing his work, it was carried on by the English physicist Henry Cavendish in his determination of *G*, the gravitational constant (a measure of the strength of gravitation).

John Milne

(b. Dec. 30, 1850, Liverpool, Eng.—d. July 30, 1913, Shide, Isle of Wight)

An English geologist and influential seismologist, John Milne developed the modern seismograph and promoted the establishment of seismological stations worldwide.

Milne worked as a mining engineer in Labrador and Newfoundland, Canada, and in 1874 served as geologist on the expedition led by Charles T. Beke, the noted British explorer and biblical scholar, to Egypt and northwestern Arabia. In 1875 Milne accepted the position of professor of geology and mining at the Imperial College of Engineering, Tokyo. He designed one of the first reliable seismographs in 1880 and traveled widely in Japan to set up 968 seismological stations for a survey of Japan's widespread earthquakes. After many seminal earthquake studies, Milne returned to England in 1894 and established a private seismological station near Newport, Isle of Wight. His attempt in 1906 to determine the velocity of seismic waves through Earth was largely unsuccessful. He served as secretary of the Seismological Committee of the British Association and organized a worldwide network of observation stations. Many of his findings were published in his books *Earthquakes* (1883) and *Seismology* (1898).

Harry Fielding Reid

(b. May 18, 1859, Baltimore, Md., U.S.—d. June 18, 1944, Baltimore)

Harry Fielding Reid was an American seismologist and glaciologist who in 1911 developed the elastic rebound theory of earthquake mechanics, still accepted today.

Reid was professor of applied mechanics at Johns Hopkins University, Baltimore, from 1896 until he became emeritus professor in 1930. His early career was mainly concerned with the study of the structure, composition, and movement of glaciers. Later he became involved in the study of earthquakes and earthquake-recording devices. He was first to develop a mechanism that explained how earthquakes were a result of faulting and not the reverse. He wrote an analysis of the 1906 San Francisco earthquake as part of the California State Earthquake Investigation Commission report, Mechanics of the Earthquake.

Charles F. Richter

(b. April 26, 1900, near Hamilton, Ohio, U.S.—d. Sept. 30, 1985, Pasadena, Calif.)

Charles F. Richter, an American physicist and seismologist, developed the Richter scale for measuring earthquake magnitude.

Born on an Ohio farm, Richter moved with his mother to Los Angeles in 1916. He attended the University of Southern California (1916–17) and then studied physics at Stanford University (A.B., 1920) and the California Institute of Technology (Ph.D., 1928). Richter was on the staff of the Seismological Laboratory of the Carnegie Institution of Washington, Pasadena, California (1927–36), and then taught both physics and seismology at Caltech (1937–70) and worked at its Seismological Laboratory (founded in 1936).

With Beno Gutenberg (1889–1960), a German-born Caltech professor, he developed in 1935 the magnitude scale that came to be associated with his name. Based on instrumental recording of ground motion, it provided a quantitative measure of earthquake size and complemented the older Mercalli scale, which was based on an earthquake's reported intensity. Richter also mapped out quake-prone areas in the United States, though he disparaged attempts at earthquake prediction. He wrote (with Beno Gutenberg) *Seismicity of the Earth and Associated Phenomena* (1949) and *Elementary Seismology* (1958). He also wrote the article Earthquakes for the 15th edition of *Encyclopædia Britannica* (first published 1974).

THE SCOPE OF TECTONIC FORCES

Earth's surface and interior are prone to the violence caused by tectonic forces. The activities of seismic waves during earthquakes and the expulsion of molten rock, explosive gases, and ash that occur during volcanic eruptions scar and deform Earth's surface. When people and their settlements occur within areas affected by earthquakes and volcanic eruptions, the potential for tremendous loss of life and property damage is always present. Secondary events spawned by earthquakes and volcanic eruptions, such as tsunamis and landslides, can add further misery. There are many examples of cities and regions falling victim to volcanic eruptions and massive earthquake events. Some events (such as the eruptions of

Mount Toba, Mount Tambora, and Mount Pinatubo) have even affected global climate patterns.

Despite the devastation caused by these tectonic forces, the activities of earthquakes and volcanoes also recycle and remake Earth's surface. At smaller timescales, ash and rock from volcanic eruptions become deposits of soil that can be used by plants, and lava extruded from volcanoes can add coastline. Across geologic timescales, tectonic forces are responsible for breaking continents into multiple pieces and for building mountains when continents, or parts of continents, collide. These processes can transcend geology since they can also strongly influence the evolution of life.

GLOSSARY

accretion The addition of material to a plate or area of land.

asthenosphere The weaker layer of Earth's upper mantle lying directly below the lithosphere and composed of plastic and partially molten rock.

back-arc basin A basin that forms behind an island arc as a result of two converging oceanic plates and the subduction of older and denser oceanic crust.

bomb Volcanic fragments larger than 64 mm (2.5 in) in diameter.

constructive margin Also called divergent margin.

continental rift A separation in Earth's continental crust caused by two diverging lithospheric plates pushed apart by magma.

convergent margin The boundary created between two tectonic plates moving towards each other.

craton Stable area of continental crust, typically composed of crystalline basement rock.

diastrophism Natural reshaping of Earth's crust leading to the formation of geological features, such as continents, mountains, or ocean basins.

divergent margin Boundary created between two tectonic plates moving apart where new crust is formed.

fumarole Vent in Earth's surface that emits steam or volcanic gas.

Gondwana Also called Gondwanaland. Name given by geologist Edward Suess to an ancient supercontinent comprised of modern-day South America, Africa, Arabia, Madagascar, India, Australia, and Antarctica.

island arc Chain of islands formed by volcanic activity near converging oceanic plates.

isostasy State of equilibrium on the lithosphere, wherein forces supporting Earth's crust balance those that push down on it. Isostasy affects continental and oceanic elevations.

kimberlite Igneous rock created in the asthenosphere that forms vertical pipelike structures in the surrounding rock as it ascends through Earth's crust.

lithosphere The rigid outer layer of Earth's surface that includes the crust and is about 100 km (60 miles) thick. It is composed of large and small plates that move and can cause seismic or volcanic activity.

mofette Also called Moffette. Fumarole containing a large quantity of carbon dioxide gas.

Mohorovicic Discontinuity Also called Moho. Border between Earth's continental or oceanic crust and mantle underneath.

obduction The thrusting of oceanic crust up and onto continental crust during the process of subduction.

oceanic trench Narrow and long depression on the ocean floor, representing the deepest part of the ocean.

orogeny Formation of mountains by way of natural processes.

paleomagnetism The study of Earth's magnetic field through observation of magnetic rocks and minerals.

Pangea Supercontinent formed from the joining of all of earth's major landmasses between the early Permian and Jurassic periods, prior to the separation of continents.

polar wandering The movement of magnetic poles over Earth's surface.

pyroclastic flow A combination of hot gases and glowing rock particles that slide down slopes as a result of volcanic activity.

rheology The study of how matter flows and deforms.

seafloor spreading The divergence of oceanic crust from midocean ridges.

seismic tomography An imaging technique that uses information from earthquakes to form three-dimensional representations of Earth's interior.

solfatara A fumarole with a large quantity of sulfur.

stratigraphy The study of rock layers, especially in relation to sedimentary and igneous rocks.

subduction The process in which one denser tectonic plate sinks below another plate and into Earth's mantle as the two plates converge.

supercontinent cycle The concept that a supercontinent fragments into pieces that can then collide and form new supercontinents.

terrane Group or formation of crustal or related rocks.

tillite Glacially deposited rock useful for determining the timing and extent of glacial episodes.

transform fault Boundary between two plates moving past each other laterally without forming or destroying crust.

Wilson Cycle The concept noting that ocean basins opened and closed.

FOR FURTHER READING

Blackwell, Susan. *Tsunami*. Surrey: Taj Books, 2005.
Bolt, Bruce A. *Earthquakes*. 5th ed. New York, NY: W. H. Freeman, 2003.
Bryan, T. Scott. *The Geysers of Yellowstone*. 4th ed. Boulder, CO: University Press of Colorado, 2008.
Bryant, Edward. *Tsunami: The Underrated Hazard*. 2nd ed. New York, NY: Springer, 2008.
Chester, Roy. *Furnace of Creation, Cradle of Destruction: A Journey to the Birthplace of Earthquakes, Volcanoes, and Tsunamis*. New York, NY: Amacom, 2008.
Erickson, Jon. *Marine Geology: Exploring the New Frontiers of the Ocean*. Rev. ed. *The Living Earth*. New York, NY: Facts on File, 2002.
Fradkin, Philip L. *The Great Earthquake and Firestorms of 1906: How San Francisco Nearly Destroyed Itself*. Berkeley, CA: University of California Press, 2005.
Francis, Peter, and Cliver Oppenheimer. *Volcanoes*. 2nd ed. New York, NY: Oxford University Press, 2004.
Hough, Susan Elizabeth. *Earthshaking Science: What We Know (and Don't Know) about Earthquakes*. Princeton, NJ: Princeton University Press, 2002.
Lutgens, Frederick K., and Edward J. Tarbuck. *Essentials of Geology*. 10th ed. Upper Saddle River, NJ: Prentice Hall, 2008.
Oreskes, Naomi, ed. *Plate Tectonics: An Insider's History of the Modern Theory of the Earth*. Boulder, CO: Westview Press, 2003.

Rogers, John J. W., and M. Santosh. *Continents and Supercontinents*. New York, NY: Oxford University Press, 2004.

Schmincke, Hans-Ulrich. *Volcanism.* New York, NY: Springer-Verlag, 2004.

Scholz, Christopher H. *The Mechanics of Earthquakes and Faulting*. 2nd ed. Cambridge, MA: Cambridge University Press, 2002.

Shearer, Peter M. *Introduction to Seismology*. 2nd ed. Cambridge: Cambridge, MA University Press, 2009.

Wilson, John, and Ron Clowes. *Ghost Mountains and Vanished Oceans: North America from Birth to Middle Age*. Toronto, CA: Key Porter Books, 2009.

Young, Davis A. *Mind Over Magma: The Story of Igneous Petrology*. Princeton, NJ: Princeton University Press, 2003.

Yuen, David A., Shigenori Maruyama, Shun-ichiro Karato, and Brian F. Windley, eds. *Superplumes: Beyond Plate Tectonics.* New York, NY: Springer, 2007.

Zeilinga de Boer, Jelle, and Donald Theodore Sanders. *Earthquakes in Human History: The Far-Reaching Effects of Seismic Disruptions.* Princeton, NJ: Princeton University Press, 2007.

Zeilinga de Boer, Jelle, and Donald Theodore Sanders. *Volcanoes in Human History: The Far-Reaching Effects of Major Eruptions.* Princeton, NJ: Princeton University Press, 2002.

INDEX

I

J

K

L

M

N

O

P

R

S

T

U

V

W

Y